LIVING IN THE MEANTIME

Concerning the Transformation of Religious Life

Paul J. Philibert, O.P.

EDITOR

PAULIST PRESS
New York / Mahwah, NJ

ACKNOWLEDGMENTS

The Publisher gratefully acknowledges use of the following materials: Excerpt from "East Coker" in *Four Quartets*, copyright © 1943 by T.S. Eliot and renewed 1971 by Esme Valerie Eliot, reprinted by permission of Harcourt Brace & Company; use of a photo of the crypt of the cathedral at Auxerre, plate 71 of *France romane: XIe siècle, 1989* (edited by Raymond Oursel).

Library of Congress Cataloging-in-Publication Data

Living in the meantime : concerning the transformation of religious life /
    Paul J. Philibert, editor.
        p.   cm.
    ISBN 0-8091-3519-1 (pbk.)
        1. Monastic and religious life.   2. Monasticism and religious orders—
United States.   I. Philibert, Paul J.
    BX2435.L58   1994
    255-dc20

                                                                              94-19036
                                                                                    CIP

Published by Paulist Press
997 Macarthur Boulevard
Mahwah, NJ 07430

Printed and bound in the
United States of America

Contents

iii

PART THREE: FACING THE SIGNS OF THE TIMES

This book is dedicated
to the Sinai generation of American religious men and women
(who made profession before 1965),
who believed in the promise of a new covenant
and walked by faith through the desert places
that opened up before us following Vatican II:
prophetarum choro decet honor et gloria!

Acknowledgments

The idea for a book on religious life drawn from the valuable contributions of speakers at recent annual assemblies of the Conference of Major Superiors of Men and the Leadership Conference of Women Religious came from Paul Hennessy, C.F.C., who was president of CMSM from 1991-93. As we discussed the possibility of preparing such a volume, we both thought immediately of precise contributions which ought to be included, and commented on their relevance to this moment just before the Roman Synod of Bishops meeting in November, 1994, when the bishops will address the status of the consecrated life in the church. I am happy to express my gratitude to Paul Hennessy who encouraged this work and who followed it with interest throughout its preparation. In addition, I acknowledge with pleasure the cooperation of Gregory Reisert, O.F.M.Cap., Executive Director of CMSM, and of Margaret Cafferty, P.B.V.M., Executive Director of LCWR, who encouraged the project.

The authors whose work is printed here have cooperated in helping me to indicate the underlying unity of essays that were prepared at different times and for different contexts than the immediate present. I thank them all, especially Mary Margaret Funk, Richard Sipe, and Archbishop Weakland, who created new material that is presented here to complement the essays that came from CMSM and LCWR conventions.

Mary Collins, O.S.B., Joseph Gallagher, Paul Hennessy, C.F.C., Robert A. Krieg, C.S.C., Patricia Livingston, and Joseph Payne, O.P., all read portions of the manuscript with critical care and offered important suggestions for its improvement. In the name of the authors of these essays, I express my sincere thanks. Dennis McManus, my editor at Paulist Press, has been a judicious and encouraging force for many months, suggesting profitable ideas for the development of the project and providing me with good critical response throughout the growth of the book. I could not have asked for a more sensitive and effective editor for the project.

Barbara Dudley and Judy Rhoades, my administrative assistants at the Institute for Church Life at the University of Notre Dame, have ably made their way through numerous revisions of the manuscript with enthusiasm and good cheer. There would be no book without them. I am happy to express my thanks.

The Lilly Endowment, Inc., of Indianapolis made a grant to support the production costs of this volume. I acknowledge this gift as an ex-

viii   *Acknowledgments*

pression of their interest in the future of religious life and a gesture of continuity with their support over many years for projects of research and education to enable the graceful evolution of committed Christian community life and service. I am happy to express my gratitude to Sister Jeanne Knoerle, S.P., Dr. Craig Dykstra, and their colleagues at Lilly for the important assistance from this grant in making this book accessible to a much wider audience.

Finally, I express my appreciation to the University of Notre Dame and to my colleagues in the Institute for Church Life who have provided both helpful resources for the execution of this project, and kind collegial support.

Contributors

LUISE AHRENS, M.M., is engaged in university work at the University of Phnom Penh in Cambodia where she assists the Vice-Rector for Language and Social Sciences. She was President of the Maryknoll Mission Sisters Congregation from 1985 to 1991.

MARGARET BRENNAN, I.H.M., is professor emerita of pastoral theology at Regis College in Toronto and a former president of LCWR. She is a frequent lecturer on the theology of religious life.

MARY COLLINS, O.S.B., is Professor of Liturgical Studies in the Department of Religion and Religious Education at the Catholic University of America. She is co-editor of *The New Dictionary of Theology* (Glazier, 1989) and of several books and many articles.

MARY MARGARET FUNK, O.S.B., is Executive Director of the Monastic Interreligious Dialogue and a member of the Board of Trustees of Contemplative Outreach; she teaches Centering Prayer. She was the prioress of Our Lady of Grace Monastery in Beech Grove, Ind., from 1985 to 1993.

HOWARD J. GRAY, S.J., is director of the Tertianship program for the Detroit province of the Society of Jesus, a former provincial superior of that province, and a frequent lecturer and writer on the theology of religious life.

PAUL HENNESSY, C.F.C., was president of CMSM from 1991-93; he concluded an eight-year term as provincial of the Christian Brothers in 1993. He was for many years professor of theology at Iona College.

DONNA MARKHAM, O.P., is director of the Southdown Center, a therapeutic facility for religious and priests, near Toronto. She was president of LCWR in 1991-92 and a member of the leadership team of the Adrian Dominican Sisters for six years.

PAUL J. PHILIBERT, O.P., is director of the Institute for Church Life and concurrent Associate Professor of Theology at the University of Notre

Dame. He concluded five years as prior provincial of the Southern Province of the Order of Preachers in 1993.

SEAN SAMMON, F.M.S., is Vicar General of the Marist Brothers of the Schools and resides in Rome. He was president of CMSM from 1989 to 1991. He is author of *An Undivided Heart* (Alba House, 1993) and *Alcoholism's Children* (Alba House, 1989) and *Growing Pains in Ministry* (Twenty-Third Publications, 1983).

R. KEVIN SEASOLTZ, O.S.B., is a monk of St. John's Abbey and professor of theology in St. John's University, Collegeville, Mn. He is editor of *Worship*, a journal of liturgical theology, and author of several books and many articles.

DONALD SENIOR, C.P., is president of the Catholic Theological Union in Chicago. He is the author of a four volume study of the Passion of Jesus in the Four Gospels (Glazier, 1984-91) and of many books and articles on sacred scripture.

A. W. RICHARD SIPE is a practicing psychotherapist who holds an appointment as instructor in psychiatry at Johns Hopkins University School of Medicine. He has taught on the faculties of three Catholic major seminaries from 1967 to 1984. His book, *A Secret World: Sexuality and the Search for Celibacy* (Brunnner/Mazel, 1990), is an ethnographic study of the practice, process, and achievement of clerical celibacy.

REMBERT G. WEAKLAND, O.S.B., the Archbishop of Milwaukee, is former Abbot General of the Order of St. Benedict and former Abbot of St. Vincent Archabbey, Latrobe, Pa. Archbishop Weakland chaired the NCCB committee that produced the Bishops' Economic Pastoral.

Editor's Introduction

Paul J. Philibert, O.P.

In the Fall of 1994, the Roman Synod of Bishops will address the topic of "Institutes of the Consecrated Life and the Apostolic Life." One certain effect of the synod will be to draw added attention to the status of religious orders and congregations. As a recent statement of the Conference of Major Superiors of Men said, "This is an occasion for hope that the Synod's examination of the status of renewal and the prospects for future growth of religious institutes will be a moment of grace and revitalization, of benefit to religious and to the whole church."[1]

The discussion of what constitutes authentic renewal is an important topic, not only for religious themselves but for the whole church. American religious have been courageous and creative in addressing the renovation of their apostolates, the restructuring of their religious formation, and the updating of the elements of their community life. Yet not all religious institutes are in accord about what stance to take relative to the transformation of their life and mission. The heightened attention given by the synod provides a moment in which some clarification of the core issues for renewal of religious life should be welcome.

The value of the papers collected in this present volume needs to be assessed in this context. Most of the chapters of this book were presented at conventions of The Leadership Conference of Women Religious (LCWR) or The Conference of Major Superiors of Men (CMSM) in recent years. I have chosen to seek their publication at this time because they appear to me to articulate well both the vision behind the renewal that has shaped the life of the majority of American religious as well as the prospects for the future evolution of religious life within North America. It is important at this moment to articulate as clearly as possible the nature of the renewal that the majority of American religious have set about achieving and to explain the reasons for the journey of *aggiornamento* that they have begun.

1

SEEKING TO UNDERSTAND THE CULTURAL DIMENSION

Religious life has a long history, made more complex by the fact that it has functioned variously in different localities and in different eras. Today we find religious life expressed in a spectrum of cultural forms and ecclesial activities that reaches from the one extreme of Carthusian hermit monks and cloistered nuns to the other extreme of apostolic societies of priests, brothers, and sisters whose very sense of corporate life is solidarity in support of a specific apostolic work. We have some institutes whose focus is fundamentally upon the spiritual evolution in contemplative discipline of the individual religious, and others whose focus is over-ridingly apostolic. We have orders with roots in the sixth century and others founded mere decades ago. Yet, despite this awesome diversity, it is still helpful to reflect upon some cultural characteristics that have helped to shape the experience of all of them.

CULTURAL ORIENTATION AT THE START

The first wave of religious life was characterized by a theme of with-drawal from the world—"world" in the Johannine sense of that which is unable to be responsive to the transforming power of the gospel. The desert fathers and mothers are a key example. Athanasius, in his life of St. Anthony, tells us that Anthony was moved to flee into the Thebaid when he heard preaching upon the gospel word, "What good is it for [persons] to gain the whole world, yet forfeit [their] soul?" (Mk 8:36)[2] From one point of view, the desert ascetics lost interest in the "world"—i.e., in business, family, power, money, property—because the real challenge for them was doing combat with the Evil One. Wrestling with the devil, as Jesus did in his forty days of fasting and temptation, was the prototypical spiritual combat. None of the desert ascetics set out to open up schools of spiritual instruction. Radical asceticism was in the air. Success bred fame; fame bred followers.

Once cenobitic (community-based) monasticism became dominant and, in the West, the Benedictine rule became the chief strain of the cenobitic life, monasticism undertook other roles. It exported faith by establishing monasteries in foreign lands. It preserved learning by teach-ing reading for the sake of *lectio divina.* It modeled a pattern of cultural order and productivity in a world torn by barbarism. The monastery was the safe harbor of peace that became the repository of art, wisdom, and technology, all the while remaining marginal to the centers of money and power in the medieval world.

The posture of the monastic existence was that of the "radical Christian," who opts for Christ and the gospel and sees all else as relatively insignificant.[3] Indeed, in the interpretation of H. Richard Niebuhr's *Christ and Culture*,[4] the radical Christian makes the rejection of secular society the counterpart of loyalty to Christ. Secular society stands for the threat of sensuality, materialism, and egotism seen as an obstacle to the embrace of the gospel. The emphasis of radical Christianity on a definite posture in behavior and action in support of the gospel tends to lead to the elaboration of precise rules, a spirit of conformity, and an expectation of heroic exertions for the sake of the gospel.[5] The radical Christian needs to create an alternative world of order and goodness within a wider world of chaos and perversity.

It is a tribute to the achievements and the cultural success of monasticism that, despite countless changes of context and pastoral needs, the core structure and attitudes of monastic spirituality continued to mark all forms of religious life in many ways through the course of centuries. In the High Middle Ages, clerics regular and mendicants responded to the church's new need for preaching and pastoral work in the emerging urban centers. Yet these groups, such as the Premonstratensians, Franciscans and Dominicans, retained an essentially monastic community and choir life.

Later apostolic orders, at the time of the Counter-Reformation and after, responded to the church's need for teachers, missionaries, and entrepreneurs of healing and social work and care for the poor. Still, for the most part, each new institute maintained a certain isolation from the Catholic public at large and nourished its members on traditionally monastic exercises like the chapter of faults, reading at table, and the great silence. The traditional shape for all forms of religious life was essentially monastic, at least in terms of spirituality and models of religious formation.

THE DAYS OF AGGIORNAMENTO

When Vatican II occurred, many religious felt that a rethinking of the cultural expressions of religious life was long overdue. They read these lines of the Council's Decree on the Renewal of Religious Life as an invitation to clean house—or renovate the structure:

> The appropriate renewal of religious life involves two simultaneous processes: (1) a continuous return to the sources of all Christian life and to the original inspiration behind a given community and (2) an adjustment of the community to the changed conditions of the times.[6]

The early days after the council were marked by polarization in the American church. There was a power struggle in many religious institutes between those who feared and avoided change, and those eager to move ahead into the process of renewal. Despite the openness of the norms of *Perfectae Caritatis*, there were many voices anxious to insist on the limits to change—most often expressed as limits to cultural expressions of dress, rites, and life-style. A great many talented potential leaders left religious life in the late 1960s and early 1970s because they feared that their bishops and major superiors would stonewall genuine and substantive renewal out of fear of losing control of the enterprise. It was not an easy time.

American religious, especially women religious, recognized that the norms of the council for renewal of religious life would carry us far beyond superficial changes of modified habits and adjusted horarium. *Pacem in Terris*[7] and *Gaudium et Spes*[8] had underlined the theme of the "signs of the times," including the specific acknowledgment that the promotion of women into new roles and positions of leadership in modern society was such a "sign" of God's continuing creation at work in our present-day world. It is not too surprising, then, that professional education and higher administrative responsibilities would become a priority for women religious in response to these prophetic norms.

In cultural terms, this post-conciliar period represents in many ways a swing of the pendulum away from the stance of the "anti-cultural radical Christian" to its opposite "culture Christian" position. Again, citing Niebuhr, culture Christians "feel no great tension between the church and world, the social laws and the Gospel, the workings of divine grace and human effort, the ethics of salvation and... progress."[9] Christ is identified with what the culture conceives to be its highest ideals.

In the United States, this swing to culture Christianity coincided with Lyndon Johnson's "Great Society" and later with the countercultural movement in opposition to the Vietnam War. The efforts of religious to achieve social justice were fed by two streams: a renewed appreciation for the apostolic roots of our institutes and a cultural sympathy for social reform felt by many liberal thinkers. It is interesting to note that many religious, having once repositioned themselves in socially engaged and challenging ministries, no longer felt any need to stay affiliated with their institutes. The work was everything, and community living paled by comparison.

A liberal and optimistic reception of the reforms of Vatican II coincided with a deep-felt concern for massive social change in U.S. society on the part of many religious in their thirties and forties. Finding themselves allied against a massive power block of conservative bishops and reactionary superiors led many in such situations to abandon ship. The fact that there were notable exceptions in such ecclesiastical luminaries as Archbishop Hallinan, Cardinal Sheehan and Cardinal Dearden, who were architects of orderly church reform, only made the situation of being caught in a reactionary power structure the more untenable. There is no impatience more urgent than that of those who imagine themselves to be on the threshold of a utopia.

Those were also the days of "the greening of America"[10]—the celebration of the alternative wisdom which young Americans were purportedly finding in earthy hedonism, drugs, massage, meditation, and Eastern philosophy. If one read "renewal" and "adaptation to the new conditions of our times" as a serious mandate, then it was easy to see how a degree of naiveté entered into the pursuit of renewal. Alas, some replaced the old Puritanism of "holier than thou" with the new Puritanism of "trendier than thou." People who are convinced that an entirely new utopian culture is inexorably emerging will label most efforts to preserve tradition as legalism, formalism, and escapism. It was during these days that lines of communication broke down between liberals and conservatives, between those for whom tradition was the marrow of their institutes' bones and those who rebelled against the imposition of otherworldly cultural accretions upon their communal and apostolic life.

It is a wonder, in retrospect, that so little disciplined dialogue has taken place in these past thirty years between "radicals" and "culturists," since both emerged from the same socio-religious origins. The incivility of public discourse in America in general, and the practice of demonizing ideological enemies encouraged by two decades of polarizing presidential leadership, modeled poorly how to address cultural differences. This makes the need for genuine dialogue still a reality if mutual understanding and healing are to follow hostility and suspicion.

The culture Christian period produced many good fruits, however. It was in great part due to the culturist posture of renewal that commitments to social justice marked so much of the energies of religious in the 1970s and 1980s. As people who took culture seriously, religious culture Christians also became vocal critics of the inadequacy of traditional secular social structures (notably cultural blindness to poverty, to immigrants, and to structural injustice to women in employment and economic benefits).[11]

Another positive contribution of the culturist period has been its openness to the new spirits of the late twentieth century. This has been a period that has witnessed an explosion of interest in spirituality and an explosion of concern for the environment. Good, enduring scholarly and pastoral work has been done, inspired by the posture of the culture Christian, in exploring the significance of the mystical heritage of our

Christian past as well as convergences between Asian spiritual traditions and our own.

Thomas Merton was the literary voice of this period, fusing both spiritual and social concerns in writings which challenged the established positions of leaders in both church and society. An American school of Catholic theology emerged which was grounded in serious research in the church's tradition but which had a practical and pragmatic edge to it as well. The moral writings of Charles Curran are a notable example. Spiritual writing marked by theological depth and appealing personal conviction came from the pens of Henri Nouwen, John Powell, and many others. A broad cultural interest in meditation was represented by excellent studies on centering prayer by Basil Pennington and Thomas Keating.

A new sense of solidarity with those who risk being marginalized by their differences—victims of AIDs, homosexuals and lesbians, new immigrants, and others whose human rights are jeopardized—marks the concerns of many religious. At present, the openness of religious institutes to the collaboration of laity not only as coworkers in ministry, but also as partakers of the spiritual heritage and charism of the religious institute, is a distinctive frontier of the ongoing evolution of religious life in our country.

But vital as many of these phenomena have been (and are), it appears fair to say that the "culture Christian" stance has not succeeded in elaborating a viable model of religious living. The weight of thirty years of renewal has borne upon the revitalization of ministries, while the domestic culture of religious community living has paid the price of neglect. Today there are some religious who are eminently successful at apostolic work, whose memories of their religious formation days are so bitter that they hope never again to live in community.

We are now seeing for the first time the phenomenon of aging religious who, having lived and worked apart for twenty years, are now being invited to come back into a religious house to feel at home again before their age and infirmity forces them to become dependent upon members of their institute for care in their last days. Because of the emphasis given by religious to the renewal of apostolic works in these past thirty years, the renewal of their forms of conversation, worship, and mutual service in the average local community has been mediocre. In my view, this is a signal of our need for a new moment. The "culturist" stance will not be the source for this needed evolution. We must look elsewhere.

An argument is nothing more than an attempt to understand and to explain. In matters as complex as this discussion, the best one can do is to open a path and follow it through. By mining many sources of reflection (including renewal of biblical understanding), the culturist attempted to demonstrate the incongruity of the radicalist position that one must renounce one's culture in order to save it. Yet the mainstream of the postconciliar renewal period—described here as the age of the religious as culture Christian—in some ways demonstrated the non-viability of the cultural model as well.

The Catholic Church's public voice is stronger today than it was in the 1950s as a result of the toil for relevant interaction with our society that has occupied so many of us for three decades. The troubling issue for most religious today is not apostolic relevance. That, for the most part, has been gained. There is still need to assure broad acceptance by the clergy of women's new roles as professionals in pastoral service. But the key issue now is supportive community life shared in obedience to the gospel, seen as an end in itself—or at least as an end equal in nobility to the apostolic mission.

THE GRIP OF NOSTALGIA

Not every aspect of the topic of renewal of religious life is out in the open. A reality that continues to be a factor in discussions about renewal is the tenacity of an old-fashioned vision of the very meaning of religious life.

Older Roman Catholics (and observers of Catholics) often cling to a deeply entrenched image of religious life that is linked to their early experiences of the church in this country. In their imagination, religious are a phalanx of somewhat odd, alien creatures decked out in black serge and starched white linen, marching in dimly lighted corridors with military precision, rapt in otherworldly silence. Formerly they could be depended upon to function as the backbone and key personnel of Catholic educational and service institutions.

This phantom brigade not only lived in a parallel universe, but was expected not to intrude upon ordinary events of family, neighborhood, workplace, or social networks. They were a band of "angels," safely fed and tended in their cloistered precincts, but whose insertion into the religious activities of the Catholic world was strategic to the church's prospering. This entrenched vision—sketchily described here—represents both the canonization of a certain nineteenth-century cultural phenomenon as well as an expression of resentment at the passing of an era of history and experience.

The odd, opposite face of the coin was the spirituality that developed in the Victorian age of religious culture, expressed in extreme form in the breviary meditations of Bishop Angrisani, who counseled priests to never let it be said that they returned from among the laity less a priest.[12] The same kind of segregation for a superior level of sanctification was held essential for the culture of religious life.

In part, this was the translation of old-world customs into the context of new-world apostolates. Many of the religious institutes that have thrived in the United States came here at the invitation of this country's first generation of bishops, who reached out to the homelands of their immigrant populations for pastoral workers to tend their ecclesial flock. It is not surprising that in this way the spiritual tendencies of these European congregations were introduced not only into apostolic work but also into religious formation here.

The majority of religious living in the church today are members of religious congregations that were founded in the nineteenth century. Two factors which contributed to their foundation were the persecution of older religious orders by the French revolutionaries (and by other northern European governments) and the missionary outreach of the church to new lands and new opportunities for evangelization. Cultural and historical changes since then have substantially modified the context of religious service and the models of Christian holiness claimed by religious today.

Recently, a friend who is an American religious woman said to me that she still remembers how confusing it was, at the time of her entry into religious life, to feel that she was obliged first to become a Bavarian peasant before she could become an authentic Sister of her order. In my view this issue of culture is very much a part of the present transition in religious life.

Although nostalgia for the colorful pageant of religious regalia and cheap apostolic labor is strong, it fails to take into account other images that belong to privileged moments of the history of religious life. A different perspective on the enterprise of religious life emerges when we meditate upon Francis Bernadone stripped naked before his wealthy family, taking a baggy tunic of sackcloth to show his contempt for dress; upon Matteo Ricci inserting himself into the traditions of Chinese manners and culture to dispel the fear that evangelization by these Western visitors meant intrusion upon the indigenous mores of an ancient culture; upon today's missioners camping with the poorest of the poor in Latin American barrios to share life as a context for sharing gospel hope; and upon Henri Le Saux and Bede Griffiths adopting prayer forms and monastic routines of the ancient Hindu world to enter into a dialogue of profound openness with one of the world's oldest traditions of contemplative discipline. Clearly, the need to put religious life in a broader cultural perspective than the vestiges of nineteenth-century religious customs is a valid exercise of searching for understanding.

THE TRANSFORMIST CHALLENGE

We stand at the edge of a frontier. What lies beyond is as yet unclear. Phrases like "refounding" and "reweaving" religious life have served to articulate eloquent pleas for a reconsideration of the form of living that religious life constitutes.[13] Perhaps the image of "getting lost" will also evoke the meaning of this moment. "Radical Christian" religious appear to have gotten lost in the paraphernalia of their alternative world and become defensive about the relevance of their traditional approach to the consecrated life. "Culturists" appear to have gotten lost in their advocacy of apostolic endeavors and dropped the thread of witness to a privileged experience of intimacy with a God who calls us into anointed silence.

In July of 1989, the Leadership Conference of Women Religious and the Conference of Major Superiors of Men met in joint assembly in Louisville and engaged in a process of identifying and discussing the "transformative elements" that they imagined would shape religious life in the year 2010. This exercise was an effort to get the major superiors of religious women and men into a mode of envisaging the future in dialogue with one another. It also aimed at fostering a deeper realization of the limited resources that each institute must confront and the awareness that we must fulfill our vocation and charism within these given limits.

It is noteworthy that two dominant themes of the transformative elements were contemplation and charism. The contemplative posture of religious men and women was perceived to be a cultural witness to the hectic society in which we live and work. More important, it was recognized to be at the heart of our authenticity as vowed religious in continuity with our institutes' history and achievements.

The functioning of charism was seen in terms of its fruitfulness for the church universal. The transformative elements speak of "liberating" and "reappropriating" our charisms. This effectively means setting them free to become engaged in unpredictable ways with the needs and possibilities of our own moment of history. The theme of the "transformist challenge," then, has roots in one of the more memorable moments of significant collaboration of American religious men and women in recent years.[14]

The transformist challenge is energized by new phenomena in the Catholic world as well. For twenty-five years, lay Catholics living ordinary lives with their families have supplied energies and talent that formerly would have come from the parish clergy and from religious brothers, sisters and priests. A noteworthy example of this phenomenon are the ranks of Directors of Religious Education in parish service throughout the country. In addition, we have long taken it for granted that those providing weekly religious education to our young people in the parish setting will be for the most part dedicated and interested lay members of the parish community. Closer to the point of the evolution of religious life, however, is the matter of the proliferation of lay associate groups as apostolic and fraternal support systems for religious institutes.

Since the High Middle Ages, there have been lay affiliates of religious orders—so-called "third orders"—whose relation to the institute has varied considerably through the ages. "Oblates" or "lay claustral brothers or sisters" have been a part of Benedictine life for an even longer time. In these cases, persons who for various reasons either could not or did not wish to become vowed religious living in a monastic setting, nonetheless entered the family of the institute as (for want of a better phrase) "canonical cousins." Sometimes their affiliation was specifically sought by the community to serve a function unavailable from members of the community, such as overseers of properties or liaison with the non-cloistered world. In other cases, such persons were following a "second career," entering a more dedicated existence after raising a family or the like.

Today the thrust is different. Many religious perceive themselves to be midwives of a new ecclesial reality. Papal teaching in this century has stressed the apostolic action of the laity. From the phrase "Catholic action" (common to the 1920s and 1930s), to Vatican II's description of laity as "witness and instrument of the mission of the church,"[15] to Pope John Paul's call for laity to "evangelize the culture,"[16] the common thread has been an insistence upon the apostolic potency of the Christian life of lay faithful. In addition, *Lumen Gentium*[17] taught the importance of recognizing the "universal call to holiness" of all the baptized. These two theological teachings, however, lay apostolic mission and a lay call to holiness, represent paradigm shifts—at least for popular Catholic thinking. It was widely believed before the council that these two themes were what identified persons as religious, as opposed to laity.

While the Second Vatican Council uncovered the theological treasure of a new expression of the meaning of the Christian life, it left to the activity of living believers the elaboration of the sociological and institutional realities that could embody this vision. If religious today serve the role of midwives, then, it is precisely to bring to birth the social and institutional forms that can enable the laity to embrace the call to mission and to holiness.

NEW LAY ASSOCIATIONS

I find it tremendously interesting that many lay apostolic associations have been formed in recent decades to open up the treasure of a dedicated Christian life to new clientele and to new cultural expressions. In Italy, the Community of Sant Egidio is a lay apostolic movement embracing as members both married and celibate persons. In Italy, also, there is the Focolare movement, which demands the living of the evangelical counsels, but for the sake of new forms of insertion in secular contexts. There is the international society of L'Eau Vive, religious women of Carmelite inspiration, who catechize in a context of offering lodging and meals to pilgrims and travelers. In France, several groups, like the Association de Cluny—a lay consecrated group of men and women who live in community for the sake of offering exemplary community experiences in villages throughout the world—have sprung up and are recruiting more successfully than most religious institutes. In the cases just mentioned, liturgical piety and the pursuit of a deep spirituality are joined to richly creative and artistic expressions of common life and prayer.

We find ourselves in the predicament of passing on the charism of our institutes to a new generation of apostolic Catholics without requiring them to go through the same cultural initiation that would insert them into our corporate life. Some significant transformation of religious structures appears needed to respond to our new circumstances.

Let us compare the options. The "anti-cultural radical" stance tends to solve cultural problems by following the instinct to create an alternative world, segregated and sanctified, as the forum for common life and apostolate. The "culturist" stance is preoccupied with relevance in terms of the culture's own agenda and standards and is thus pushed into a preoccupation with action and apostolic goals that appear to meet the culture's needs. A new alternative "transformist" position would insist that we can no longer indulge a radical escapist tendency or an overemphasis upon apostolic focus. Our religious charisms as treasuries of living spirituality must be viable within our culture but also faithful to their origins. To some degree, that is what we see happening in the new forms of community that are arising in so many places around the world.

A prominent reality which faces us now is the growing hunger for spiritual nourishment among lay Christians. While many religious have lived for decades in reaction against the legalism and empty formalism of religious formation from the time before the Second Vatican Council, their reaction was also a rejection of centuries-old means of corporate identification and spiritual development: daily mental prayer, silence, *lectio divina,* chapter of faults (or—in renewed form—house meetings for spiritual growth). Despite resentment and bad memories of some about early formation that appeared to demand pointless subjugation of the intelligence and will of religious to their superiors, religious must ground their authenticity in spiritual experience that is developed by traditional patterns of prayer and discipline.

The heart and soul of religious life is intimacy with God. As the council phrased it: "... as [religious] seek God before all things and only [God], the members of each community should combine contemplation with apostolic love."[18] The renewal of the contemplative dimension of religious life will be a key factor in the transformist challenge for the future. The sense of how a contemplative life should be lived, however, is quite different today from some decades ago. Ideas from Eastern spirituality and from Hindu and Buddhist monastic traditions, as well as insights from twentieth-century communitarian movements, promise to extend the boundaries of sharing of Catholic monastic communities.

Too often the rejection by religious of traditional observances was followed by an uncritical appropriation of media and recreational distractions from the popular culture. This means that we now need a serious and creative project of critically examining the dehumanizing and de-Christianizing elements of the media and the popular culture. It means applying the genius of talented leaders to the discovery of life-giving expressions of the interior life appropriate to our new cultural possibilities. It means orientating energy, conversation, and accountability by religious to attend to this dimension, making it a much higher priority than it has been in recent decades. And it will mean that some—still in reaction against their preconciliar formation—will have to grow beyond their reactive resentment and be guided less by their fading psychohistory than by the future of their evolving and self-renewing institutes.

All this is still vague. Only living out the mystery of God's call today will produce the viable reality. Contrary to our customary way of thinking in our highly rational contemporary culture, "rules" are not *a priori* plans for a possible future, but the distillation of the shared reality of common life. The transformist frontier that I have evoked here is the object of consideration of the authors whose chapters follow in this volume. Using different images and different categories, each in some way is talking about crossing the border between radical and culturist options and moving beyond into a new life of transformist possibilities.

It would be wrong for readers to imagine that I favor a "back to the drawing board" approach to renewal. For institutes that are in some cases centuries old, it would be a great naiveté to imagine that the spiritual wisdom of the last decade of the twentieth century is somehow superior to that of previous ages. The most basic fact about religious life in the Catholic Church is its multiplicity and diversity. The dynamics of monastic groups will be considerably different from those of apostolic groups. The role of the spiritual heritage of a founder or of the writers and theologians of an institute will vary from case to case. But, given that inescapable diversity, some fundamental challenges will remain common to all groups. It is these that I am concerned to describe.

SPECIAL CONSIDERATIONS

By chance, I happened to attend Sunday mass at a large Trappist abbey on the very day that I was sketching out my ideas for this essay. For more than twenty-five years, I have visited this monastery from time to time at irregular intervals—in part because it is near to where friends live. As before, I was pleased and moved by the beauty of the liturgy, the intelligent adaptation of the chants to English with new musical compositions in the ancient Gregorian modes, and the ethos of eternity that is symbolized by so many details of an ancient form of monastic life.

In the last few years, I have noted an interesting change. Laity are welcomed into the monastic enclosure and sanctuary area for the eucharist, bringing them closer to the liturgical action and linking them symbolically with the monks' community at prayer. I remember years ago having to climb up high into a remote tribune in the back of the abbey church to watch the eucharist from a distance.

The new arrangement was a great change, then, for this monastic household. At the same time, I noted that the monks have withdrawn a bit more into their cloistered environment. Visitors are not so easily allowed to visit within the monastery buildings as before. The core dimensions of their life—penance, recollection, an environment of continual prayer—have come again more clearly to the fore. I went away feeling that the monks had chosen carefully and well how to relate themselves more realistically to the world that comes visiting.

This anecdote helps me to explain an important message about the whole challenge that lies before American religious at this threshold to a "transformist" future. I don't imagine that the forms of religious life of the future will be any more homogeneous than they have been heretofore. Contemplative life will continue to be a special example of consecrated discipleship.

While I think that contemplative religious need to think through the same challenges as others, their call and their style will be distinct. What they contribute to the witness of the Christian life is the fruit of their unusual environment of reflective silence. Their way of being open to the new impulses toward mission and holiness among the laity will be decidedly different from the way of active, apostolic religious. Yet they, too, will have to sort out the excesses of "radicalist" formalism and possible deviations of "culturalist" trendiness. My point, however, is that the church will always need their witness to intimacy with a God who beguiles us into listening in silence and peering into the darkness.

It is also true that the authenticity of apostolic zeal is manifest in fruitful contemplative prayer. While the context of their prayer is different from that of contemplatives, apostolic religious also derive their spiritual sustenance from contemplation. It is interesting to note as well the apostolic fervor of a contemplative like St. Thérèse of Lisieux whose thoughts and prayers were focused so frequently on the activity of foreign missionaries.

Other forms of life, such as that of the small communities of the Little Brothers and Little Sisters of Jesus of Charles de Foucauld, attest to what is essentially a ministry and witness of presence. Like the Brothers of Taizé, this form of life finds its most dynamic exchange with the surrounding world through sensitive and generous moments of hospitality. Their unusual life refracts the light of our common calling so that we can see the potential for all forms of religious life to renew themselves in hospitality. Again, this is hospitality as an instrument of faith and conversion. These religious open up their houses, their chapels, their moments of prayer, and their conversation to bear witness to their own vulnerability to God's Holy Spirit.

"The problem of culture is . . . the problem of its conversion, not of its replacement by a new creation; though the conversion is so radical that it amounts to a kind of rebirth."[19] The transformist religious does not center upon a cultural superego dating to the origins of the institute's foundation, nor upon the expectations of the popular culture. Rather, the transformist faces squarely the available reality of this moment and the "signs of the times" as these can be hesitantly discerned within the chaos of the world. God is not withdrawing from the church the gift of a dedicated or consecrated life, described in the preaching of Jesus and received in so many different ways through the centuries. But God may be calling us to reshape its cultural configurations in ways that are surprising. That, at least, is my conclusion. Within such a perspective, there is energy and hope.

Tolerance or enthusiasm for change of the kinds described will vary considerably, depending upon the history and spirit of the institute in question and depending as well upon the pressures for survival. Many religious are experiencing a severe crisis in recruitment. Some appear to be facing their institutional demise. A comparison of the response of the American bishops to the vocations crisis with that of most religious institutes gives food for thought. Many bishops appear to be still in denial of the reality or the dimensions of the vocations crisis. Religious by and large have begun to assess their options for maintaining their apostolic mission even in the face of declining numbers of vowed members.

The point of my reflection in these pages is not to advocate an ideological position, as though somehow I could persuade readers that a vast institutional transformation of religious life-style was philosophically or culturally desirable. The point, rather, is to face up to and respond to the shifting currents of events. This can be done only if we are able to understand them better than we have in the recent past.

The cultural analysis which I propose here is an effort to provide perspective. We can see to what degree we are still instinctively dependent upon ancient cultural forms—some of which may be anthropologically congenial for any age or culture, but others of which may be effective obstacles to our wholehearted response to the *kairos* (the graced genius) of this particular moment of the church's life.

This very point is worthy of extended discussion—something not reasonable to attempt in this focused context. But sooner or later, decisions about cultural reality mature, i.e., they ripen to the point that something must be done about them. Just as I believe that the church may finally suffer from the denial that has characterized some responses to the vocations crisis, so also do I believe that special graces of guidance will be given to those dioceses and institutes that acknowledge the shape of available reality. Grace will allow us to open our hearts to respond to what is really before us, rather than manipulate things in an effort to maintain past solutions.

A precious heritage is at stake, of course. It is an agonizing judgment to decide that some aspect of an ancient order of life is no longer viable as it was lived by generations of sisters or brothers of one's institute. Yet it is not impossible that we have an agenda of deferred maintenance now laid upon our shoulders and that business as usual just cannot be sustained.

THE PROJECT OF THE BOOK

In turning to the contents of this book, I can offer you a variety of rich expressions of the new vision and the new hope which I have called the "transformist option" for religious life. In Part One, Sean Sammon describes a more hopeful way to imagine the three decades of "renewal" that have occupied us since the council. He notes that it has taken substantial effort for us to arrive at the point of even perceiving what the true agenda for renewal may be.

Howard Gray offers perspective to superiors (especially major superiors) about where their energies belong. In a time of profound change, it is all too easy for administrators to spend all their time tidying up, managing the chaos. He clearly explains *why* this can't be the approach for today.

Part Two is devoted to spelling out "the form of life" that is religious life. Donald Senior's powerful reflection on the biblical roots of religious life shows us that our fundamental challenge from the word of God is not to refine our legal understandings of the vows, but to appropriate a vision of life "in the meantime." Kevin Seasoltz explains the fundamental meaning of religious obedience as the radical listening of the whole community to the word of God as a source of life and a call to fruitful witness. Luise Ahrens puts poverty into the perspective not of asceticism, but rather of generous response to God's call and of functional availability to the apostolic mission.

Richard Sipe offers helpful insights into the gradual process of becoming celibate—an inescapable project for everyone who receives a celibate vocation. My own essay on celibacy and prayer compares the parallel between the discipline required to enter into the ineffable mystery of prayer and the discipline needed to orientate one's affective life to the reality of God's love, and the implications of this for religious consciousness. Mary Margaret Funk reports on a study done of women monastics and their efforts to reappropriate their Benedictine tradition in terms of present-day realities.

Part Three attempts to sketch out some of the guideposts for the future development of religious life. Margaret Brennan expands the understanding of what religious life and apostolate contribute to a world with so many social and moral ambiguities, and how religious perform a service of moral witness that is decisive in many ways. Donna Markham addresses the qualities of successful religious communities and holds that an essential quality is their capacity to shed light and hope on the humanity of those who need support in finding community in an alienating society.

Paul Hennessy addresses the issue of charism and charges us not to think of this "gift" as a possession to be hoarded by those who at present preside over the religious institutes that embody the charism historically, but to actively seek to share the charism in religiously and apostolically fruitful ways in the broader Catholic world. Mary Collins addresses one central question touching the alienation that many women religious experience in Catholic sacramental life, and proposes a theological challenge to lead us beyond the pain of the present. Archbishop Weakland contributes a summary review of the renewal of religious life in the United

States since Vatican II—a helpful assessment by a distinguished American archbishop who is himself a religious.

In addition to the general sense that our title, *Living in the Meantime*, has for the whole Christian world, clearly here it applies as well to this moment of transformation that I have been attempting to describe in this introduction. But now it is time to turn to the illuminating contributions of our authors. In the maps that follow may all of us who are living in the meantime find helpful indications of where we are going.

NOTES

1. CMSM, "Religious Orders Amid Cultural Realities," *Origins* 22:42 (Apr. 1, 1993), 724.

2. St. Athanasius, *The Life of Saint Anthony* (Westminster, Md.: Newman Press, 1950).

3. John Boswell's study of the "oblation" of children in the High Middle Ages offers a telling perspective on the flexibility and variability of monastic culture in differing times and places. See John Boswell, *The Kindness of Strangers: the Abandonment of Children in Western Europe from Late Antiquity to the Renaissance* (New York: Pantheon, 1988), ch. 8. "Oblation," i.e., the turning over of children to the care and service of the church, "accounted for a high proportion of monks from the tenth through the end of the eleventh century, and only began to decline in the twelfth" (297). Boswell cites Constable's study of Cluny in the first half of the eleventh century where "boys constituted between a third and a fifth of the whole community" (297 n. 4). Peter the Venerable, an abbot of Cluny, "himself an oblate, forbade further reception at Cluny without express permission of the abbot, because of the great number—practically a majority, he felt—of peasants, infants, old men, and mental defectives the monastery had been receiving" (299). Ulrich of Cluny, half a century before Peter, complained that the monastery had been wrongly used by greedy parents who "commit to monasteries any hump-backed, deformed, dull or unpromising children they have . . ." (cf. *Patrologiae cursus completus*, ed. J.P. Migne, Series latina [Paris: 1844-55], 149.635-36; in Boswell, 298). Note here that this "use" of the monastery as a refuge for the unfit and the unwanted is a sort of demonstration of one aspect of the "radical" Christian posture, viz., the creation of a separate, sacralized world which operates mythically as a space outside ordinary considerations of utility and social convention.

On the other hand, some monasteries became the protégés of royalty or of the nobility who gave their abbots or abbesses privileged access to the court and abundant sources of wealth for libraries and monastic buildings. See David Knowles, *The Religious Orders in England* (Cambridge: University Press, 1959).

4. H. Richard Niebuhr, *Christ and Culture* (New York: Harper & Row, 1951), 47–48.

5. *Ibid.*, 79–80.

6. *The Documents of Vatican II*, Walter M. Abbott and Joseph Gallagher, eds. (New York: Guild Press, 1966): "Religious Life (*Perfectae Caritatis*)."

7. *L'enciclica "Pacem in Terris,"* Card. Pietro Pavan, ed. (Rome: Editiones Academiae Alphonsianae, 1988), 31. The Italian translation used the phrase "Segni dei tempi," known to be a formula chosen by Pope John XXIII, as the heading for §19. English translations replaced this formula with the phrase "the contemporary scene." See *Pacem in Terris: Peace on Earth* (New York: American Press, 1963), 13, §39.

8. See *The Documents of Vatican II*, "The Church Today," 201, §4: "... the church has always had the duty of scrutinizing the signs of the times...."

9. *Christ and Culture*, 83.

10. Charles A. Reich, *The Greening of America* (New York: Random House, 1970).

11. Note that in Niebuhr's account of culture and Christianity, it is the culturist tendency that is most sensitive to justice issues. See *Christ and Culture*, esp. 91–101. The culturist period of religious life saw a reawakening of the justice agenda as it resonates with the charism of most religious institutes. See note 14 below.

12. Joseph Angrisani, *Daily Breviary Meditations* (New York: Benziger Brothers, 1954), Vol. III: "If your foot wants to carry you to places of dissipation or to private homes, where your honor and sobriety have nothing to gain there, cut it off" (52); "You have divided your heart and your life between God and creatures: externally you preserve the garb of the priest, the name and functions; internally you are the slave of Satan and of creatures" (267); "Are we not forced to say that a priest's ruin is a foregone conclusion when, called as he is by nature to a life of sanctity, he shuts up and imprisons his high ideals with such narrow and material confines as are those that put him on a par with easy-going laymen...?" (414).

13. See, e.g., Gerald A. Arbuckle, S.M., *Out of Chaos: Refounding Religious Congregations* (New York: Paulist, 1988) and Mary Jo Leddy, *Reweaving Religious Life: Beyond the Liberal Model* (Mystic, Ct.: Twenty-Third Publications, 1990).

14. "Transformative Elements for Religious Life in the Future," developed by the 1989 Joint CMSM/LCWR Assembly in Louisville, KY. (private publication). The first five elements are: prophetic witness, contemplative attitudes toward life, poor and marginalized persons as the

focus of ministry, spirituality of wholeness and global interconnectedness, and charism and mission as sources of identity.

15. *The Documents of Vatican II,* "The Church," 60, §33.

16. John Paul II, *The Lay Members of Christ's Faithful People: Christi-
fideles Laici* (Boston: Daughters of St. Paul, 1989), §34.

17. *The Documents of Vatican II,* "The Church," 66, §40. Note that
the council explicitated that the commitment of religious life is rooted
in baptismal grace (§13, §44). The council's teaching is a critique of the
nineteenth-century ecclesiology that dominated the canons of the First
Vatican Council and that maintained the imagery of a church that was
hierarchically divided into more and less holy categories and roles. It
should be obvious that the development of lay roles for spiritual leadership and apostolic ministry flows from Vatican II's teachings. It should be
equally obvious that religious have a special opportunity, if not even a
responsibility, to assist laity to assume this leadership and ministry.

18. *The Documents of Vatican II,* "Religious Life," 470, §5.

19. *Christ and Culture,* 194. Let me recommend to those eager to
reflect more thoroughly upon the cultural analysis of this chapter that
they read carefully the whole of H. Richard Niebuhr's *Christ and Culture.*
Beyond this, it will be in the articles that follow that readers will find more
concrete expressions of possible renderings of a "transformist" incarnation
of religious life for days to come.

PART ONE:

Continuing Issues for Renewal

The Transformation of U. S. Religious Life

Sean Sammon, F.M.S.

What are the first fruits of any revolution? Surely not a sense of well-being and new order. In its early days, a revolution does little more than sweep away the old; it clears the ground for something new.

American men and women religious have learned that lesson well in recent years. Typical of those who survive an upheaval, they have suffered through days of uncertainty, confusion and loss; many now long for the freshness of a new order, a sense of direction and purpose, some hope for the future.

Antonio Gramsci captured well the present state of religious life in the U.S.; he wrote in his *Prison Notebooks:* "the crisis consists precisely in the fact that the old is dying and the new cannot yet be born; in this interregnum a great variety of morbid symptoms appear."[1]

With the passage of time, this sad truth about the recent revolution in American religious life has become more evident: the old has been cast aside; the new "something," however, has escaped our grip. What about the "in-between-time" that faces us today? It provides an opportunity to shed illusions about the past; it also challenges us to put our energies into preparing the way for something new.

This chapter will discuss the recent revolution in U.S. religious life. It will also try to describe consecrated life's present state of affairs and suggest some steps that need to be taken to insure its future.

At the outset, two points need to be made. First of all, to understand what has happened to American men and women religious during the last quarter century, we need to attend not to this or that particular change, but to the process of change itself. In retrospect, as they entered renewal U.S. religious were unprepared for this fact: no matter how much they welcomed it, change would disorient them, leaving many demoralized, self-absorbed, and full of mistrust.

Second, today many of us run the risk of being unprepared to recognize religious life's future when it emerges among us. Unfortunately, like Israel of old, we long for a king, a Messiah of human making; like our forebears we may end up rejecting the Suffering Servant who comes instead.

A CONTEXT FOR OUR DISCUSSION

Whenever we are moved to despair, contexts provide welcome relief. They help us frame a question or topic and give us perspective on an issue. How can we put the past twenty-five years of U.S. religious life into context? Church historian John Padberg, S.J., proposes that religious life has experienced three major periods of upheaval during the last four hundred and fifty years.[2]

To begin with, starting around 1517, religious life was dramatically influenced by the Protestant Reformation: Luther, Calvin and the other reformers rejected the whole notion of religious life. It had lost its credibility; religious life's reputation had become so bad that more than once the Holy See received proposals that all but four orders of men and most orders of women be suppressed. In spite of this sorry state of affairs, a Catholic reformation later took root and spread. Part of its fruit was the rise of new religious orders and the reform of some already existing ones.

Almost two and a half centuries later, the French Revolution and its aftermath brought chaos to the church and to religious life. Many orders were officially abolished in countries touched by the upheaval. The lands upon which they depended for their support were also secularized and sold to the highest bidder.

Two facts may bring home the widespread devastation that took hold of religious life during this period. First of all, in 1789, there were approximately 2,000 Benedictine establishments in Europe; by 1815, only twenty were still functioning. Second, of the many religious orders of men in existence prior to the French Revolution, only two, the Brothers of the Christian Schools and the Jesuits, have ever grown to be as large or larger in number than they were prior to that time. The nineteenth century, however, also witnessed the foundation of a large number of new service congregations as well as the reform of many already existing orders.

Finally, the third major period of upheaval got underway around the time of the Second Vatican Council. Marist Father Albert DiIanni points out that there has been a period of shakeout after each ecumenical council; approximately twenty-five years are needed for the spirit of a council to take root and begin to bear its best fruits.[3]

He cites three stages in the development of religious life surrounding

Vatican II: 1) a rigid period prior to the council; 2) chaos immediately following the historic meeting; and 3) a current time of sober reassessment marked by conversation and the hope of refounding.

Without doubt the council gave rise to profound changes for U.S. men and women religious. When asked to compare the mid-1960s with the late 1980s, for example, sisters participating in research conducted by sociologist Maria Augusta Neil, S.N.D., reported shifts in these areas of their lives: decision-making structures, "particular friendships," personal/communal finances, Great Silence, Chapter of Faults, horarium, activities and relationships outside the community.[4]

During the past quarter century, a number of U.S. religious men and women also moved from living within a "total institution," a place where all needs were met, to having membership in a number of communities. These new groups? Family, networks of friends and colleagues, apostolic and civic groups. Sociologist Patricia Wittberg, S.C., puts the matter another way; she reports that some Roman Catholic congregations have shifted, since the council, from the structure of an "intentional community" to more bureaucratic and associational forms.[5]

Intentional communities make extensive demands on their members and ask them to cede control over some or all aspects of their public and private lives; the transcendent mission or goal of the group takes precedence over the needs of individual members.

Bureaucratic and associational structures make comparatively fewer demands on members. While individuals within a bureaucracy cede some control over their public lives to their work group, they remain largely independent when the work day is over.

Associations differ in significant ways from intentional communities and bureaucracies. In associations, members exercise personal choice over their degree of involvement with the larger group; they retain complete control over their personal lives, meeting together periodically because of common interest, or for some task or event. This shift on the part of some U.S. congregations from the structures of an intentional community to more associational forms has given rise to questions about religious life's identity and the meaning of membership.

During the last twenty-five years, North American religious men and women have also suffered staggering losses in membership. From the mid-1960s, for example, to the mid-1980s, the U.S. Catholic population increased by approximately ten million people. During the same time period, women religious witnessed an approximately forty percent decline in membership; religious brothers, forty-four percent; diocesan and religious priests, eleven percent.

Change and upheaval, then, are no strangers to consecrated life. When tempted to despair about the state of contemporary religious life, we need only to look at our history to regain some perspective.

THE LIFE CYCLE OF RELIGIOUS ORDERS

Writing during the late 1970s, Lawrence Cada and his colleagues described five separate stages in the life cycle of any religious order: foundation, expansion, stabilization, breakdown, and critical period.[6] First, there is a time of foundation; this period usually coincides with the founding person's last years of life. During this stage, that person's vision provides the focus for the life of the group.

Following the time of institutional origin, most religious congregations experience a fairly lengthy period of expansion; it can last for two to three generations or longer. This stage has two characteristics: the group's members appear to have endless energy: the church and society begin to recognize the group's founding vision and the world's need for it. This is followed by the period of stabilization.

STABILIZATION

Prior to Vatican II, most U.S. provinces and congregations of men and women religious were experiencing a time of stability. It had lasted for a few generations or more: membership continued to grow and geographic expansion, while more modest than during the group's earliest days, was still evident.

This period of stabilization was quite seductive; during it *the identity of religious life was clear and clearly accepted by all*. Groups were accomplishing their self-evident purpose; most were pervaded by a feeling of success. If the congregation's mission was health care, its members strove to build bigger and better hospitals; if education was the focus of its efforts, larger and more successful schools were the order of the day. During this period, interior commitment was also cultivated by emphasizing conformity to standards of external behavior. People everywhere assumed that religious life had always been this way and always would be.

Two hidden crises began to emerge near the end of this period of stabilization: activism and a failure to adapt. First of all, overwork began to overshadow many other aspects of the life of the members of religious congregations. Some people lost sight of the spiritual and apostolic underpinnings of their work. Second, many groups became resistant to change as rules began to take the place of custom. Changes needed within the province or congregation were often enough not made.

The stable period in religious life that came to a close around the time of Vatican II was a mixed blessing. Author Mary Jo Leddy points out that a common vision, symbols and a shared system of meaning ordered its form.[7] Its image was capable of commanding sacrifice, commitment, and greatness of heart. At the same time, it was susceptible to pettiness of spirit and trivial pursuits of piety. Stated simply, while the old days of religious life were not always good, sometimes they were great!

A PERIOD OF BREAKDOWN

Beginning in the 1960s and continuing for almost three decades, religious life in the United States lived through a period of breakdown. We dismantled institutional structures and discovered that belief systems that arose during the periods of expansion and stabilization had outlived their usefulness.

The "founding experience," by now long distant from the membership, had little effect on most. Members of many congregations became dissatisfied with their group's status and questioned its function and purpose: authority and decision-making procedures became confused. In some instances, the group's service to the church began to lack direction and became haphazard. The resulting collective decline gave rise to stress and doubt among the membership. Departures increased; the number of new entrants declined.

What crises marked this period of breakdown? Some long established works were abandoned and "business as usual" came to a stop. Polarization increased in many provinces and congregations and the morale of members took a nosedive. Today you often hear a number of priests, sisters, and brothers asking this question with concern: Is my province or congregation dying?

With so many aspects of our lives changing significantly, many provinces and congregations lost their sense of identity and mission. The changes also brought about other losses; psychologist Bill Bridges divides them into six categories: loss of attachments, turf, structure, a future, meaning, and control.[8]

LOSS OF ATTACHMENTS

As the present transformation in religious life got underway, many U.S. sisters, priests, and brothers lost the feeling of being connected in a larger sense. Peer and hierarchical relationships were disrupted. Some also suffered a loss of attachment as long-established apostolates were closed, novitiates scaled down, and familiar properties sold because they no longer served a purpose in the new order. People dealt with these losses in a variety of ways. Those members whose identity was based largely on relationships, however, seemed more vulnerable to changes.

Ritual can be an important means for dealing with change. Unfortunately, many provinces and congregations failed to use it and, as a consequence, never sufficiently mourned the losses of the past quarter century.

Several years ago, for example, my province closed its novitiate. A lack of novices, as well as several other factors, led to the decision to disband the novitiate community and dispose of the building and its furnishings. Understandably, a number of the brothers who made up this community found the decision difficult to accept.

To help ease their transition, our assistant provincial and Director of Formation developed a ritual for closing the novitiate. While quite simple, it proved to be very effective. First of all, members of the provincial administration gathered with those brothers still living in the novitiate community. The group began with a prayer service in the chapel and then processed from room to room in the house, incensing each and pausing to talk about the men who had lived there. Particularly poignant were stops in the dining and community rooms. Brothers talked about leisurely and conversation-filled meals, about many humorous moments and an equal number of sad and touching ones. Finally, the group ended its procession in the chapel and later concluded the ritual with a meal of celebration.

What did this process accomplish? It provided many of the brothers who lived in the community with an opportunity to talk more fully about their experience of loss in all its dimensions. It also helped bring to a close an era of formation in my province. We now have a new joint novitiate with another of our provinces. This new venture has gone as smoothly as it has because we took time to mourn when we closed the old place.

LOSS OF TURF

When people are faced with any change-caused ending, they experience a loss of turf. Any change that involves how or where things are done within a group can lead to this outcome. For example, while moves toward greater collaboration with other groups within the church have been welcomed by many men and women religious, they have also resulted in the loss of turf for a number of members. Once again, groups need to be sensitive to the experience of their membership in this situation. Why not ask: how has this change exacted a price from our group? It is very important to talk through the losses experienced.

LOSS OF STRUCTURE

When structure is lost, people feel as though they have been exposed to a world that is empty and chaotic. The structures referred to are more psychological than physical. The policies, schedules, and understood ways of doing things within a group protect members from the chaos of living without a structure.

Bill Bridges provides a helpful analogy when he compares people who experience the loss of structure to deep-sea divers who depressurize too quickly.[9] Men and women religious who lost familiar structures too quickly or who depended upon those external structures for a sense of identity, were often incapacitated by a case of the psychological "bends" when dramatic change came to religious life during the last twenty-five years.

LOSS OF A FUTURE

The loss of a future caused by change can be particularly painful for many people to bear. Change does not mean that the group has no future, but rather that the future many members expected will probably not come to pass. Witness the loss experienced by a number of men and women religious when a good friend withdraws from the congregation; the possibility of growing old together in a way previously anticipated is no longer possible. For the "dreamers" in any group, a new future may be more easily generated; for those who lack this gift, however, many months and even years may pass before a new future can be embraced.

LOSS OF MEANING

Change within a group always gives rise to a loss of meaning. When one meaning within an organization breaks down, a number of new ones rush in to fill the vacuum. For some people, meaning is threatened when attachments are lost; for others, the loss of turf or a future puts meaning in doubt. When people lose faith in their province or congregation, they often feel as though an important part of themselves is gone.

Communication is vitally important when the members of a religious order experience the loss of meaning. The word communication refers not only to the official transmission of information. Memos, for example, are among the most ineffective ways of communicating when meaning is threatened. Instead, personal letters and contact on the part of leaders are much more helpful in assisting people to reestablish meaning in their lives.

LOSS OF CONTROL

Finally, when a group changes, its members experience a loss of control; they are no longer "in charge" as they once were. The loss of control hits some people harder than others. Who is most at risk? Those among us whose well-being depends on being in control at all times. All of us, however, feel this loss when everything appears up for grabs and our attempts to influence the outcome of events seem to count for little.

Taking time to attend to endings and the losses they entail is the first, the most necessary, and often the most frequently overlooked step in managing the transformation of any group. Many men and women religious failed to avoid this pitfall when dealing with the recent endings in their lives. The consequences of this failure are striking.

OUR PRESENT DILEMMA

There is some "good" news and some "bad" news in what has happened to U.S. religious life since 1965. The bad news? Its present transformation is just now getting underway.

Any time of transformation has three distinct parts. First of all, it usually begins with an ending. Then a prolonged period follows during which people feel "up-in-the-air." Finally, a new beginning gets underway. During the last quarter century, we have been completing the first stage of religious life's present transformation; an era has come to an end.

Christian Brother Michael Horan gives a poignant description of our present situation.[10] We are like adult children whose parents have died; the family home has been sold; familiar relationships and guidelines are gone. We are no longer even sure where we can go to celebrate the holidays.

What about some good news? The losses and uncertainty of the last twenty-five years have helped us to begin to ask some important questions about religious life's identity and mission; they have also given us the possibility of refounding provinces and congregations.

This fact has become evident during the past several years: the present renewal of religious life is not nearing completion; indeed, it has hardly begun. A critical period is just now getting underway for many groups;

the manner in which they negotiate this stage will be indicative of their long-term health and vitality.

CRITICAL PERIODS

Critical periods in the lives of religious congregations give rise to three possible outcomes: extinction, minimal survival, or refounding. First of all, some religious congregations in existence today will go out of existence in the not too distant future. This outcome should not be surprising: 76 percent of all men's orders founded before 1500 and 64 percent of those founded prior to 1800 no longer exist.

The second, and perhaps least attractive, outcome facing religious congregations today is minimal survival. Some groups will change but fail to renew themselves; they will modify dress, reform language, and restructure community and apostolate. They will, however, also fail to capture religious life's prophetic character; eventually people will ask: what do they stand for?

What about those groups that choose refounding? They will be marked by three characteristics: a transforming response to the signs of the times; a reappropriation of their founding charism; and a profound renewal of their life of faith, prayer, and centeredness in Christ.

First of all, refounding groups accept the contradictions that emerge during the breakdown period. As early as the late 1970s, Cada and his colleagues were pointing to several: individualism versus the group's common goals; personal choice of ministry versus the needs of the community's institutions; traditional church work versus a response to new needs.[11] By accepting these contradictions, the group admits that its structure and life-style fail to satisfy the membership. Acceptance, however, does not mean approval; these contradictions must be addressed and resolved for the group to remain vital.

More recently two psychologists, David Nygren, C.M., and Miriam Ukeritis, C.S.J., completed a comprehensive study about the future of U.S. religious life. They, too, cite a number of contradictions present in U.S. religious life today: one, lack of understanding on the part of many priests, sisters, and brothers about their role and function in the church versus concern for the mission of the church and the extension of the charism; two, racism versus the need to adapt to the multiculturalism required by heterogeneity in a congregation; three, assimilation by the mainstream U.S. culture versus simplicity of life, and a response to absolute human need, marked by joy in serving God; four, living out religious life's prophetic role versus assimilation into parochial structures; five, leadership that transforms versus leadership that manages; six, corporate identity versus an emphasis on individual ministry; and seven, confusion about the exercise of authority versus communal empowerment.[12]

Second, personal transformation is at the heart of the refounding experience. Following a period of personal darkness and exploration, members develop a new relationship with Jesus, greater depth in faith and prayer, and a genuine openness to the Lord's call.

The real crisis in religious life today is not vocations. No, it is our lack of spirituality and of a sense of significance. A vibrant life of personal and communal prayer must be at the heart of our life; otherwise, we run the risk of being nothing more than associations that give little witness to the presence of Jesus in the world.

Jesus came to bring life; religious life must be the church's memory of that fact. The distinct character of religious life is its public profession, recognized, appreciated and legitimized by the church, of the will to live fully and radically the gospel plan, as the object of one's life.[13] Striving to live this ideal today would surely say something of significance to our wider world.

Finally, the refounding experience gives groups an opportunity to explore variety in their life and apostolate. Keep in mind that this search will result initially in more failures than successes. We need to be comfortable with our mistakes and learn from them. The process of exploration has an important lesson: it will help us rework our group's charism, to free it from its historical trappings.

Marist Father Gerald Arbuckle identifies a refounding person as a central character in the process of transformation that leads to a group's conversion.[14] Others point to refounding groups or "seed communities" as the impetus for change. Whether it be an individual or a small group, both need to have the gift of prophecy: to share the founding person's vision in a world that is vastly different from that in which their congregation was founded originally. While, in the final analysis, refounding is the work of the Lord, some understanding of the process of change and transformation will help us comprehend what many religious orders are facing today.

CHANGE VERSUS TRANSFORMATION

What is the greatest fallacy we have accepted about change? If it is necessary and explained carefully, we will be able to handle it! Bridges points out that planned change is almost as disruptive as unplanned change.[15]

Change and transformation are not the same. Change happens at a point in time; transformation happens over time. Change is a new beginning; transformation begins with an ending. While change can require people to undergo a transformation, the latter allows for the spiritual and psychological reorientations that need to take place before people can find meaning in any changed situation.

A number of factors influence our experience of any transformation. First of all, our personal and collective history with change plays a role. How have we been taught to react to change? With fear and apprehension? By denying that anything new is happening? With a sense of welcome relief?

Second, the life phase in which we find ourselves also influences our experience of transformation. For example, sisters, priests, and brothers facing midlife questions about the meaning and purpose of their own lives may have a far rougher time with the change that accompanies any transformation than others who are experiencing a more stable period in their lives.

Temperament also plays a role. Some of us are sensate or present-oriented; we get our data about the world from the details of the actual situation. Others of us are intuitives or future-oriented; the general pattern of possibilities found in any situation is our information source. While sensates need a step-by-step plan of action to get from here to there, intuitives embrace strategic planning and get excited about visions of the future.

Despite factors that influence our experience of transformations, most people report some common feelings during these periods of change and reorganization. Many talk about being disengaged; for them, the system has stopped working. Others report a feeling of disenchantment; their world is no longer real.

Still others lose their sense of self-definition; having broken their old connections to the world, it becomes harder for these men and women to answer this question: "Who am I?" Finally, a number of people become disoriented. Dante said it well: "In the middle of the journey of my life, I came to myself within a dark wood where the straight way was lost. Ah, how hard it is to tell of that wood—savage and harsh and dense—the thought of it renews my fear; so bitter is it that death is hardly more." People who are disoriented feel a bit shipwrecked.

When the first stage of any transformation has run its course, most of us hope that a new beginning will follow quickly. Instead, we experience a rather prolonged period called a "neutral zone." Like Erik Erikson's "moratorium," this neutral zone or desert experience is a "time-out." It teaches us that the process of rebirth is not one of mechanistic modification, but rather one of death and resurrection.

WHAT ABOUT THE FUTURE?

Students of midlife know quite well that a person's shadow side often comes to the fore during this time of life change. Personas or public images start to break down. What emerges? Those parts of our identity that are suppressed and denied in the name of living up to some ideals.

Groups and organizations have the same experience during times of transformation. Bridges defines an organization's shadow in this way: the mirror image to the official culture that everyone in the group espouses; for example, the suppressed greediness behind the altruistic facade of a not-for-profit organization or the hostility behind a hospital's public image of loving care.[16]

Religious life has been no stranger to this experience during its current time of transformation; some people wonder if it has lost its soul. In the United States men and women religious need to reassure themselves with this knowledge: they can always count on the emergence of some elements of the shadow of any group during its time in the neutral zone.

Life in the "in-between time," however, also presents tremendous opportunities. Bridges points out that while the vacuum of the neutral zone draws out the suppressed shadow and some forgotten fears, it also provides an empty place where the new and creative can come to life. The "in-between times" call us to return to the bedrock of our existence.

Religious life today, like Israel of old, is wandering in the desert; it is faced with a situation similar to the wilderness experience of Native Americans. Stated simply, religious life has not been called to change, but rather to die so as to be born anew.

We need to be careful not to miss the opportunity that such a situation presents or to forget this fact: the desert, in many ways, is a fertile place; its very emptiness, the source of so much anxiety, is also a precondition for a new vision.

SOME PRACTICAL STEPS

David Lloyd George once said, "The most dangerous thing in the world is to leap a chasm in two jumps!" Men and women in the United States need to develop a plan of action to help them exploit this time of change and transformation. Two elements should be apparent in its makeup. One, some strategies for supporting people through this period when "business as usual" has come to a stop; two, others that give them access to the innovativeness, vision and Spirit of God that are always part of any "neutral zone" period.

First and foremost, we need to educate ourselves and one another about the characteristic features of a time of transformation. Sometimes just identifying and naming them can bring a measure of relief. However, more than just formal education is needed. We must also talk about the distress that haunts us. When you discover that you are not alone, your anxieties lose much of their power over you. Talk will help us realize that we have a lot of company in the stormy waters of these "in-between times."

Second, we need to develop mechanisms for monitoring the course of change within our provinces and congregations. Not all our members will embrace with equal enthusiasm the challenges of a time of transformation. How can we learn about difficulties before they take on a life of their own or fester and poison some segments of our group? What means can be set up to feed into decision-making processes from otherwise silent elements within our provinces and congregations?

Third, new channels of communication need to be created and used. Information exchange should be simple, constant, and repetitive; some things need saying over and over again.

When anxiety is high and uncertainty and confusion are the order of the day, people have difficulty understanding what they are hearing. Memos get lost on bulletin boards; an avalanche of paper discourages rather than invites average readers to expand their knowledge. "In-between times" place heavy burdens on those "in-charge"; it is a time for highly visible and supportive leadership, one that communicates a sense of evolving purpose to members.

Bridges cites Moses as a good example of a transformational leader.[17] He climbed the mountain to talk with God and then came back into the camp and shared what he had learned and experienced. Moses walked around and talked with people in front of their tents; he reminded them why the strange but attractive gods of the quick fix would not work. Leadership in the "in-between times" alternately pushes and pulls people along the wilderness path to a new beginning; Bridges calls this "management by walking around."[18]

Fourth, during a time of transformation it's important to encourage cohesion within the group. When people feel threatened, they tend to fragment and look out for themselves. Leadership needs to pull them together and find ways to enhance solidarity.

Provincial, regional or congregational gatherings are one means to encourage cohesion. Over the past two and a half decades we have lost many of the once-familiar ways of building solidarity. In addition, the members of some groups are scattered over a wide geographic area. Well-planned and executed gatherings will go a long way toward helping people pull together.

Fifth, expect the group's old and unresolved issues to surface during a time of transformation. Most of us sweep our conflicts under the rug. "In-between times" have a way of lifting the rug's corners and exposing the mess. Don't try to curtail discussion of difficult or tedious issues; rather, view a time of transformation as another opportunity to put some old and unresolved issues to rest.

Sixth, ritualize endings and keep the reasons for them in the forefront of people's minds. Otherwise, their anxieties and confusions will tempt them to escape the chaos of the present by trying to return to a simpler past.

After all, the Israelites were not in the desert for very long before they began to murmur. They told one another, "Egypt wasn't really so bad compared to this place. Why did we ever leave there anyway?" Moses was an effective transformational leader because he had great faith and did two things: presented the people with a clear view of the opportunities of the Promised Land and provided them with an accurate memory of what Egypt was really like!

Seventh, create temporary structures for governance and temporary lines of authority and responsibility shaped by the needs of these "in-between times." These are not normal days; they call for innovation and courage on the part of all of us.

A FINAL CHALLENGE

Men and women religious in the United States have been blessed with the ancient Chinese curse: May you live in a time of transformation! These are crisis days: filled with danger while also rich in opportunity.

We need to be bold and courageous in response to this gift of God in our time. We must also help our provinces and congregations to dream new dreams about how they will live out the gospel of Jesus Christ in this age and culture and have the courage to bring those dreams to life. We have to be filled with the same fire as our founders and foundresses; their passion needs a new form for our new age.

Theologian Donald Senior points out that we also need to dialogue with some of the positive aspects of values in American culture as we renew religious life in our age.[19] What are some of those values? They include personalism, freedom and self-determination, pluralism, democratic self-criticism, egalitarianism, and an emphasis on productivity and success.

Many U.S. men and women religious were educated for a church and a religious life that were dying by the time they reached maturity. The notions they learned early in life were meant for another age and a different understanding of the world. The religious life of the first half of this century and earlier was developed for a church and world that no longer exist. While we need to mourn their passing, we cannot return to them. To do so would be to deny grace, growth, and the possibility of a future.

The Second Vatican Council caused a huge shift to occur in what was once thought to be a secure and immobile landscape. When it was over, we were all left standing in a different place. The results of this earthquake are the reality we need to address today. When frightened, we may think about returning to older forms for security or to get things in order once again. We need to resist this temptation.

Real renewal has not yet come to U.S. religious life. This failure has not been due to ill-will nor the lack of effort; rather, the time has not been right. No one can rush the movement of a time of transformation; it has a life of its own.

The stage of transformation that American men and women religious are entering today is an important one in the process of their renewal and the renewal of their provinces and congregations. It will help them critique the changes of the last quarter century and to ask some difficult questions.

The religious life we hoped for with expectation just twenty-five years ago will be a longer time in coming. The events of the last quarter century, though, have been quite important. They helped us fall apart. They also prepared the way for something new.

We needed the current transformation in U.S. religious life more than we realized. It has roused us from our sleep, helped us surrender the past, and caused us to ask, once again, this faith question: On whom or what do we set our hearts? As we search for an answer, let us rely on faith to guide us, hope to sustain us, and the love of our God and one another to support us on our journey.

NOTES

This chapter was presented as the author's presidential address to the annual assembly of CMSM in San Antonio, Texas, in August, 1991. It appeared in *Origins* 21:12 (Aug. 29, 1991), 185–191 and in *Review for Religious* 51:1 (Jan.-Feb., 1992), 64–77 in slightly different form.

1. Antonio Gramsci, *Selections from the Prison Notebooks of Antonio Gramsci*, Quintin Hoare and Geoffrey Nowell Smith, trans. and eds. (London: Lawrence & Wishart, 1971), p. 276.

2. John Padberg, "The Contexts of Comings and Goings," in *The Crisis*

in Religious Vocations: An Inside View, Laurie Felknor, ed. (Mahwah, NJ: Paulist, 1989), pp. 19-31.

3. Albert DiIanni, "Religious Life and Modernity," *Review for Religious*, 50:3 (May/June, 1991), pp. 339-351.

4. Maria Augusta Neil, *Catholic Sisters in Transition: from the 1960s to the 1980s*. (Wilmington, DE: Michael Glazier, Inc., 1984).

5. Patricia Wittberg, *Creating a Future for Religious Life* (Mahwah, NJ: Paulist, 1991), esp. 61f.

6. Lawrence Cada, Raymond Fitz, Gertrude Foley, Thomas Giardino, and Carol Lichtenberg, *Shaping the Coming Age of Religious Life* (New York: Seabury, 1979).

7. Mary Jo Leddy, *Reweaving Religious Life* (Mystic, CT: Twenty-Third Publications, 1990).

8. William Bridges, *Surviving Corporate Transition* (New York: Doubleday, 1988), pp. 40-52.

9. *Surviving Corporate Transition*, p. 44.

10. Michael Horan "Creating the Unknown ... Vocation Awareness Ministry in a Changing Church" presentation given at the National Religious Vocation Conference: Atlantic Area Assembly, Savannah, GA, September 8-12, 1989.

11. *Shaping the Coming Age of Religious Life*, pp. 98-99.

12. David Nygren and Miriam Ukeritis, "The Religious Life Futures Project," *Review for Religious* 52:1 (Jan./Feb., 1993), 6-55.

13. Marcello Azevedo, *Vocation for Mission: The Challenge of Religious Life Today* (Mahwah, NJ: Paulist, 1988).

14. Gerald A. Arbuckle, "Participative Leadership for Refounding: Reflections," *Review for Religious* 50:3 (May/June, 1991), pp. 357-367.

15. Bridges, *op. cit.*, pp. 3-16.

16. *Ibid.*, 60-61.

17. *Ibid.*, 76.

18. *Ibid.*, 76.

19. Donald Senior, "A Biblical Perspective on Why They Left" in *The Crisis in Religious Vocations, op. cit.*, pp. 141-151.

The Challenge to
Religious Leadership:
Maintenance or Mission?

Howard J. Gray, S.J.

In his extraordinary examination of adolescence, *A Separate Peace,* John
Knowles uses the metaphor of World War II to explore that moment when
the human moves from innocence to the pain of shared human guilt.[1]
Knowles' novel has become a modern classic because it speaks to us about
how historical moments have the power to represent realities which transcend chronology, moments which speak to us about our deepest values,
emotions, and inspiration.

For most Roman Catholics over forty, the Second Vatican Council was
such an historical moment, a moment which has become a metaphor
for renewal or regression, for progress or loss, for change or chaos, depending on how one responded to what happened to us Catholics between
1963 and 1965.[2]

Vatican II had a special metaphoric power for religious because it
invited them to be free enough to reconsider their lives according to a
fresh set of priorities—fresh, not new, because the priorities were but a
discovery of our deepest Christian heritage.

The appropriate renewal of religious life involves two simultaneous
processes: (1) a continuous return to the sources of all Christian life and
to the inspiration behind a given community; and (2) an adjustment of
the community to the changed conditions of the times.[3]

The Decree on the Appropriate Renewal of Religious Life spelled out
the principles of this renewal. These principles were the following of
Christ, a loyal recognition and safekeeping of each community's special
character and purpose [its charism], participation in the life of the church,
an awareness of the contemporary human condition and the needs of the
church, and an internal renewal of the spirit.[4]

If the American religious' cooperation with the recent reflective process inaugurated by "Essential Elements in Church Teaching on Religious Life" has done nothing else, it has reaffirmed for most religious their desire to continue the work of Vatican II: to make the gospels credible, to be our own people graced by a charism of service to the human family and to the church, to have an effective voice in our church's life and direction, and to continue to promote that life in Christ's Spirit, which will make us free enough to serve out of love and not out of fear or ambition or a desire to master anyone.[5]

Consequently, when I say that Vatican II is a metaphor for decision, I mean a decision to struggle in this world for the kingdom of Christ, by denying neither the reality of the world nor the reality of Christ's kingdom, by learning from each how to interpret the other, and by a radical commitment to serving Christ's kingdom. This decision to bring world and kingdom together is a bold decision, one with risks and one with marvelous exhilarations. Vatican II is a metaphor for renewal which summons us from maintenance to mission.

This is background for my reflections here. I emphasize Vatican II, because that council was the last great universal church effort to talk about the challenges which modernity and cultural-social changes have brought to the church. I also believe that there are subtle efforts to weaken the spirit of Vatican II, a reactionary movement which would push church and religious communities back into a concentration on the accidentals of religious life and not on its essentials.

If we are to face the challenges offered to contemporary religious leadership, then we must see leadership as one for mission not just for maintenance. Let me explain this distinction. By "mission," I mean the call to work for the establishment of God's rule over creation. That work "will come to fullness only at the end of history as we know it, on the Day of the Lord." That day will mark the kingdom. The kingdom "will have arrived when all creation acknowledges God's reign and sin is no more. But the Kingdom is also (at least in part) a present reality. The healing and teaching activities of Jesus constitute its inaugural aspects."[6] Mission is, then, work for the kingdom of God proclaimed by Christ. This mission involves being sent, a moving into the world to preach, to teach, to confront, and to heal.

By "maintenance," I mean treating the kingdom as if it were already fully possessed, identifying the kingdom with *these* apostolates, *these* constituencies, *this* economic system, *this* present church, so that one is preoccupied with preservation not evangelization, with conventional rectitude not God's justice, with resisting changes not discerning their origins nor their direction.

Now all those who are major superiors must do some maintenance. They must sustain the good; they must give responsible stewardship to what people have bestowed on their communities: they must give effective security to their sick and aged so that they can live in simple but real dignity. Additionally they must structure a careful, ordered process of formation and education of our young. But all this is done for the sake of the more radical call to work for the coming of God's kingdom. Our apostolic efforts are not substitutes for the kingdom. Our goods are authentically good only if they are open to be used for the kingdom. Our stewardship is a genuine stewardship when it looks to spending its resources prudently for the greater work of the kingdom.

Our security is not meant to provide a pampered retirement, but to give all members the apostolic freedom they need to choose for the kingdom and not solely from any set of economic criteria. Our formation is not oriented "to finding ourselves" whole, happy, educated, or relevant, but rather to becoming people who can respond to the needs of our times with competence and Christ-like dedication to the kingdom. In other words, we do maintenance in order to be on mission for the sake of the kingdom: we do not go on mission to maintain a work, a house, or even a religious community.

I emphasize this because just as I think that there are persistent contemporary efforts to enfeeble the spirit of Vatican II, I likewise think that there are persistent contemporary efforts to enfeeble the missionary priority of religious life, calling us from the work of the kingdom to the work of maintaining a safe, domesticated version of religious life where everyone is properly attired, properly regulated, and properly assigned to works which challenge no one's *status quo*.

Thus what I want to say by way of introduction is: (1) That Vatican II called us to repossess our authentic evangelical and community charisms, (2) in order that we might respond to the needs of our times and of our church, (3) especially through a renewal of spirit. (4) Consequently, Vatican II for most of us U.S. religious became a metaphor for contemporary religious commitment to the mission of the kingdom. (5) The subtle enemy of the missionary commitment is the temptation to make maintenance its own end or to allow the imposition of maintenance concerns on us from outside. This erroneous focus on maintenance threatens to domesticate the very charisms Vatican II invited us to recognize, develop, and exercise.

Given this background, let us consider two concerns: Where have we been? And where are we going? Or as I phrase them here: *From What?* and *To What?*

FROM WHAT?

To get a handle on what changes have touched us since Vatican II and because of Vatican II, I am going to focus on two distinct chronological periods. The first chronological period is from 1940 to 1965, while the second is from 1965 to 1980, i.e., the years preparatory to Vatican II and the years following Vatican II and prior to the document *Essential Elements.*

Between 1940 and 1965, just as the church was defined by an institutional model of her identity, so too were religious communities. We grew up with clearly defined lines of authority, with standard sets of rules and regulations, with emphases on conformation to approved past ways of doing things, with regulated community life, with an almost sacramentalized daily order, and with an apostolic orientation to specific institutions and/or professions which we termed "our works." We were members of a definite sociological sub-group called religious, which, in turn, meant men and women whose identity, conduct, and future were easily anticipated.

Let me now consider what impact such an institutional model had on four key areas of religious life: (1) the symbolic, (2) the existential, (3) the reflective, and (4) the apostolic.[7]

By "symbolic" I mean those concrete realities which signify something beyond themselves. For example, the crucifix stands for a rich conglomerate of Jesus, sacrifice, love, forgiveness, redemptive death, and the victory of Jesus over sin—to list only some of the connotations and meanings which the crucifix can inspire. Another example would be clasped, upraised hands which can inspire images of prayer, petition, human need, and an outpouring of self to God. Our symbolic world has always been important, including the words we use, sacred signs, gestures, and special people.

Symbols have an especially rich field in Roman Catholic tradition. Our religious communities from 1940 to 1965 were peppered with symbols: cassocks, long black lines making their way to chapel or to the refectory, silences, cloister, bells, the Motherhouse. You can go on and on. Just trace out the formation which you and I have had and recall how much our education has been linked to assuming the right symbols of Dominican, Franciscan, Marist, Redemptorist, Benedictine, or Jesuit life. We were formed and incorporated into our affective community by a series of symbols of testing, of proving oneself, of acceptance, and of union with the older, symbol-bearing group we called the "the professed."

These 1940-1965 symbols were so amazingly consistent that the novices of 1948, the year I entered the Jesuits, could converse easily with the men who entered ten and twenty years earlier, sharing radically and extensively a common symbolic life. Frequently, to be a particular kind of religious meant to be a symbol-carrier. For example, doing the right symbolic actions led one to being characterized as "a good monk," "a good religious," "a good community man," or "a man of the rule." The lives of our community members and our apostolic works were structured by these same symbols, allowing us to pass from community to community with a minimum of trauma and adjustment.

Second, let us consider the experiential reality in religious life from 1940 to 1965. By "experiential," I do not mean empirical, i.e., "primarily concerned with data, the factual, the description of inner and outer phenomena." Rather, by "experiential" I mean that reality which "draws on sense and other experiences with a frank acceptance of 'the reasons of the heart.' [The experiential] reveals what is unique, personal, subjective."[8]

Experiential reality was carefully moderated in the religious communities of 1940 to 1965. In that period, our experience emphasized universal norms and values, abstracted from particular realizations of those values or norms. Let me take an example from my own personal history. When most of us entered religious life between 1940 and 1965, we were told to break off past relationships. We were ushered into a world which was almost ahistorical. Our ecclesiastical studies, with few exceptions, emphasized the tradition we were to guard but not contribute to. Our deepest, subjective insights were saved for informal get-togethers or for personal prayer. Hence, a kind of secondary experience developed where we cultivated social and devotional coping mechanisms to harmonize our monitored, formal experiential data with our hearts. Many of us lived, peacefully and effectively, with a two-tiered experience of religious life: what we were taught to expect and what we actually experienced.

Third, let us consider the way we reflected on our symbols and our experiential lives. For some the symbols became the reality. The garb, for example, was holy; not just a sign of consecration but somehow the place of consecration. The rule became not a means to charity, but the virtue itself for which one would lay down his or her life. Daily order and established apostolates became the only way to live and to work as religious. Thus the ahistorical, monitored experiential became the critic of all other experiences.

Consequently, whatever challenged the official, ahistorical experience was dismissed as deviant, radical, or even heretical. In short, because all norms were set, reflection was seen as the task of putting subsequent, personal experience into an already assumed context. To think about one's religious life was basically an act of conforming one's ideas to the accepted patterns of symbolic values and acceptable behavior.

Finally, out of this came an emphasis on group apostolic works: schools, hospitals, parishes, mission stations. Fitting into the approved works was expected.

This style of religious life was characteristic of the years 1940 to 1965. Great men and women emerged from this era—talented, generous, inventive, and holy. Nonetheless, it was a style in need of radical review and change. Vatican II did not prompt those changes, but Vatican II did prompt a radical review and hasten the worldwide implementation of long overdue changes. Let us consider those changes by turning to the period of 1965 to 1980.

THE CONCILIAR MOMENT

If the earlier pre-Vatican II period was dominated by an institutional model of the church, the period following Vatican II was one dominated by a plurality of models of the church. The model which one employed depended on the pastoral needs of the situation. In developing a pastoral ecclesial response, the U.S. church relied heavily on the psychological sciences:

> For to see the Church as mystery or as people of God or as Sacrament or as *communio* or as herald or as servant or as disciple was also to see the essentials of the Church as far more plentiful than those enunciated in the institutional model of Church. The implicit invitation to find that model which best met one's graces, temperament, apostolic inclination, and personal history was also an invitation to trust one's own experience of God.[9]

All this had an impact on the four areas of the symbolic, the experiential, the reflective, and the apostolic.

The symbolic shifted from images of order and continuity with the past to those of experimentation and preparing for the future. Far from relinquishing a symbolic world, religious after Vatican II were engaged in a sometimes feverish enterprise to create a new symbolic world. Religious garb became more eclectic; daily orders yielded to new flexibilities; in a formation rural setting gave way to moves to cities and university centers.

Cloister surrendered to hospitality and the open dining room. The good religious became the one who responded generously to a new asceticism of meetings, consultations, communal discernments, and faith-sharing. U.S. religious went through a tremendously complicated symbolic-shift between 1965 and 1980, a shift which many religious found to be disintegrating. Thus some religious retreated into a stubborn rejection of Vatican II and into a nostalgic longing for "the good old days." Others interpreted this symbolic shift as the abandonment of religious priorities and found leaving religious life a logical next step. We have been and continue to be in a process of profound symbolic change which has not left any one of us unchallenged or untouched.

In the area of the experiential, a strong personalism was asserted. Personal history—at once psychological and social—influenced our experiences. Interpersonal communication, feelings, a stress on community togetherness through dialogue, shared autobiographies, shared homilies, shared prayer—these created an environment of high affect.

Reflection was raised to the level of a theological process. New emphases were given to the rules of memory, imagination, and story-telling. With this came an emphasis on the particular as primary: *this* pastoral case, *this* local church, *this* fundamental moral option, *this* conversion experience, *this* moment of evangelization. Reflection shifted its focus from texts, confessional statements, and "proofs" to personal experience. Reflection shifted its goal from continuity with the past to witnessing to the present reality of Christ, church, community, or whatever was the immediate religious concern.[10]

Finally, from 1965 to 1980 we saw a similar shift in apostolic priorities. Religious questioned traditional works—if not their existence, then at least the way they were operated. With more attention being given to personal history, personal temperament, personal graces, and personal talents, there was less demand that one "fit into" an established corporate apostolate.

Most of us have retained many of our schools, parishes, hospitals, retreat houses, and centers. But we have also seen these apostolates change their structures, their clientele, and their staffs. We have all seen a growth in new ministries, both in the U.S. and in the Third World. It would be hard today to cite any one work or any one apostolic location as having an undisputed apostolic claim on our corporate loyalties, our personnel, or our finances. The reevaluation has been universal.

THE EFFECT OF CONCILIAR RENEWAL

Let me bring these reflections into synthesis. If we talk of today's challenges, then we have to see that these challenges are rooted in our immediate past. Just as the institutional priority of the church gave way to a plurality of models of the church, so did the symbols, experience, reflection, and apostolic works of religious congregations move into a new plurality. From a clearly defined symbolic world, we moved to a process of change as the controlling symbol of post-Vatican II religious life. From institutional experience guided by norms, we moved to norms guided by personal experience. From conformity to the tradition, we moved to the creation of a new tradition of witnessing, story-telling, and sharing of experience. From the identification of particular works or places as the community priority, we moved into an apostolic critique of assumed priorities and into the establishment of new apostolic works and new apostolic locales.

This is a quick and sweeping overview of where we have been. It is, I believe, an accurate one. This survey brings us to today. Briefly put, I think our first job as religious leaders is to understand our immediate contemporary history. We have come to a point where diminished personnel, ever-increasing secularity in our culture, a social and religious neoconservatism, and the rise of qualified lay people committed to ministry in the church prompt a reassessment of our responses and our directions.

What the periods from 1940 to 1965 and from 1965 to 1980 have in common is that both were taken up with questions of maintenance. We did change; but most of these changes were changes in life-styles, in formation, and in apostolic commitments. I think that the future lies with those religious leaders willing to shift their energies from maintenance to mission.

In saying this, I am not urging the abandonment of responsibility. As major superiors we have to care for our men, young and old; we have to exercise a faithful stewardship over our resources; we have to work with the people who have been benefactors. But we have to do all these tasks in terms of the kingdom. We need to choose carefully symbols, experiences, reflection, and apostolic works which move us from being caretakers to being leaders. This leads to the second major part of this chapter: To What?

TO WHAT?

Religious life needs symbols. It needs affective and effective realities to spell out that we are gospel people, Christ's people, the church's people, the kingdom's people. Let me suggest areas where we can create a new, mission-oriented, symbolic world: in our life-styles, our communities, and our relationship with the U.S. church and U.S. society.

Society here is increasingly dichotomized between those who have much and those who have little. Consumerism is a reality which has developed its own set of symbols: possessions beyond necessities, leisure without labor, and waste. Our society is highly competitive in business, in advertising, and in education. Far too many in our society are being victimized by violence: on the streets, in the work place, in schools, and in the home. Our society is increasingly committed to the pursuit of pleasure. Much is splendid in our country, but consumerism, competition, violence, and pleasure-seeking work against the fraternity, reconciliation, and purity of heart enunciated in the Sermon on the Mount.

How do we symbolize, as American religious leaders, both a love for our country and a critique of those values within our culture which resist all that the kingdom means? We do not lead by becoming part of the system. Neither do we lead by a simplistic withdrawal from the system, becoming a kind of irrelevant sect. We need symbols of apt, prophetic critique.

Our life-styles must be simple, hospitable, reconciling, and humanely ascetic if our presence is to be interpreted as a relevant prophetic critique of consumerism, competition, violence, and a preoccupation with pleasure. Similarly our communities must become locales where those looking for leadership in forming alternative life-styles can find support. We have to see our charisms in terms of calling the church to this kind of mission of profound witnessing to the kingdom.

You will note that I have said nothing about garb, daily order, or cloister. These are secondary symbols. The primary symbol is to put life-style and community in a dual relationship with the kingdom and with U.S. church and U.S. society. Leadership means having and promoting a spirituality which calls our religious brothers and sisters to become symbols of the priorities of the kingdom in the very quality of their lives.

In terms of experience, religious leadership calls us to promote mutual accountability and not just conformation to old norms or self-expression in the present. We must promote solid formation for commitment to the kingdom, ongoing formation as updating and renewal for the sake of the kingdom, and interpersonal relationships as the charity of the kingdom.

In terms of reflection, religious leadership calls us to bring norms and personal experience together into a profound synthesis. We review our experiences of mutual accountability in order to learn how we can be one in promoting the kingdom.

Finally, in terms of apostolic action, we move from promoting or adjusting our works to the serious effort at ecclesial, intercommunity, and transcultural collaboration. We will be working toward an effective network of apostolic commitments for the sake of the kingdom.

THE FOURFOLD CHALLENGE

The challenge to religious leadership from a changing U.S. society and U.S. church is the challenge to become authentically religious, in the spirit of the kingdom preached by Christ. This is a fourfold challenge: (1) To create religious life-styles and communities recognized as counter-cultural in their simplicity, hospitality, reconciling power, and humane asceticism; in short, to create a new symbol of/out of religious life. (2) To create a structure throughout our initial and continuing formation where communication among members is oriented toward accountability to the values of the kingdom. (3) To create a discerning community which moves from accountability to a new level of synthesis, i.e., of recognizing new apostolic possibilities and needs arising out of our mutual communication. (4) To create a collaborative model of apostolic service where we trim away duplications, encourage joint projects, and enter into partnership for the kingdom.[11]

CONCLUSION

Two practical considerations follow from this analysis: What questions can lead us to respond to the challenges from U.S. society and church so that we move from maintenance to mission for the sake of the kingdom? And what spirituality supports this new style of religious leadership?

First, the practical questions which I would suggest.

1. Regarding Recruitment and Formation:

Do we look for men and women capable of apostolic risk who show creativity and who exhibit an ability to learn from their experiences—both those of success and those of failure? Do we look for people comfortable in working with both men and women, and with lay people? Can they live with a minimum of comfort? Do they see authority as a way to organize energies for a common good and not as an imposition nor as a security against personal responsibility? Do they see consecrated chastity as an orientation toward a love people can trust?

Or are we accepting safe, security-seeking, conventional or even reactionary women and men because we are worried about staffing our schools, hospitals, parishes, retreat houses, and international centers.

Even more radically do we see the need for creative cosponsorship of joint formation programs? Do we see our future in creative union with lay women and men and in joining our formation, in as many ways as possible, to theirs?

2. *Regarding the Education of Our Personnel:*

Do we put a premium on a collaborative model of ministry whereby we have our personnel work with religious of other communities, with lay students, with non-Catholics? Do we have ongoing evaluations of our personnel precisely in terms of their ability to work in union for the kingdom? Do we evaluate their pastoral skills and their ability to communicate the gospel? Do we emphasize an educational process which promotes justice as a constitutive element of the gospel? Is there a steady effort to help those new to religious life to integrate their academic, pastoral, and spiritual formation into apostolic service?

3. *Regarding Our Communities:*

Do we live in isolation from or in openness to other people and to one another? Is community for us a place of mutual support, healthy challenge, ongoing discernment about effective apostolic service, and hospitality? Do we see community as the locale where we can invite lay colleagues to come to share a meal, eucharist, or a weekend of prayer? Do we put priority on comfort or on communication? What do people see when they look at how we live together?

4. *Regarding Our Apostolates:*

What is our commitment to the poor and to the others marginalized in our society: the African American poor, Hispanics, the divorced, gays? What apostolic planning—province-wide or community-wide—has been done to address the problems of consumerism, of unhealthy competition, of violence and of the pursuit of pleasure?

Is there any ongoing assessment within your community about duplication of works, i.e., where a number of religious communities serve the same people in the same area? If so, is there any consideration of meeting with other religious to consolidate apostolic efforts and thus free our communities to work in neglected areas?

How seriously do we consider phasing out our control of successful apostolic ventures and putting these into the control of qualified lay personnel and then moving into new areas of service, especially of the poor and marginated? Do we commit men and women from our communities precisely to train lay men and women to replace us?

Finally, have we faced our possible deaths? Do we see at least the possibility of our being a remnant, and the major apostolic work of the kingdom passing into the hands of a new religious entity: committed, trained, and available lay people? Are we helping our fellow religious to see the priority of the kingdom even over our institutes?

These are not easy questions. But the pattern of our responses—about formation, community, and apostolate—will indicate a trend either toward maintaining ourselves or giving ourselves to mission. Leadership means helping people move toward life and love. These are gifts only Christ can give.

Discipleship spirituality can be described in many ways. Let me indicate one classic description, found in Luke 10: 25-37, the parable of the Good Samaritan. In that familiar narrative, what distinguished the Samaritan from the priest and the levite was a fourfold process of seeing, feeling, doing, and sustaining. This is also a fourfold process of discipleship.

The Samaritan really saw the Jew as brother and as victim. Likewise, our process of discipleship must be based on a contemplative viewing of our times. Prayer must be an engagement with the world of suffering, aspiration, and struggle to overcome all the evils which inhibit the kingdom.

The Samaritan really felt for the Jew as brother and as victim. Likewise our process of discipleship must be based on a human caring for and identification with all the suffering, aspirations and struggles of our society and church.

The Samaritan really did the practical helping deeds. He stopped, he bound up the wounds, he put the Jew on his own mount, he interrupted his plans, he spent his time and his money. So, too, our process of discipleship must move from contemplative compassion to contemplative action, i.e., we must move into doing the good at hand.

The Samaritan really found a way to sustain his contemplative compassion and action by creating a structure to continue his ministry when he left to continue his journey. So, too, we must create enduring structures to do our work as we move along the journey God gives us.

Christ supports us not by taking us out of today's and tomorrow's challenges, but by the abiding gift of his Spirit who teaches us how to become men and women on a mission—contemplative, compassionate, practical, and generative. This, I submit, is a spirituality of discipleship.

We do need a new paradigm to meet the challenges of our day. Yet the paradigm which I have explored here is eternal. It is the paradigm of God's mission given to Jesus. But it calls us to hear with new hearts the summons: "Go into the whole world and proclaim the good news to all creation" (Mark 16:15). Central to that good news is the priority of mission over maintenance. Mission looks at what is the enduring good we wish to accomplish which will implement the priorities of peace, justice, and love established by Jesus and preached by the early church.

Mission looks at the initial challenges which inspired our founders to risk their lives, reputations, and energies to bring a new way of living the gospel to the church and to the world. Mission looks at the life people live around us, at how people act toward one another, at what causes fear, enmity, and violence and at what causes confidence, union, and mutual care. Mission asks *why* we run a school or a hospital or a parish or a social center and *how* we can maintain each work only insofar as it genuinely promotes the values of our charism and meets the most universal needs of our times. Consequently, maintenance is a part of mission but never its substitute.

To live and to lead with that conviction is worth a life—ours in leadership and those of our sisters and brothers who labor with us. Let us, then, be about that mission, not as a moralizing imposition from above and not as one more agenda item, but as the heartfelt expression of our religious call to continue in our way the work begun on this earth by Christ.

NOTES

While I have emended some sections of this 1985 CMSM presentation, the substance remains the same. So, too, do the end notes below. However, I do want to indicate some evolution in my argument about the centrality of mission in the life and work of apostolic religious and some places which offer a more recent bibliography.

Today I would emphasize the place of apostolic service in the spirituality of religious women and men. Mission involves a charismatic autonomy and the power to initiate just as much as it involves the ability to work in support of episcopal priorities. If religious have an ineffective voice in their mission, this has serious ramifications for their identity, morale, and creativity.

Second, I would add to the term "mission" the words "in solidarity." Mission-in-solidarity involves: continued fidelity to the Vatican II summons to renewal, to an evangelical faith that finds expression in works of justice, to heightened communication and colleagueship among all church membership but particularly between lay people and religious and to the development of a theology and spirituality of the Spirit.

I have elaborated these ideas in a series of presentations which also provide additional bibliography on this topic of mission: "Shift in Theology" *The Way Supplement* 65, 1989, 54-65; "The Structure of the Document," *The Way Supplement* 71, Summer, 1991, 29-40; "Continuing Summons to Renewal and Reorientation," *Origins* 23(8), July 15, 1993, 115-120, and "Religious Life's Spirit of Solidarity," *Origins* 23(10), August 12, 1993, 173-176.

1. John Knowles, *A Separate Peace* (New York: Dell, 1959).
2. Bishop James Malone, "Evaluating Vatican Council II," *Origins* 15,

(July 4, 1985), 97; 99-102. This represents a thoughtful appreciation of the achievements and limits of Vatican II. Cf. also: Andrew M. Greeley, "The Failures of Vatican II, Twenty Years After," *America*, February 6, 1982, and "The Failures of Vatican II Revisited," *America*, June 12, 1982, 454-461.

3. "Decree on the Appropriate Renewal of Religious Life," #2 in *The Documents of Vatican II*, Walter M. Abbott, S.J., General Editor (New York: Guild Press [1966], 468).

4. *Ibid.*, 468-469.

5. The best single English-language volume containing the pertinent ecclesiastical documents and a series of excellent commentaries is *Religious Life in the U.S. Church, the New Dialogue*, ed. Robert J. Daly, S.J., et. al. (Ramsey, New Jersey: Paulist Press, 1984).

6. Daniel J. Harington, S.J., *God's People in Christ* (Philadelphia: Fortress Press, 1980), 17-32.

7. In a different context, I discussed many of these features in "Religious Formation: Evolution to Revolution," *New Catholic World*, 226 (Sept./Oct., 1982), 235-238.

8. Thomas E. Clarke, S.J., "A New Experience," in *Tracing the Spirit*, ed. James E. Hug, S.J. (New York: Paulist Press, 1983), 13-37.

9. Gray, "Religious Formation: Evolution to Revolution," *New Catholic World*, 236.

10. Robert L. Kinast "Theological Reflection in Ministry Preparation," *Tracing the Spirit*, ed. Hug, 83-99.

11. There are two recent studies on leadership, one secular, the other scriptural, which say many of these same things: Warren Bennis and Burt Nanus, *Leaders: The Strategies for Taking Charge* (New York: Harper and Row, 1985); Helen Doohan, *Leadership in Paul* (Wilmington, Del.: Michael Glazier, 1981), esp. 11-25.

PART TWO:

Understanding the Form of Life

Living in the Meantime: Biblical Foundations for Religious Life

Donald Senior, C.P.

It is the right instinct and the proper Christian impulse to turn to the scriptures in order to reflect on the meaning of vowed life. Returning to our biblical roots is always a source of renewal for the church.

But almost all of the questions which drive us to the scriptures have to be recast and reframed as we enter the biblical world. The Bible speaks of "vows," but not exactly the kind of "vows" we refer to. The Bible surely knows of religious people and religious experience, but the state of life we call "religious" or the vowed life had not yet been established in Israel or the early church.

So as we enter the Bible's marvelous world of symbol and story, of powerful history and poetic language, we must be prepared, like some respectful visitor to another culture, to lay aside, at least momentarily, some of our assumptions and expectations, and allow ourselves to be immersed in the biblical way of understanding and expression. Then, refreshed, we can return to our own land and our own time.

The questions that I would like to bring to the biblical world are three: (1) What is the fundamental connection between what we call religious life or the vowed life and the Bible? (2) More specifically, what are credible biblical foundations for the classical expressions of the religious vows: obedience, poverty, and chastity? and (3) Can the Bible assist us in reviving our sense of the meaning of religious life for today?

THE BIBLE AND THE VOWED LIFE: FINDING THE FOUNDATION

Let us try a first probe of the biblical frontier with a direct question about vows. The Bible is no stranger to solemn promises made to God.

55

When Jacob lays his weary head on a stone at Bethel and dreams his haunting dream of the angels of God ascending and descending a ladder between heaven and earth, he awakens with a sense of God's presence and makes a vow that if God would walk with him then he would make his pillow stone into a temple and give a tithe of all he possesses (Gen 28:20). Or there is Hannah's vow at the shrine of Shiloh, that if God would breathe life into her barren womb, then she would give that son to God and, as a sign of this, no razor would ever touch his head (1 Sam 1:11). David in his psalm vowed that he would not enter his house or get into his bed until the Ark of the Covenant had found a resting place (Ps 132:2).

And there are some vows the Bible probably would like to forget. Jephthah, a zealous son of Gilead and a great warrior, vows to God that if the Ammonites would be defeated, he, Jephthah, would slaughter for a sacrifice the first person who came out to greet him when he returned home! Unfortunately for Jephthah, the first person to greet him, dressed in her ribbons and dancing with a timbrel, was his beautiful and only daughter! (Judg 11).

Most of the vows in the Old Testament are like this: payoffs—promises to do something if God comes through. In fact, most of the references to vows in the Hebrew scriptures are found in the legislation governing sacrifices offered in fulfillment of such vows.

The New Testament is relatively silent on vows. Paul, we know, makes one; but we don't know about what. In Acts we learn that he cut his hair as a sign of a vow at the port of Cenchreae before sailing to Ephesus (Acts 18:18). Later in Jerusalem, the Christian elders counsel Paul to go up to the temple and purify himself with four other men who have taken a vow—but, again, we learn nothing about the nature or content of their vows.

So entering the biblical world through this port does not yield much. The Bible knows the terrible power of a promise and knows, too, of solemn promises to God, but they are narrow in gauge and usually conditional promises: I will do something if God does something else. These sorts of vows have little, if anything, to do with what we mean by the vowed life. To find a credible biblical connection we need to shed the explicit language of vow and turn elsewhere in the biblical landscape.

LOVE DEEPER THAN A BARGAIN: THE CALL TO HOLINESS

Religious vows, I suggest, are not a conditional promise but an expression of a far deeper reality. Religious vows are not a plea that God enter my life in some specific way, but practically the reverse—an expression of the fact that God has already taken hold of me with a grip so strong and so mysterious that I cannot turn away. It is here, in the fundamental biblical conviction that God enters human life, seizes and even torments it with God's powerful enticements, that the true scriptural foundation for religious life is to be found.

Israel's whole history can be spun out in this way. The first biblical impulse about God is told in the exodus event. The Israelites, mired in slavery and without hope, are invaded by God. God wrests them from Egypt, purifies them during a desert sojourn, breathes new life and identity in them at Sinai, and finally gives them a land and a destiny.

The first and fundamental biblical "vow," if you like, is the covenant: Israel's solemn response to what God had done to and for them. They would be holy as God is holy; they would listen to God and obey God. They would be faithful because God had proven faithful.

At every turn in the biblical saga, such exchanges between a saving God and a responsive people take place. When God prompts Joshua to lead the people across the Jordan and on to Shechem, the covenant is renewed as desert nomads took on the responsibility of land and governance. Each moment of Israel's history is read by biblical faith as God's loving and powerful intrusion into the heart of Israel. When the period of the Judges had run its course, Israel's will faltered and political chaos boiled. God, through the prophet Samuel, would pass over all of Jesse's sons until his eye fell on the youngest: a shepherd—ruddy, handsome, with "beautiful eyes," the texts says—David. God would make him a king whose dynasty would rule Israel forever (1 Sam 16). And centuries later, when all hope seemed shattered—with Jerusalem destroyed, the temple razed, and the people deported—God would intrude again: moving Cyrus, King of Persia, to return the people home to build the temple, to build a new people and new hope.

The true vows of Israel, deep promises of conversion and new life, come not as conditions laid on God but as responses to God's own initiative. That exchange can chart the history of Israel as a people, just as it characterizes the experience of its individual leaders. The Bible sees the lives of the patriarchs precisely in this way: Abraham, the cattle baron from Mesopotamia, leaves home and clan and sets out on a journey of faith because God mysteriously lays claim to him. Moses becomes the firebrand liberator of a reluctant people, not ultimately because of his own political ambition, but because he treads near the burning bush and God who is holy sends him to redeem the Israelites. So the roster goes: Deborah called by God to confound the people's enemies on the plains of Meggido; Isaiah haunted by God's voice in the temple and so becoming a prophet; Samuel roused from sleep at Shiloh; Jeremiah doomed to prophecy because, as he says, God burns like fire in his bones.

If there is anything that the Bible extracts from its history, it is that God acts first. Therefore, the proper and primordial religious response is an ear cocked to hear God's voice, an eye open to see God's footprint in the strange sands of Israel's tortured and wonderful history.

NEW TESTAMENT IMAGES

The New Testament canvas is narrower but the drama etched on it is very similar. The first religious impulse of the disciples is not their self-directed religious quest but the intrusion of Jesus into their lives. Casting nets into the sea, counting tolls at the tax collector's booth, drawing water at a Samaritan well, tormented, sick and alone in the Gadarene hills, sitting under a fig tree in Galilee or perched in a sycamore in Jericho—into each of these unlikely places, Jesus intrudes with a call to holiness and mission.

In fact, one might first trace this same type of experience in the very life of Jesus himself. The Galilean is drawn mysteriously to the Jordan, to the desert prophet who proclaims a message of repentance. As Jesus immerses himself in the waters of the Jordan, the Spirit descends on him, and then, literally in Mark's gospel, "hurls" Jesus into a desert confrontation with the power of evil and leads him to Galilee where he begins his mission of proclaiming the advent of God's rule. Jesus himself is the prototype of the one in whom God works uniquely, the one who responds with every fiber of his being. Jesus, we could say, takes the primordial biblical vow.

What happens to the disciples during Jesus' ministry is continued with even greater force under the impact of his resurrected Spirit. Like some driving storm, the Spirit of the risen Christ breaks into locked doors, throws Jerusalem crowds into chaos, knocks zealous persecutors from their horses, turns upside down the well-ordered households of Roman centurions, and troubles the journey of an Ethiopian eunuch. In each instance, a new relationship and a new way of life result.

I would suggest that if religious life is to have a biblical foundation, it will ultimately rest here in that profound transforming bond between God and the believer. Religious life, the vowed life, is an expression of the biblical call to holiness; it is a public enactment of an ancient quest: the quest to respond to the God who has already touched us and haunted us. It is no less than the quest for holiness.

Note what is *not* my starting point for finding the biblical foundation for religious life: it is not rooted in a distinctive type of ministry; not rooted in the witness of the common life; not rooted in the distinctive spiritualities and modes of life that dot the spectrum of the vowed life in Christian history; not rooted in the ability of religious life to respond to human need or human ideals. Rather, it is rooted in the fundamental biblical call to be holy as God is holy. Take away the God intoxication that characterizes the history of Israel and of the early community, and one takes away the biblical rationale for any life we can truly call "religious."

THE BIBLICAL CALL TO HOLINESS AND THE VOWED LIFE

Not only does the call to holiness form the biblical basis for the vowed life and, indeed, all Christian life, but it also gives to each of the vows and to religious life as a whole its characteristic content, spirit and mission.

One of the remarkable and often noted qualities of a biblical perspective is that the believer is called to imitate God. The words of Yahweh to Moses in Leviticus 19 put this motif in its classical form: "Say to all the congregation of the people of Israel, You shall be holy; for I the Lord your God am holy" (Lev 19:2). The demands of the covenant are to be understood in this fashion. Because God adopts Israel as a people, they are to respond by keeping God's commands. Those commands—reverence, fidelity, honesty, purity of heart and intention, compassion—reflect the very qualities that mark Yahweh's relationship to Israel. Two of the classical virtues associated with covenant fidelity fit this same mold: *hesed* and *emeth*. *Hesed:* that wonderful word so hard to translate—faithful, enduring, loving-kindness. *Emeth:* truth, justice, a God who is totally trustworthy. These virtues are word portraits of the God of Israel and these same virtues are to mark the Israelite who is in communion with this God through the covenant.

The epic story of Israel demonstrates this time and time again. The great characters of Israel are ultimately proven for their God-like virtues: Abraham for his faithfulness; Moses and Deborah because of their zeal for the people's freedom; David for his enduring strength; Hosea for remembering God's compassion in the midst of marital collapse; Elijah because he was driven by God's spirit. The role call goes on.

New Testament theology moves this notion to its zenith. *Imitatio Dei* becomes *imitatio Christi*. It is most explicit, perhaps, in Johannine theology where Jesus the Word incarnate becomes the embodiment of God's love for the world. The programmatic text of John 3:16 (now frequently displayed in the end zone of NFL games) says it clearly: "For God so loved the world that he gave his only Son, that whoever believes in him should not perish but have eternal life. For God sent the Son into the world, not to condemn the world, but that the world might be saved through him" (Jn 3:16-17).

The word that God whispers to the world through the very humanity of Jesus is love. And with startling force, John's gospel recognizes
that the most eloquent articulation of that word was Jesus' death on the
cross, which John interprets as an act of friendship love: "No greater
love than this, than one lay down one's life for a friend" (15:13).

If God is love, then in Johannine thought the life response of the
believer must itself be love; and that, in fact, is the blunt force of Johannine ethics. "By this will all know that you are my disciples, if you have
love for one another" (Jn 13:35). All other ethical injunctions seem to
drop out of sight for John or, more accurately, are subsumed in this core
intuition.

But it is not only John's gospel that makes this point in the New Testament. In the synoptic gospels, for example, the disciple is to "follow"
Jesus; "following" does not mean simply tagging after the Master but being
guided by his way, faithfully obedient to his person and teaching. The
way and the teaching of Jesus come ultimately from God.

One of the most eloquent expressions of this can be found in the
Sermon on the Mount in Matthew (and in its Lukan parallel). When the
Matthean Jesus gives the zenith point of his teaching—love of enemies—
that call to the most demanding ethical expression ever asked of humans,
this is motivated precisely by the *imitatio Dei*. In loving your enemy,
Jesus says, you will thus show that you are children of your heavenly Father, "who makes his sun rise on the evil and the good, and sends rain on
the just and on the unjust." God's love, in other words, is lavish, completely
gratuitous and gracious. The true disciple is to be "complete as your heavenly Father is complete" (Mt 5:48) or in Luke's version, "merciful, even
as your Father is merciful" (Lk 6:36).

Therefore, if we conceive of the vowed life as a response to God's
loving presence in our life, then the meaning of the vows—the very spirit
and content of religious commitment, if you will—must reflect God's own
character. Those caught up in God's embrace will reflect God's Spirit in
their lives. This, I am convinced, is the proper gateway through which
religious life can find its homeland in the biblical world. Let us test this
out on each of the vows and on some of the defining characteristics of
religious life.

THE BIBLICAL ROOTS FOR THE VOWS

As I think we all appreciate, the vows are not really autonomous
entities. Each attempts to lift up a distinctive facet of gospel values and
Christian existence, but each vow is intimately related to the other. In
some religious traditions, all of the vows can be subsumed under one. This

interrelationship of the vows will become evident as we try to trace more firmly their biblical foundations.

THE VOW OF OBEDIENCE

I choose to take first the vow that may be the least appreciated today, but the one with the strongest and most evident biblical roots.

If we understand obedience in its most radical form as faithful listening to God's voice as it comes to us through the community, through our teachers and leaders, and through the events of history, then we tap into a characteristic of faith most blessed by the Bible. The very creed of Israel—recited twice daily in the synagogue from at least the first century of the Christian era, and surely in Jewish homes and places of prayer centuries before that, and still enduring as a sign of Jewish faith until our own day—is the perfect expression of the biblical virtue of obedience:

> Hear, O Israel; The Lord our God is one Lord; and you shall love the Lord your God with all your heart, and with all your soul, and with all your might. And these words which I command you this day shall be upon your heart; and you shall teach them diligently to your children, and shall talk of them when you sit in your house, and when you walk by the way, and when you lie down, and when you rise. And you shall bind them as a sign upon your hand, and they shall be as frontlets between your eyes. And you shall write them on the doorposts of your house and on your gates (Deut 6:4-9).

This creed, the famous *Shema,* expresses the Bible's great God-intoxication, the experience that stands at the heart of what I am trying to convey here. Because Israel is so convinced of God's loving presence in history, because it is so swept up by the reality of God, the deepest instinct of the believer is reverent obedience, trusting openness to God's loving direction in everyday life.

Biblical faith, we are all aware, is not naive, not serendipitous. Raw biblical faith in the reality of God's presence can coexist with baffled anguish at God's silence and seeming absence. Thus, Moses who takes off his shoes in complete awe before the burning bush and the voice of the living God, can also smash God's tablets in frustrated rage at the stupidity of God's people and God's confusing ways. The psalmist who hymns God's loving presence in every corner of the universe, who praises in some of the Bible's most lyrical poetry the Spirit of God that tracks down the beloved from loftiest heavens to the darkness of sheol, can be matched by the unvarnished and near despairing lament of the believer who cries out, "My God, My God why have you forsaken me?" Jeremiah the prophet, whose strength is like a brass wall and who speaks of God as a raging fire in his bones, can also call God a treacherous brook which streams into the desert only to vanish in arid waste.

Once again *imitatio Dei* becomes *imitatio Christi*. Even Jesus knew the whiplash of biblical faith. Jesus was the unique Son in whom God abided, one who was drenched with the Spirit of God, the one who ranged the mountaintops alone for communion with his Father, one who lifted up his voice in ecstasy in his sure confidence that he knew God and God knew him. Yet before the mystery of failure and death, Jesus, too, obedient Son of God, raged against the darkness and the stillness of God's voice.

In other words, biblical obedience is played out in real life. Suffering, dashed hopes, spiritual fatigue, all take their toll. But the Bible clings fiercely, tenaciously to its faith in the reality of God's presence in history, *its* history. And therefore the person of biblical faith stands ready to hear God's voice and binds the phylacteries of that vow of obedience on the forehead and on the arm and fastens it to the doorpost.

Without this substratum of faith, religious obedience simply has no meaning worthy of our concern. Issues of authority structures, freedom and responsibility, balancing communal demands and individual initiative—all of these are important but quite secondary, and even capable of making us lose our way in understanding the authentic character of the obedience we vow. What we vow is to listen with all our heart and all our soul and all our strength to the living voice of God. Kevin Seasoltz explores the implications of this vision of obedience further in the following essay.

THE VOW OF POVERTY

Unlike obedience, one has to dig a bit, but not too far, to find the biblical roots for the vow of poverty. Obedience is a common biblical word; the abstract word "poverty" is hardly ever used. But the key to this vow, as we have suggested above, is the realization that it must flow intrinsically from the bond of faith and love that ties us to God. In fact, from the biblical perspective, what we mean by obedience and poverty are closely related. If we understand obedience as the commitment to listen to the voice of God, then the vow of poverty commits us to the freedom necessary to respond to that voice.

In general, the Bible takes a pragmatic view about possessions. Basically they are good, part of Israel's birthright, God's gift to humanity at the moment of creation, the bounty of milk and honey promised for their land of destiny. Poverty and destitution, on the other hand, are evil—a wound on human dignity, the fingerprints of oppression and exploitation. Therefore, one of the solemn obligations of the covenant was that all of the people were to be cared for; no one was to be in need. No one was, in fact, to be "poor." When Luke portrays the post-Easter community of Jerusalem, he describes it precisely in these terms as the fulfillment of the ideal community longed for by Israel: all were of one heart and one mind; all things were possessed in common so that no one would be in need.

But Israel and the New Testament churches also knew the abusive power of too many possessions. Beginning with Solomon, Israel's national experiment seemed to go sour because of the lure of wealth. Solomon broke down the protective community shield of the tribal system and, in its place, established administrative units for taxation purposes. Divisions between the wealthy and the poor began to emerge and the clan spirit of early Israel was diminished.

Eventually prophetic voices from Elijah to Jeremiah would rail against the rich and powerful because they abused the defenseless. Amos and Hosea would excoriate the wealthy "cows of Bashan" who lounged on their ivory couches while the poor lived miserably. And Isaiah would not hesitate to ridicule the temple liturgy itself when it was performed by those whose hands were red with the exploited blood of the poor.

Thus, two biblical instincts about possessions emerge in the Hebrew scriptures and carry over into the New Testament. First, possessions are good when they serve as instruments for and expressions of the human dignity one holds as a child of God. Second, in a community based on faith in a God who is gracious and compassionate, no one should suffer need, all should be at peace.

The New Testament follows this pragmatic, thoroughly religious view of possessions. Great wealth is viewed warily, not because of some ascetical impulse, nor out of any romantic notions of poverty, but with the suspicion born of experience. Jesus and the early church lived in a time and place where disparity between the wealthy and the poor was quite visible. Too many possessions lure your heart and make material things your treasure. "Where your treasure is, there your heart is." The man with too much harvest is likely to make the mistake of building too many barns instead of thinking about the destiny of his soul. The one who steps over Lazarus and his sores to enter his banquet hall is probably also too preoccupied to recognize the voice of prophecy, even when his own life is at stake. The one who finds solace and power in what he owns may soon find himself worshipping mammon as if it were his God.

These, of course, are Jesus' own examples about wealth and possessions. They are practical, wry, experiential. Some of Jesus' most explicit
instructions on possessions are set in the context of travel metaphors. Too
much wealth is simply too much baggage; those that carry too much baggage do not have the freedom to move. So the rich young man turns
away sad—too much luggage. And Zaccheus, seeking approval from Jesus,
notes that he gives half of his riches away.

The journey that beckons is the journey of faith and service, ultimately the journey to God. It will lead, Jesus knows, inevitably through
suffering and hardship and conversion of heart. The synoptic gospels put
before us the indelible icon: Jesus walking in the lead, his face set with
determination for Jerusalem—for the giving of his life out of love. The
disciples stumble along behind, not fully comprehending, half fearful,
half ecstatic.

For this journey one must be free. This fact shapes the sayings on possessions that begin to come from the Master:

> If any one would come after me, let him deny himself and take
> up his cross and follow me. For whoever would save his life
> will lose it; and whoever loses his life for my sake and the gospel's
> will save it. For what does it profit someone, to gain the whole
> world and forfeit their life? (Mk 9:34-36).

And when the disciples pause on the journey, wondering if they have
risked too much, the call of freedom is sounded again:

> Peter began to say to him, "Lo, we have left everything and fol-
> lowed you." And Jesus said, "Truly I say to you, there is no one
> who has left house or brothers or sisters or mother or father or
> children or lands, for my sake and for the gospel, who will not
> receive a hundredfold now in this time, houses and brothers and
> sisters and mothers and children and lands, with persecutions;
> and in the age to come eternal life (Mk 10:29-31).

The logic is clear again. What we call evangelical poverty is what the
gospels call putting aside whatever keeps you from following Jesus. Jesus
was supremely free, free to follow the lead of the Spirit, free to roam the
margins of his society, free to be in communion with the dispossessed,
free to touch those in need of healing, free to absorb anger and violence,
free to hear the voice of God.

The Bible never speaks positively of "poverty" (and so we do have a language problem here). It does, however, speak positively of the "poor": they are the object of God's compassion and, therefore, must be the concern of a covenant community. But the "poor" also, in the eyes of the Bible, have one advantage over the rich: they are, by definition, less likely to be seduced by an abundance of possessions. They are defenseless and vulnerable by all human accounts and so their only defense, their only bulwark, can be God.

And so a probe of the biblical roots of the vow of poverty leads us back to the foundation we described above. Blessed are the poor for theirs is the kingdom of God. Blessed are they who are so smitten by God and the vision of life with God that they put aside all encumbrances, all baggage, and travel with Jesus to the fulfillment of their hope.

In the history of the church a number of motivations for the vow of poverty have developed, some of them reflecting an ascetical ideal of stripping oneself of material things in order to clarify one's spiritual vision. Additionally, poverty is taken as a spiritual state of total, humble dependence on God, and therefore one can embrace Lady Poverty. These and other traditions can certainly claim some biblical roots.

But the most apparent biblical motivations for laying aside possessions are two: the freedom to put the excess of our goods at the disposition of those in need, and the freedom from those possessions that would encumber us in following Jesus.

THE VOW OF CHASTITY

To find the biblical roots of the vow of chastity, we must also scan carefully the biblical landscape. As in the case of poverty, the close relationship among all of the vows becomes apparent.

From the beginning of Christian history, those who have chosen celibate chastity have appealed to the famous text in Matthew 19 as the biblical foundation for their decision. After Jesus has proclaimed his teaching on marriage and apparently revoked the possibility of divorce, the stunned disciples ask him, "'If such is the case of a man with his wife, it is not expedient to marry.' But he said to them, 'Not all can receive this saying, but only those to whom it is given. For there are eunuchs who have been so from birth, and there are eunuchs who have been made eunuchs by men, and there are eunuchs who have made themselves eunuchs for the sake of the kingdom of heaven. The one who is able to receive this, let him receive it'" (Mt 19:10-12).

Allow me for just a moment to reflect a bit on this passage. As I suspect you have heard many times in recent years, the immediate applicability of this passage to celibate chastity has been put in question by modern biblical scholarship. The immediate issue in the passage is the question of marriage, not celibacy, and the state of being a "eunuch" in this text probably applies to those who, because of Jesus' teaching, chose not to remarry.

While this is true, I think this text remains an important lead for discovering the biblical roots of the vow of chastity. We should be clear from the outset that the Bible has a most positive view of sexuality, not in a romantic sense, but as a vital human expression of God's creative power. The biblical injunction was to "increase and multiply." So children—particularly sons, in a patriarchal and clan culture—were not only a sign of blessing and security but an expression of obedience.

Barrenness and sterility, on the other hand, were a curse and reason for ridicule. Even in Jesus' saying—a "eunuch" for the sake of the kingdom—we catch the biblical perspective. How interesting that Jesus should use this word. No one was more contemptible from a Jewish perspective than the eunuch. The Bible has no hymns to virginity and few words of praise for the celibate life. More typical is the wrenching picture of Hannah, tears streaming down her face as she prays before the shrine of Shiloh, begging God to deliver her from the shame of barrenness. When Isaiah wished to portray the utter abjection of Israel in exile, he chose the image of the virgin, one who is barren: "Sing, O barren one, who did not bear; break forth into singing and cry aloud, you who have not been in travail!" (Is 54:1)

In the passage from Matthew, the latch that opens the door to the biblical meaning of celibate chastity is the phrase: *dia ten basileian ton ouranon.* It is often translated, "for the sake of the kingdom," but we should carefully note what we mean by the phrase, "for the sake of." The notion implied in the Greek is not that one "makes oneself" a eunuch in order to set out toward the kingdom, but rather that the *kingdom* has done something to make a person become a eunuch. The translation should more precisely be: "*because of* the kingdom of heaven." In other words, God's rule—God—seizes a person with a passion so strong, so commanding that it takes over one's life, leads one to a decision the Bible can hardly contemplate (and before which the disciples flinch).

We might note, parenthetically, that the other favorite passage used as a biblical foundation for the vow of chastity is 1 Corinthians 7, where Paul says that in view of the approaching endtime all should stay put in their state of life, but that his own preference is to be unmarried. Why? Because, Paul says, "the unmarried man is anxious about the affairs of the Lord, how to please the Lord." He says this, he assures them, not to lay any restraint upon them but "to secure your undivided devotion to the Lord" (1 Cor 7:32-35).

The same note is struck here as in the passage from Matthew. Celibate chastity becomes a Christian option only because consuming passion for God takes over one's life.

This fits the biblical picture we noted above. The barren who lament their emptiness and sterility find that God alone fills their life. God brings life to the dead womb of Sarah; God removes Hannah's shame; God breathes life into the womb of Elizabeth; and God's Spirit renews creation in the body of Mary. For the Bible and for genuine Christian tradition and, I believe, human experience itself, the only passion that can eclipse the passion of sexual love is the passion of faith. So, the Bible suggests that the vow of chastity, like the vows of obedience and poverty, takes its radical meaning from the vibrant primordial bond between God and the believer.

Without a consuming passion for God, a celibate life remains, in the Bible's view, just that: a solitary, impoverished life. If we can speak of the witness value of celibacy, then here is a witness that comes from the heart of the scriptures—a consuming passion for God is the core of human existence. Any child of God, celibate or married, who substitutes any other passion (even one like sexuality which the Bible prizes) as the defining center of human life is, in the biblical view, doomed to disillusionment.

The passages we have considered, especially the one from Paul, throw light on another dimension of celibate chastity that has strong biblical roots. One becomes a eunuch because of the overwhelming experience of the kingdom, or one becomes filled with passion for God, or one has "undivided devotion to the Lord" for the sake of the mission. Here Jesus himself becomes the proper model. The restless, itinerant mission of Jesus was "for the sake of the kingdom." The driving force of Jesus' mission, the target of his energy and authority was his love for others. He was not a solitary figure. His life was characterized by self-transcendence—laying down his life for his friends; giving his life in ransom for the many; losing his life in order to save it.

Paul, too, was no solitary. His letters reveal a man with an incredible number of friendships and apostolic partnerships strung across the Mediterranean world.

Thus the celibate life may allow the same freedom to travel that poverty is meant to foster. The gospels continually portray Jesus as free from his family: "Who are my mother and brothers and sisters . . . ?" His new family became the community of his disciples, of those he served and empowered for mission.

From the biblical perspective, the vowed life of chastity has meaning only when coupled to an evident passion for God and an apostolic passion for others.

THE BIBLE AND THE WITNESS OF THE RELIGIOUS LIFE

Let us pause for a moment and take stock. The vowed life, as the Christian life itself, is rooted in the call to holiness. Christians are called to be so bonded to God in faith and love, that the character of one's life and values and commitments takes its shape from the very life of God. "Be holy as I am holy."

What we have traditionally called the vows find their spirit and content in this call to holiness. Obedience is reverent listening for God's voice. Poverty is freedom from the encumbrance of possessions in order to follow God's call and to insure no one is in need. Chastity is making way for the passion of faith and being free for the new family of Jesus.

These gospel values are not the preserve of vowed religious, but should, in fact, characterize all authentic Christian life. Before we ask what is distinctive about religious life, we must see what it holds in common with all Christian life. Only then, not before, should the question of distinctive features be raised. Once raised, what, if any, would be the biblical foundations for the distinctive role of religious life, with all of its variety of forms and expressions, within the church?

There are two special features—both based in strong biblical values— that give religious life its distinctive role and public witness within the church. The first is the call to a common life and the second is a consciousness of living in the meantime. Allow me to briefly comment on each.

THE COMMON LIFE

Biblical vision couples faith in God with life in community. The closer we move to the blazing heart of the biblical God, the closer we move to each other. From the theophany of Sinai comes a covenant people who are responsible to each other, particularly to the vulnerable—the widow, the orphan, the sojourner. And the storm of the Spirit at Pentecost forges one people from many different nations and many tongues. That people is bound in a covenant of love and justice. Judaism knew and Christianity underscores the insight that love of God is inseparably bound to love of neighbor.

Paul's own life enacts this same experience. Once he has encountered the risen Christ he is, by his own testimony, driven—often at terrible personal cost—to draw within the boundaries of God's people those who before had been condemned to stand beyond its frontiers. Paul's vision was the vision of the covenant community with its arms flung open as wide as the heart of the biblical God: "neither Jew nor Greek, neither slave nor free, neither male nor female but all one in Christ Jesus."

For Paul the ultimate witness to the presence of God's Spirit within history was the formation of adult communities of faith and love, his churches that he planted on the rim of the Mediterranean world from Antioch to Rome. These communities, even with their wrangling and imperfections, were still the body of Christ for Paul. They were temples of the Spirit and living testimony to the reality of a gracious God as well as genuine signs that the world was capable of being transformed. He fretted over them, was anxious about them, and spent his life planting them and building them up.

The biblical basis for the communitarian witness of religious life is, indeed, the basis for the purpose of the church itself. Religious life, as a Christian institution, is rooted in the life of the church and takes its mission from this source. If in some fashion religious life does not reflect in an intensive, visible way the Christian reality of what it means to be called together as God's covenant people, then it is difficult to know, from a biblical basis at least, what rationale the common life would have.

LIVING IN THE MEANTIME

I come, finally, to a dimension of the biblical perspective that I think has particular relevance today for the witness of religious life in the church, namely the biblical sense of history. The Bible perceives human reality as standing in time between the present condition and future reality. The Bible has a strong future orientation. Strangely it believes that the future—because it is God's future—is more real and more enduring than the present. The future is not the projection of our imagination, but a God-shaped destiny toward which we move.

Although the creation story begins the biblical saga, the deepest instinct of the Bible is not paradise lost but paradise to be gained. The onrushing movement of biblical history is from slavery to freedom, from death to life. Creation, for much of biblical tradition, is an ongoing, future-oriented act, itself an act of redemption: "For behold, I create new heavens and a new earth; and the former things shall not be remembered or come to mind" (Is 65:17).

Jesus, likewise, sets his face toward the endtime when the dragnet would be sorted, the wheat freed from the tares, the harvest abundant, and the Son of man would come to gather his community from the four corners of the earth. But even now, the poor are blessed and those who mourn can take comfort because their joyous destiny with God is secure.

Paul, too, has a fierce commitment to this future. Life with God, when death would die and all things would be given over to God (1 Cor 15), is so compelling, so true, that this future destiny breaks in on the present.

This promise compels one to live now by the future that one so earnestly desires to see. You *are* the body of Christ; you *are* the temple of the Spirit; you *are* the redeemed children of God—even now while the Spirit still groans within the limitations of created reality.

Christian existence for Paul and for much of the New Testament is life *in the meantime;* life, as it were, played out between the present and the future. Life in the present brings its human heritage of pain and limitation and even death itself. But living in faith means that one chooses to have the present defined not in terms of a dead past but of the living future, God's future. Therefore, awareness of God's illuminating presence breaks into the spiritual dullness imposed by the past. The spirit of justice and liberality and graciousness that will characterize the future community with God breaks into the instinct of self-preservation and control. Offsetting the low-grade despair that drives us to expend everything now is the tonic of hope in our human destiny. Into the present narrow gauge of our capacity for love and the thin span of our relationships comes the ecstatic joy and inclusiveness of God's manner of loving.

This is certainly Paul's vision, one he sustained throughout his life. He was a mystic, but he was also a pastor. Paul realized that the redeemed future not only had to coexist with the limitations of the present but, at times, seemed to be smothered by it. Nonetheless, the role of the Christian community was to acclaim again and again God's future by living, even in snatches, its amazing reality now.

Religious life, if it is to find a biblical foundation, cannot escape grappling with this biblical perspective. The eschatological motivation for religious life (a more technical name for what I have been describing) has slipped from vogue in many current discussions about the rationale for the vowed life. But without this faith perspective on human destiny, the distinctive witness of the vowed life is muffled or lost altogether.

The ideal for which the vowed life strives is a community of human beings whose lives are rooted in a passionate love of God, directed by obedient listening to God's voice in history, free from the encumbrance of possessions, sustained by the passion of faith, and bound together as an adult community where no one is in need. Our Christian faith drives us to believe that this portrayal, even with all of its idealism and despite the awkwardness of our efforts to incarnate it, is indeed the destiny to which *all* human beings of whatever culture or whatever age are called. Without this driving conviction, religious life will not have the greatness of purpose and the strength of truth to sustain it in history.

One can and should say that such an anthropology should characterize all Christian life—and that is true. But religious life has the capacity to live it in a fully intentional, manifestly visible way so that it can become a sign to the wider church and to the wider world of its own nature and of the capacity of the human spirit before God.

CONCLUSION

I will conclude with three brief words of wisdom that struck me as I reviewed the biblical materials:

1. If the roots of the vowed life are to be found in the quest for holiness, then this should be the focus in discerning an authentic vocation to the vowed life. Ultimately, attraction to a religious community because of its characteristic ministry, or because it offers a haven from solitude or from the rigors of the marketplace, or because it provides an ascetical subculture will prove inadequate and transitory if a fundamental hunger for God is not the real itch.

Perhaps if religious life has become a bit flaccid and not a compelling option for serious minded young people, it is because it does not seem like a place where one has to wrestle with God.

2. If the biblical picture we have sketched seems true, then we may need to take ourselves more seriously. What the evangelical ideals of the vowed life have to say are crucial for human existence; they are not esoteric values. As religious people, we should remember that without faith, without a passionate commitment to the other, without the proper use of possessions, without hope in its future, humanity will die. There are signs of this all through history and they are quite apparent today. The events of recent history—both the explosion of freedom and religious renewal in Eastern Europe and the gnawing self-doubt in the heart of Western culture bespeak gospel truth. Quite literally, the world needs visible communities of human beings who live in the meantime in a way that gives credible witness to the spiritual nature and capacity of the human person. Renewal of religious life is not just a responsibility to and within the church. Even more importantly—because this is the ultimate purpose of the church itself—it is a responsibility to the world.

3. Finally, a suggestion about the catechesis of the vows. I think the religious vows are eminently biblical in nature. We would do ourselves and those who seek a religious vocation a favor if we would use more biblical images and symbols in reflecting on the meaning of the vows in our lives. The vows have to do, ultimately, not with a set of proposals, but with commitment to a way of life, a way rooted in faith. The biblical language, biblical symbols, and biblical stories have passion; they carry religious feeling as well as religious thought.

Surely it is important to continue what we have done during the past few years: steep ourselves in the histories of our founders and the characteristic spiritualities of our communities. But let's not forget that, first and foremost, authentic religious life must be authentic Christian life. The perennial touchstone of any authentic Christian life is its symmetry with the word of God, the living word expressed in the scripture and reflected in the wisdom of the church.

NOTE

This chapter was first presented as an address at the annual assembly of CMSM in Newport, R.I., in August, 1990.

Religious Obedience: Liberty and Law

R. Kevin Seasoltz, O.S.B.

Christians in general and religious in particular are called to listen to the word of God and to respond by laying down their lives for God and others just as Jesus laid down his life for his Father and for all of God's people. Women and men religious live in a context where they are presumably formed by the word of God day in and day out; they are also publicly committed to be obedient to that word and to bear prophetic witness to the meaning of Christ's paschal mystery through the profession of vows, including the vow of obedience. What difference does that profession really make in the way they exercise obedience to God's word in Jesus Christ through the power of the Holy Spirit and in the way they attempt to live a life of justice and charity by laying down their lives for God and for others?

There is little doubt that obedience as a virtue and a vow collides with values highly prized by many people in our modern world, including many of those professed as members of institutes of consecrated life. The practice of obedience is, to say the least, countercultural, for it is often felt to be at odds with the achievement of personal autonomy, independence, self-actualization, self-determination, freedom, personal responsibility, success, personal initiative, and professionalism. All of these are in some sense positive goals widely esteemed in many sectors of the modern world, especially by those in the middle and upper classes of society.[1]

If obedience is accepted merely as a functional necessity to achieve the execution of some project, it is apt to be tolerated almost as a necessary evil rather than espoused as a virtue. In other words, many people tend to resign themselves to the need for some obedience in their lives, realizing that without it social life would be next to impossible, but they want it reduced to a minimum. Most people instinctively feel that one's primary goal in life should be the maximum amount of self-determination.

BIBLICAL BACKGROUND

The word for obedience, both in Semitic and Indo-European languages, is derived from the root word meaning "to hear." It has consistently meant a readiness to listen and to attend to what is other than oneself. More precisely, it has come to imply a willingness to fulfill the will of another. The foundation for all obedience is authority, either divine or human. The adjustment or alignment of one's will to the will of the one in authority is obedience. By obedience the authority figure's determination is embraced by the will of the one obeying and so becomes a basis for action leading to the effect desired by the one in authority. A stable readiness to submit to legitimate authority in this way is the virtue of obedience. In institutes of consecrated life this disposition has regularly been confirmed by promise or vow.[2]

Special value has been attributed to obedience in both the Old and New Testaments. Throughout Christian history the practice has been given prominence through the development of what has come to be called religious obedience. During the centuries described in the Old Testament, obedience to God was exercised above all within the framework of the covenant, which required that the people should obey the law as divine revelation and hence as the primary norm of life. The law laid the foundation for religious observance, for ethical behavior, and for civil life. All authority figures, both religious and civil, were to be obeyed so long as their authority was thought to have derived its power from God.[3]

Of all the books in the Bible, Deuteronomy contains the most reflections on obedience. Sometimes the texts are stern: "If you obey the commandments of the LORD your God that I am commanding you today, by loving the LORD your God, walking in his ways, and observing his commandments, desires and ordinances, then you shall live. . . . But if your heart turns away and you do not hear, but are led astray . . . I declare to you today that you shall perish. . . . I have set before you life and death, blessings and curses" (Deut 30:16–19). The choice, however, is made more attractive by an invitation to love: "Choose life so that you and your descendants may live, loving your God, obeying him, and holding fast to him; for that means life to you and length of days" (Deut 30: 19–20).[4]

Obedience expresses a response to the most basic law of human existence: "Choose life!" But when the Deuteronomist counsels us to "choose life," he does not mean to seek a narrow, self-centered, self-preoccupied form of existence, but rather a life of compassionate concern and outgoing help toward one's neighbor. Deuteronomy's laws are marked by exquisite thoughtfulness; they invite people out of their narrow worlds into the broad arena of heaven and earth.

At the center of the New Testament stands Jesus whose whole life was a submission to his Father's will. He tells his disciples, however, not to choose life but to lose life: "If any want to be my followers, let them deny themselves and take up their cross daily and follow me. For those who want to save their life will lose it and those who lose their life for my sake will save it" (Lk 9: 23-24). The synoptics indicate that Jesus obeyed his parents and other legitimate authorities as a matter of course. He in turn was obeyed by the forces of nature, by demons, by disease and even by death.[5]

Jesus expounded the true meaning of the law for his disciples in a binding way and called them to imitate his obedience and to submit their wills to his. However, above all, the categories of love and faith were used to express the relationship of the disciples to their creator and savior more often than obedience. In the Johannine writings love for God is expressed by obedience to the divine will; that love involves love for one's neighbor, a love which often involves obedience.

Obedience to human authority is legitimated in the Pauline and other epistles as a fulfillment of Christ's directive to the Pharisees that they should "Render to Caesar the things that are Caesar's and to God the things that are God's" (Mt 22:21).

In the New Testament the emphasis is primarily on obedience to God, and secondarily on obedience to human authority figures, provided their will is in accord with God's will.[6]

HISTORICAL DEVELOPMENT OF RELIGIOUS OBEDIENCE

"Hearing God's word" and "the obedience of faith in God" are early descriptions of the Christian response to God's offer of salvation in Jesus Christ. Christian obedience is basically a response to Christ's paschal call to die to self-preoccupation and self-centeredness and to lay down one's life for God and others. Out of the New Testament a distinctive concept of religious obedience gradually developed. It seems that the earliest Christian anchorites were not drawn to their desert hermitages by a formal intention of binding themselves in obedience to a particular human superior, but rather by a strong desire to imitate Christ. They went to the desert to do battle with the demons through a life of asceticism and unceasing prayer. They sought above all to renounce sin and Satan.[7]

Trust in the success of certain eremitical figures, however, led many individuals to submit themselves to the direction of such desert fathers and mothers. Their submission was not based on a juridically structured authority system but was rather rooted in a conviction that charismatic women and men of professed holiness could be effective channels through which God could mediate a clearer understanding of the divine will and the consequent achievement of holiness.

Submission to such a holy man or woman was freely undertaken and was not formalized by vow; it was in fact revocable and not presumed to be for life. Linked with the hermit's trust in the holiness of another was a distrust of one's own disordered will; hence, renunciation of one's own will and submission to the will of a spiritual father or mother seemed highly virtuous.[8]

In fact the solitude of the hermit allowed a fair amount of scope for the exercise of self-will. Hence the cenobitic way of life with clearly defined hierarchical structures came to be looked upon as a more effective way to eliminate self-will on a daily basis. Furthermore the cenobitic way of life affected the spiritual development not only of individuals but also of communities as a whole. Submission in a monastery meant entering a cloister and living under a rule and superior who was also bound by the rule and whose authority was delineated in the rule. Obviously there was something very primitive, even inhuman, about this concept of authority and obedience, for it left no room for personal judgment about the soundness of commands.[9]

Gradually the concept was modified and mitigated due to a greater respect for initiative, a refined sense of personal dignity, and a need to respond effectively to the demands of work and what we would today call ministries or apostolates. However, it should be noted that the early history of cenobitic monasticism was characterized by a basic distrust of the human will, personal conscience, and human initiative.[10]

Religious rules tended to assume an air of divine authority, suggesting that any violation of the rule meant a contravention of the will of God. For example, the author of the Rule of the Master clearly claims divine authority for his rule as he prefaces each section with the words, "The Lord's answer through the Master".[11] Gradually there developed a refined understanding of the power of human authority, which is never absolute but always relative to Christ whose relationship to his disciples was primarily one of love and invitation rather than one of command and coercion. In the writings of Augustine, for example, we find an insistence on the use of discretion in the exercise of authority: "The superior must not think himself fortunate in his exercise of authority but in his role as one serving you in love;... in fear before God he shall be as the least among you."[12]

It was, above all, Benedict who made explicit provision in his Rule against rigid authoritarianism and an excessive insistence on uniformity. There we find an extraordinarily rich treatment of both authority and obedience. It is God who is the primary author of life for Benedict's disciples; hence the monk's obedience is above all to God and God's word, which the monk finds mediated into his life through a wide variety of persons and experiences—in the Rule, in the abbot, in the community as a whole, in the young and the old, in the sick and in guests, in the liturgy of the hours and in personal prayer, in *lectio divina*, in work, and in silence.[13]

Benedict's community might well be called a formation community in which all, including the abbot and other superiors in the community, are in the process of being formed all of their lives into the likeness of Christ by attentive listening to the word of God, and a loving response to that word mediated into the life of the community by Christ's own offer of friendship through the communication of his Holy Spirit. Hence, conversion to Christ and response to his love through the power of the Holy Spirit are the goals of obedience. It is likewise through that response that one becomes free to be and develop as the person one is called to be. The ideal of this pattern of conversion is meant to be incarnated in a special way for the community in the abbot, who is expected to be a symbolic center exercising a centripetal force that draws individuals into a truly Christian community of life for God and others in Jesus Christ through the power of the Holy Spirit.[14]

THE DEVELOPMENT OF AN INSTITUTIONAL PERSPECTIVE

Only gradually did a vow come to be annexed to the practice of religious obedience. Basil required an explicit oral promise of virginity, but that promise has been interpreted as so all-embracing that it would have included a commitment to obedience; there is, however, no clear indication of a specific vow of obedience in his writings.[15] For Pachomius, the life of a monk simply involved the full execution of one's baptismal promises; he did not, however, provide for the taking of any vows.[16] But one of his successors, Schenoudi, did introduce a solemn promise of obedience to be made in writing.[17] In that tradition, Benedict required a promise of obedience to be taken by his monks in the oratory in the presence of God and the saints.[18]

As monastic life became increasingly institutionalized in the Middle Ages, the humane approach to both authority and obedience was often eroded as communities became more and more impersonal because of size and involvement in secular affairs. Likewise, constitutions became increasingly detailed concerning liturgical observances as well as other monastic practices. The predominant influence in this regard was that of the Cistercians, whose detailed constitutions left a deep imprint on the many new congregations of canons. As the laws governing religious communities increased, the free personal giving of one's life to God often seems to have been eroded.[19]

Systematic reflection on the nature of institutionalized religious life eventually resulted in the description of religious communities as communities of the perfect, and the religious life as a state of perfection.[20] The rules and constitutions of communities were thought to exhibit the pattern of behavior appropriate to a community of saints. By their vows, and in particular by their vow of obedience, religious were thought to have committed themselves to a way of life appropriate to perfection. In other words, religious were to act as if they were perfect.

Given the presumption that the rule and the constitutions proposed a pattern of perfect behavior, it was inevitable that authority was often exercised in an authoritarian way. It was thought that the most effective way to protect individuals from sin and self-will was to take away all right to initiative and to minimize possibilities for personal judgment. This was often done by filling the horarium with many detailed duties and by requiring religious to seek permission from the superior to do anything that was not covered by the community's rule or customs.[21]

This approach to both authority and obedience lacked any sound foundation in the Bible and resulted in a distortion of the priorities set out in the gospel. The existential witness to Christian faith, hope, and love that provides a sound foundation for institutionalized religious life was endangered by this distorted understanding of authority and obedience; it identified conformity and uniformity with free and responsible union of mind and heart with Christ and others in the community.[22]

When religious, either as communities or as individuals, undertook missionary or other ministerial work in the world, religious obedience had to take into account not only the sanctification of individuals and the welfare of communities, but also the exigencies of the works undertaken. From the Middle Ages down to the present, most religious institutes, including many monastic institutes, have engaged in such work or ministry, much of it outside the enclosure. Obedience, then, consists in more than doing what the rule or superior explicitly commands. Certainly a rule cannot provide for all concrete instances, nor can a superior foresee them and by anticipatory commands chart the course of action to be followed in each case. There is a regular need for personal decisions by the individual religious in accord with the spirit of the community's rule and understanding of what one would be expected to do.[23]

With the development of the mendicant orders in the thirteenth century there was an attempt to rethink the meaning of religious obedience and to return to the gospel understanding of both obedience and authority. Franciscan obedience, for example, was firmly rooted in the bond of mutual love. Within the context of the gospel, it entailed the stripping away of one's own self-centered will and all that clutters one's life for the sake of Jesus. Open to the Spirit of Jesus dwelling within each member of the community, Franciscans were meant to become as mothers, sisters, brothers and spouses to Jesus. Their obedience, then, had both a vertical and horizontal dimension. Obedience to God was facilitated through obedience to a human instrument. This was accompanied by obedience to the others in community in a spirit of charity, so that the community established by Christ might be built up and strengthened. Those who functioned in roles of authority were first of all brothers and sisters to the other members of the community.[24]

Likewise, Dominican obedience involved a rethinking of the tradition that had been derived from the monastic and canonical inheritance. From the outset, Dominic wanted his order to be committed to a disciplined cenobitic life, but all members, both lay brothers and clerics, were to be personally responsible for the life and mission of the community.[25] St. Thomas maintained that every act of obedience must be a free, deliberate, rational act; hence, no superior could ever claim authority over the conscience of any of his subjects.[26]

The nature of Dominican obedience is reflected in the vow formula: "I, N., make profession and promise obedience to God and to blessed Mary and to you, N., Master of the Order of Preachers and to your successors, according to the Rule of blessed Augustine and the constitutions of the friars of the Order of Preachers, that I will be obedient to you and to your successors until death."[27] This unusual formula emphasizes obedience to God and obedience to Dominic and his successors; hence, the promise entails a willingness to give one's life to God and to the mission of the order.

By the end of the Middle Ages, basic patterns of religious obedience and authority were firmly in place. Minor modifications were made in those patterns in subsequent centuries, but in general they remained firmly entrenched in religious institutes until the Second Vatican Council.

Serious difficulties can certainly arise if a religious community loses sight of its primary character as a formation community and becomes primarily an action-oriented or functional community. In the latter focus the individual takes second place to the work of the community.

If the religious community thinks of itself primarily as dedicated to getting work done, it is inevitable that authority figures will consider themselves responsible for guaranteeing that the work is in fact effectively accomplished. Individuals are apt to be assigned at times to positions for which they have no particular ability, training or attraction, simply because the job needs to be done and there is no one else to do it.

The suffering that such assignments cause individual religious is sometimes justified as the practice of sound Christian asceticism which purifies one's motives and eradicates pride. In such situations there may be as little dialogue between the superior and the individual religious as between military officers and their subordinates. The comparison is apposite, because in the past the constitutions of many religious congregations were strongly influenced by the concept of the church militant; hence, they set out a militaristic concept of both authority and obedience.[28] The bald fact remains, however, that frequently in human life individuals must take on tasks and responsibilities for which they have been poorly prepared, for which they have little liking, and about which they have not been consulted. This is often the case in family life and in other basic social institutions.

RECENT DEVELOPMENTS

In the past thirty years, biblical, historical and theological studies of Christian authority and obedience have brought about a clearer understanding of the distinctively Christian foundations for both authority and obedience. We more readily grasp the meaning and practical implications of the assertion that God alone has absolute authority and that God alone is to be rendered absolute obedience.[29] We see more clearly how that assertion relativizes all human authority and conditions all human obedience. Pedagogical obedience is acknowledged as legitimate, not only in the education of children, but also for purposes of initial and ongoing formation in religious institutes. Mutual obedience—obedience to one another in the community—for the sake of community work and service and for solidarity has been generally accepted as a basic component of religious cenobitic life.

Collegial obedience has been increasingly affirmed for the sake of implementing communal decisions and in order to achieve ministerial effectiveness. At the same time compassion has led men and women religious to be more obedient to the weaknesses and woundedness of individuals both within and outside the religious institute. They are hearing and responding to the gospel of Jesus Christ by obedience to the poor and by obedience to their own poverty. In this way the primacy of obedience to God has been affirmed, as religious understand that Jesus came to bring salvation to those who are poor, not to those who simply serve the poor.[30]

In exercising these various forms of obedience, men and women religious have stressed the authority of personal conscience and the obedience due to one's own conscience in imitation of Jesus who always submitted personally to God in perfect obedience, but who did not submit to human authority figures when their will conflicted with God's will. The right to exercise obedience to one's own conscience, especially when it conflicts with the directives of those in authority, carries with it the responsibility to develop a conscience that is well formed and informed by the Spirit of the Lord Jesus, who is active not only in human hearts but also in the complex channels that we know as the teaching and learning church.

During the last thirty years there has been a paradigm shift in many religious institutes affecting both the understanding of Christian authority and the exercise of Christian religious obedience. The shift has been characterized by a move away from a rigid hierarchical exercise of authority to collaboration among adults presumed to be both gifted and responsible.[31] In other words, the shift has been away from religiously motivated submission to authority figures in an almost blind and automatic way, to responsible cooperation among the members of the group, including the authority figures. The shift has been characterized by a move away from the tendency to hear God speak almost exclusively through the authority figures in the community, who are thought to speak for God, to an effort to hear God speak in and through all the members of the community and in and through both personal and communal experiences.

This paradigm shift has had a number of important effects on religious institutes and on the lives of men and women religious. New forms of government have developed on all levels of various institutes. There have been changes in the understanding of mission and ministry and the way ministries are chosen by both communities and individual religious. Personal discernment and responsibility have been emphasized with the result that there is a better understanding of the need for ongoing spiritual and theological formation as well as for professional training among religious. The role of the superior in religious institutes has often been desacralized while the role of personal conscience has been resacralized. As a result, efforts have been made to emphasize the responsibility of individual religious to and for the institute as a whole.[32]

The human rights of individuals have been extolled. Even the 1983 Code of Canon Law seems to protect the rights of individuals more than the rights of religious institutes. This emphasis stands in rather marked contrast to the 1917 Code. Prior censorship of correspondence and other writings exercised by religious superiors has been both questioned and often rejected. Canonical actions have been taken to end unilateral dismissals from religious institutes.

Efforts have been made to abandon secrecy in elections, assignments, and the investigations of individual members. There has been an insistence on due process and a rather widespread use of arbitration. Personal and communal freedom has been championed in the areas of speech and communication, regarding the right to assemble, to take initiatives, and to take action. These developments have often been interpreted as spelling the end of totalitarian authority in religious institutes and the recovery of patterns of authority and obedience that are fundamentally Christian and appropriate for mature individuals.[33]

There is no doubt that many of these developments over the past thirty years have been positive; they have been in accord with the best strains of the gospel, Christian tradition, and the positive contributions that have been made to humanity by the behavioral sciences, especially psychology. But human beings seem to have a penchant for correcting imbalances with other imbalances, for correcting abuses with other abuses. Several questions need to be asked at the present time.

First of all, has the role of superiors in religious institutes been so desacralized that they no longer have any role other than that of coordination? Are they expected simply to accede to the wishes of individuals in their communities and to confirm the decisions that others have made? Are they often made the scapegoats on whom religious pile the blame for all the problems and mistakes that exist in institutes? Has personal freedom been allowed to degenerate into license, enabling it to take such an overriding possession of religious institutes that they are no longer communities but only collections of individuals often vaguely attached to a group and even more vaguely committed to a religious ideal, provided it does not collide with an individual's personal ambitions? These questions deserve serious attention.

CONTEMPORARY ISSUES

Vatican II's Decree on the Renewal of Religious Life *Perfectae Caritatis* counseled religious to "subject themselves in faith to those who hold God's place, their superiors.... They should be humbly submissive to their superiors, in a spirit of faith and of love for God's will, and in accordance with their rules and constitutions. They should bring their powers of intellect and will and their gifts of nature and grace to bear on the execution of commands and on the fulfillment of the tasks laid upon them, realizing that they are contributing towards the building up of the Body of Christ, according to God's plan" (§14).[34] Before the Second Vatican Council when religious were socialized into the institute by their superiors, the representative character of authority figures was usually not questioned;

it was an integral component of the social construction of the institute and an important factor in the development of a sacralized worldview. But as religious persevered in their institutes, the conviction that superiors were God's special representatives and that their will was God's will was often eroded by much contrary evidence.

If religious superiors should seriously perceive of themselves as God's special representatives in the institute and act out of that conviction in the exercise of their authority, then obviously their role should be marked by a very distinguished constellation of attitudes and characteristics. It must be noted, however, that the exercise of authority in any community will be determined to a great extent by the basic character of the community itself.

As already noted, there are different types of religious institutes, each possessing a distinctive type of authority. When a community is constituted mainly along functional lines, it is not primarily a personal community, since it is made up of individuals who are bonded together, not because of the relationship they have to each other as persons, but rather because they are agents or functionaries who work together to achieve a goal which is external to the individuals in the group.

For example, teachers are united in a school faculty in order to educate students; workers in a factory are united in a goal of efficiently producing a product. The authority figures in such groups have directive power over the members of the group because they are acknowledged implicitly or explicitly to embody the normative intention or goal of the group. Consequently, such superiors are both obliged and entitled to specify functions and commands so that the common intention or goal may be achieved with the maximum amount of efficiency.

A community that is presided over by God's representatives certainly falls short of its intended nature and potential if it is only a network of functions. It is, in fact, contrary to the Christian understanding of creation that God should give us life as human persons and communities made in the image and after the likeness of God, and yet expect nothing nobler from us than the investment of our time and energy in the execution of functions. God's business as the Trinity involved actively in creation is primarily the creation and promotion of life in persons and communities.

We mature into the beings we are called to be only through the experience of relating and responding to other persons, and being taken into account and loved by others who relate and respond to us as persons. The communities intended for us by God are personal communities, formation communities, not constituted simply by the execution of functions for the sake of efficiency and production, but rather by maximum reciprocity for the sake of human transformation. The formation of persons and communities in this way seems to be the ideal that comes closer to God's primary intention for us than any other ideal.[35]

Certainly the promotion of reciprocity is a very demanding task, for reciprocity prevails among people who have ceased to put their center of gravity within themselves and who are not driven by competition and need for success. When people become each other's center of gravity, they care for one another. They are called to be obedient to one another in their strengths and weaknesses.

In the light of the gospel, people become aware that God is not just a powerful Lord commanding obedience, but God is a family of three persons loving one another; God is communion. And this loving God calls all people into that life of love. God's greatest desire is that all people be one, but as individuals they must first of all die to all the powers of egoism in themselves in order to be reborn to that unity and communion where uniqueness and personal gifts are not crushed but cherished, and where wounds are healed through acceptance and love.[36]

That being the case, difficult existential questions surface immediately: Do individual religious submit in obedience to the strengths of others in the community or are they threatened by the gifts that others have so that they are seen as competitors? Do individual religious really submit with tender compassion to the weaknesses of others in community? Are they obedient to the burdens that others sometimes are?

The example of such loving obedience in the superiors is both indispensable and effective. Superiors who consistently show sincere reverence in their relationship with the members of their communities are apt to evoke in others a wholesome sense of the primacy of persons over work, and the primacy of people over things.

MUTUAL MINISTRY OF CONSENSUS

Another distinguishing characteristic that should be found in authority figures is the ability to promote consensus, to foster mutual obedience in arriving at community decisions. Good order and the ability to promote order are blessings in any community, since the alternative is anarchy. However, in a community of persons living under God and God's representatives, authority figures should not entertain the false idea that their major objective is to tame the instinctual drives and desires of the individuals in the community in order to preclude chaos.

The achievement of consensus is often very difficult, but it is something that should be fostered. It should be noted, however, that the personal community, the formation community, is never a matter of accomplished fact; it is always a matter of intention. Persons and communities spend their whole lives becoming the persons and communities they are called to be.[37]

Human beings, however, achieve some degree of fulfillment and self-actualization in their lives, not only by relating to other persons, but also by relating to their material environment. Human persons are themselves works of a creator God, and they express and are constituted as their true selves through their activities. The main activity to which most people devote a substantial amount of time and by which they normally earn their living is work.

Meaningful work is one of the ways by which people express themselves as well as the nature of our creator God. On the one hand, instinctive drives to power, success, and prestige can be opposed to the proper relationships that human beings should have to God, but on the other hand, these drives can be consciously shaped so that they conform to God's command that human beings should possess the earth and master all that is in it. The creative and fulfilling functions of work, however, can often be spoiled by wrong attitudes. When human persons do not see work in a proper relation to God, it can be used as an alternative to reliance on God. It can become a frustrating, painful activity motivated by ambition which increases the gap between human hopes and their final fulfillment in God.[38]

To some extent, then, religious communities are not only formation communities but also functional communities with authority figures in place to see that tasks are carried out efficiently in order that work might be accomplished. Tensions often develop in communities between authority figures who are primarily responsible for the community's work, and authority figures responsible for the personal development of community members. This tension is apt to be reflected in the members of the community who feel pulled in two directions—one toward personal development and the other toward productive work.[39]

AUTHORITY AS AUGMENTING LIFE

If superiors are God's representatives, it means that they must make God's business of creation and redemption their own. God's business is, above all, the promotion and transformation of life and the healing of wounds. Hence, human authority is authority in the most basic sense of the word, namely, the power to start, to augment, to author life, to promote life and to allow life to be and to become. Authority figures must try to engage the members of the community in productive work, while keeping in mind that their primary responsibility is the ongoing formation of individual members and the community as a whole in the image and after the likeness of God.

Obedience to such authority obviously implies a willingness on the part of religious to change, to grow, to be healed, to be challenged, to work and to be transformed by God through a life in community. Docility, then, is a quality that must characterize both authority figures and others in a religious community. The docility in question is above all docility toward God. What counts in a religious community is not primarily the superior's will or tastes or preferences, nor even the will, tastes, or preferences of individual members of the community. It is God's will that counts.

As God's special representatives, superiors should make sure that they impress the members of their community with the one direction toward which their lives should be oriented, namely, toward God. It obviously requires great strength of character to face, day in and day out, the responsibility of approaching God in prayer in order to discern what it is that God wants of the community and of individual members of the community. And since God, whose will really counts, does not communicate in words that can easily be understood, tentativeness and doubt are more properly at home in the exercise of religious authority than the decisiveness of a military officer.

Superiors who are responsible for formation communities ought to allow themselves, and they ought to be allowed by their communities, the right not to know, or to know with the benefit of much doubt. People who cultivate a holy reverence for the mystery and otherness of God rarely trust themselves to speak in God's name. If and when they do, they recognize that the tentative mode is the only one that is appropriate. The situation is often quite different in the case of authority figures who are responsible for various functions or works in the community. The work to be done is often quite clearly defined. While maintaining reverence for the workers, superiors in functional communities have the responsibility to see that the work is done and done as well as possible.

Authority figures are called to appreciate not only the sacredness of God whom they represent but also the sacredness of the individual members of the community who are temples of the indwelling divinity and members of the body of Christ. The constitutive element of human dignity is God-likeness, which Christianity so strongly affirms and which secular society often tends to ignore today.

Human beings who emerge from God's creative hand are made in the image and after the likeness of God, or as the Bible also affirms, they share in God's own vitality, God's own breath. And so together with God, human persons belong within the sphere of the sacred and are entitled to the awesomeness, the fascination, and the inviolability that are the hallmarks of the sacred. As God's representatives, authority figures must strive to remember that the sacredness of God, whom they represent, is already present in the members of the community, and that this presence affords the members of the community immunity from unconditional demands.

This means that authority figures must refrain from playing the role of pseudo-psychoanalyst or spiritual guru by putting pressure on community members to reveal their inner lives. At the present time this is a danger, when so much emphasis is put on psychological counseling and spiritual direction. Christian anthropology affirms that every human person has a sacred center. One should not climb into that center uninvited. Superiors should surround the members of the community with signs of reverence and concern but never intrude. The Holy Spirit might move individuals to reveal themselves to their authority figures, but such revelation must not be coerced: and if self-revelation does happen, appropriate norms of secrecy and confidentiality are to be observed.[40]

Authority figures who are conscious of the sacredness of the members of the community will not feel that they can enter into dialogue with the community members with the expectation of meeting what is predictable, unambiguous, and predetermined. Sacredness is by definition ambiguous, elusive, fascinating, frightening, always partially revealed and partially concealed.[41] Hence, the normative way to proceed in dialogue in a religious community is to perceive it as a genuine risk, that is, as an encounter whose final outcome does not preexist in the minds of any of the participants, but which is to be engineered through the encounter itself, resulting in a synthesis of what has been shared by all parties, superiors and others alike.

Clearly both authority figures and other members of a religious community must learn to listen without defensiveness, in order for genuine listening, authentic obedience, to take place on the part of both the superiors and the other members of the community. Religious institutes as well as Christian communities in general need to be exorcised of that defensiveness which seems to go into action instinctively when people encounter one another in a threatening way.

It is only against this background, appropriated in Christian faith, that religious will be able to see authority figures as representatives of God in the community. But what should have become clear in the discussion is that authority figures must also live in so much Christian faith that they are able to see the others in the community, their so-called subjects, as God's representatives too.

WESTERN CULTURE IN CONFLICT WITH TRADITION

The other important area of concern focuses on the major collision that occurs between the Christian concept of obedience and the contemporary spirit of much of Western culture. Whether we consider obedience as attentive listening for the will of God or selfless service responsibly rendered, its exercise is either implicitly or explicitly considered absurd by many in our world who lust for power, independence, and dominance. Life in many parts of the modern world is characterized by intense individualism, strident competitiveness, gross consumerism, and a passionate struggle for personal success—all of which tend to erode the practice of Christian religious obedience.[42]

There is certainly a keen interest in spirituality among many people today, but one must ask: Is this spirituality in any sense communal or is it simply individualistic? Is it really ecclesial and liturgical, or is it simply devotional and private? The language in many contemporary books on spirituality is often a language far removed from the language of the Bible and the liturgy. It is often a language focused on personal growth and fulfillment, a language of recognition and affirmation, of feeling good about oneself. It often shies away from the themes of transformation through suffering and of death to oneself so that others might live.

While the behavioral sciences, and psychology in particular, have made important contributions to the development of personal and communal religious life, they can nonetheless reinforce the contemporary drive toward individualism and create a fascination with oneself, leaving one in the end alone with that fascination. The paradoxical wisdom of the Bible and the liturgy can subtly be displaced by the strategies and stages of the psychological paradigm. A language that is at once very large and awesomely beautiful can be corrupted into a language that is very self-centered, very small, very individualistic, and very private. One might be left with obedience only to one's own desires and one's personal agenda.[43]

Many assume that the individual, rather than social institutions and traditions, is the origin and focus of meanings and values. Such ontological individualism maintains that the individual has priority over society which is looked upon as a second-order, derivative or artificial construct. This individualism is usually accompanied by a loss of trust in history as well as in social and cultural institutions. Hence, the structures and institutions that regularly embodied meanings and values in the past no longer are considered to have much positive mediating power. The resultant narcissistic individual becomes a minimal self, uncommitted to social relationships and public life. Personal energy is then focused on the relentless pursuit of selfish wants and needs; the public world of the community is scorned as irrelevant.[44]

This excessive subjectification of reality has had profound effects on the conception and practice of religion in the modern world, including institutionalized religious life. Religion becomes a radically private affair. Doctrines are considered irrelevant and morality is thought to be generated simply in personal consciences with little or no reference to tradition, law or virtue. This excessive subjectification of reality has devastating effects on a whole range of Christian institutions. The Bible, the liturgy, ministry, doctrine, ecclesial and religious structures, and community life are looked upon as useful only to the extent that they enhance one's experience of inner meaning and thus foster an individualistic encounter with the divine.[45] Needless to say, corporate religious commitments to public institutions such as schools, hospitals, and parishes are placed in jeopardy because they are apt to interfere with individual careers.

So long as individuals are treated as isolated entities, living and surviving on their own, societies will oscillate between fragmented individualism and collectivism. This has been one of the tragedies of the twentieth century. It has also been a tragic experience of some contemporary religious institutes. Professionalism, careerism and competitiveness have at times eroded the experience of religious life as essentially cenobitic. Within the church today and within religious institutes, it is easy for careerism to masquerade under the guise of ministry; one can develop a sense of proprietorship concerning the work and service that one does in the church and in the community, as though one owns the job or turf when one exercises one's training and gifts.

This expression of individualism undermines community life and the religious obedience that must characterize that life if it is to be truly Christian. The counsel that Benedict gives to craftsmen in his Rule might well be adapted and appropriated by all members of religious institutes: "If there are craftsmen in the monastery, let them practice their crafts with all humility, provided the Abbot has given permission. But if any one of them becomes conceited over his skill in his craft, because he seems to be conferring a benefit on the monastery, let him be taken from his craft and no longer exercise it unless, after he has humbled himself, the Abbot again gives him permission."[46]

To what does the profession of religious obedience call Christian men and women today? Personally, it calls them to grow in Christian freedom understood not as the ability to do simply what they want to do, but rather to be and become what they ought to be and become. It should call them to responsibility, to spiritual sensitivity in discerning God's will in their own lives and in the lives of others; especially those who, like authority figures, play important roles in their lives. It should help them discern God's will in the Bible, in the liturgy, in tradition, in the community, in work, and in the world. It should call them to responsible generosity as they go outside of themselves to cooperate in the life and mission of their religious institutes. Obedience can be a great challenge. It can stretch people to accomplish what they did not think possible.[47]

Communally, the profession of religious obedience calls men and women to the reform and renewal of their institutes so that they become models of the possibilities of genuine Christian community structured by freedom, responsibility, love, and a truly gospel practice of obedience understood as attentive listening for God's will everywhere and always.

Like most Christian virtues and vows, obedience can really be subsumed under the heading of love—God's love for us inviting us to listen with our minds and hearts and to attend to divine love mediated into our lives in many ways. Love invites us to be people who imitate Christ through the power of the Holy Spirit as we go out of ourselves in order to relate, to give, to respond and to lay down our lives for God and each other.

NOTES

This chapter was prepared as an address to the annual assembly of CMSM in Newport, R.I., for the summer of 1990. The author has considerably developed his initial presentation for the present publication.

1. See Christopher Lasch, *The Culture of Narcissism: American Life in an Age of Diminishing Expectations* (New York: Warner Books, 1979); also Lasch, *The Minimal Self: Psychic Survival in Troubled Times* (New York: W. W. Norton, 1984); Robert N. Bellah et al., *Habits of the Heart: Individualism and Commitment in American Life* (Berkeley: University of California Press, 1985); also *The Good Society* (New York: Alfred A. Knopf, 1991).

2. The history and theology of religious obedience are summarized in excellent articles by Jean-Marie Tillard, "Aux sources de l'obéissance religieuse," *Nouvelle Revue Théologique* 98 (1976), 592-626; 98 (1976), 817-37; "Obéissance," *Dictionnaire de Spiritualité*, LXXII-LXXIII (Paris: Beauchesne, 1981) 535-63. See also K. V. Truhlar, "Obedience," *New Catholic Encyclopedia* X (Washington, D.C.: The Catholic University of America, 1967) 602-6; G. Odoardi, G. Rocca, J. Gribomont, A. de Vogüé, C. Capelle, A. Gauthier. "Obbedienza." *Dizionario degli Istituti di Perfezione* VI (Roma: Edizioni Paoline, 1980) 492-552.

3. Xavier Léon-Dufour (ed.), "Obedience," *Dictionary of Biblical The-*

ology (New York: Seabury Press, 1973), 397–98; Raniero Cantalamessa, *Obedience: The Authority of the Word* (Slough: St. Paul Publications, 1989).

4. P. Jacquemont, "Autorité et obéissance selon l'Ecriture," *Vie Spirituelle Suppl.* 21 (1968), 340–50; C. M. Carmichael, *The Laws of Deuteronomy* (Ithaca, New York: Cornell University Press, 1974).

5. Tillard, "Aux sources de l'obéissance religieuse," 817–32.

6. See Jerome Murphy-O'Connor, *Becoming Human Together* (Collegeville: The Liturgical Press/Michael Glazier Books, 1982); B. Holmberg, *Paul and Power: The Structure of Authority in the Primitive Church as Reflected in the Pauline Epistles* (Lund: Gleerup, 1978); J. H. Schutz, *Paul and the Anatomy of Apostolic Authority* (Cambridge: Cambridge University Press, 1975).

7. D. J. Chitty, *The Desert a City: An Introduction to the Study of Egyptian and Palestinian Monasticism under the Christian Empire* (Oxford: Blackwell, 1966); Jean Gribomont, *Aux Origines du Monachisme Chrétien* (Beyrolles-en-Mauges: Textes Monastiques, 1979); K. Heussi, *Der Ursprung des Monchtums* (Aaten: Scientia, 1980).

8. See I. Hausherr, *Direction Spirituelle en Orient Autrefois* (Roma: Herder, 1958).

9. Philip Rousseau, *Ascetics, Authority and the Church in the Age of Jerome and Cassian* (Oxford: Oxford University Press, 1978); David Knowles, *From Pachomius to Ignatius: A Study in the Constitutional History of the Religious Orders* (Oxford: Clarendon Press, 1966), 71–72.

10. Knowles, 72–76.

11. *The Rule of the Master*, trans. Luke Eberle (Kalamazoo: Cistercian Publications, 1977).

12. *The Rule of Saint Augustine*, with intro. and commentary by Tarcisius van Basil (London: Darton, Longman and Todd, 1984), 23–24; Athanase Sage, *The Religious Life According to Saint Augustine* (New York: New City Press, 1990), 91–99; Theodore Tack, *If Augustine Were Alive: Augustine's Religious Ideal for Today* (New York: Alba House, 1988), 105–22.

13. Knowles, 73–76; Daniel Rees et al., *Consider Your Call: A Theology of Monastic Life Today* (London: SPCK, 1978), 192–96.

14. Rees, 89–91.

15. Cornelius Justice, "Evolution of Teaching on Commitment by Vow from New Testament Times to the Ninth Century," *Cistercian Studies* XII (1977), 24. See also Joel Rippinger, "The Concept of Obedience in the Monastic Writings of Basil and Cassian," *Studia Monastica* 19 (1979), 1–18.

16. Justice, 23.

17. *Ibid.*

18. *St. Benedict's Rule for Monasteries*, Leonard Doyle, trans. (Collegeville, MN: Liturgical Press, 1948): [hereafter RB], ch. 58.

19. Knowles, 76.

20. Jerome Murphy-O'Connor, *What Is Religious Life?: A Critical Approach* (Dublin: Dominican Publications, n.d.), 18-21.

21. Knowles, 76.

22. Murphy-O'Connor, *What Is Religious Life?*, 21.

23. Rees, 310-12.

24. Cajetan Esser, *The Rule and Testament of St. Francis*, trans. Sister Audrey Marie (Chicago: Franciscan Herald Press, 1977), 167-76.

25. *Early Dominicans: Selected Writings*, ed. with an introduction by Simon Tugwell (New York: Paulist Press, 1982), 20.

26. IIa IIae q. 104 a.1 ad.1.

27. *Early Dominicans*, 23.

28. Murphy-O'Connor, *What Is Religious Life?*, 21.

29. Yves Congar, "The Historical Development of Authority in the Church: Points for Reflection," *Problems of Authority*, ed. John M. Todd (Baltimore: Helicon Press, 1962), 119-56; Karl Rahner, "Authority," *Theological Investigations* 23 (New York: Crossroad, 1992), 61-85; Jean-Marie Tillard, "The Paths of Obedience," *Lumen Vitae* 21 (1976), 281-315; 483-515.

30. Jean Vanier, *From Brokenness to Community* (New York: Paulist Press, 1992), 20-21. See also his other works: *Community and Growth: Our Pilgrimage Together* (New York: Paulist Press, 1979) and *The Broken Body: Journey to Wholeness* (New York: Paulist Press, 1988).

31. Sandra M. Schneiders, *New Wineskins* (New York: Paulist Press, 1986), 137-67. See also *Paths in Authority and Obedience: An Overview of Authority/Obedience Developments Among U.S. Women Religious* (Washington, D.C.: Leadership Conference of Women Religious, 1978); Barbara Fiand, *Living the Vision: Religious Vows in an Age of Change* (New York: Crossroad, 1991), 108-38; Gerald Arbuckle, *Strategies for Growth in Religious Life* (New York: Alba House, 1987), 91-151.

32. Schneiders, 106-111.

33. *Ibid.*, 136-67.

34. In this part of the article I want to acknowledge my dependence on the unpublished work of Roger Balducelli, a former colleague at the Catholic University of America.

35. Murphy-O'Connor, *What Is Religious Life?*, 21-23; Parker J. Palmer, *To Know as We Are Known* (San Francisco: Harper and Row, 1983), 1-17.

36. Vanier, *From Brokenness to Community*, 1-20, 26-52.

37. Rees, 91-92.

38. Joe Holland, *Creative Communion: Toward a Spirituality of Work* (New York: Paulist Press, 1989), 18-42; M. D. Chenu, *The Theology of Work* (Chicago: Henry Regnery Co., 1963).

39. Murphy-O'Connor, *What Is Religious Life?*, 64-69.

40. Henry E. Horn, *Worship in Crisis* (Philadelphia: Fortress Press, 1972), 66-67.

41. Thomas F. O'Meara, *Fundamentalism: A Catholic Perspective* (New York: Paulist Press, 1990), esp. 5-35. See also Louis Dupré, *Transcendent Selfhood: The Rediscovery of the Inner Life* (New York: Seabury Press, 1976), 18-29.

42. Dupré, 42-49, 66-78. See also Mark Searle, "Private Religion, Individualistic Society, and Common Worship," *Liturgy and Spirituality in Context: Perspectives on Prayer and Culture*, ed. Eleanor Bernstein (Collegeville: The Liturgical Press, 1990), 27-46. For a competent analysis of contemporary American culture and its effects on religious experience from a sociological point of view see Robert Wuthnow, *The Restructuring of American Religion* (Princeton: Princeton University Press, 1988), and *Rediscovering the Sacred: Perspectives on Religion in Contemporary Society* (Grand Rapids: William B. Eerdmans, 1992).

43. Peter E. Fink, "Liturgy and Spirituality: A Timely Intersection," *Liturgy and Spirituality in Context*, 47-61. See also Philip Rieff, *The Triumph of the Therapeutic: The Uses of Faith after Freud* (Chicago: University of Chicago Press, 1987).

44. M. Francis Mannion, "Liturgy and the Present Crisis of Culture," *Worship* 62 (1988), 102-13.

45. *Ibid.*, 102-107.

46. RB ch. 57.

47. Rees, 197-204.

The Vow of Poverty: Our Challenge to Integrity

Luise Ahrens, M.M.

In beginning my reflections upon the theme of poverty as vowed commitment, I was uncertain where to go, what to read, or whom to talk to. T.S. Eliot's apt sentences in *Four Quartets* looked like a good beginning as he says:

> So here I am, in the middle way, having had twenty years—
> ... Trying to learn to use words, and every attempt
> Is a wholly new start, and a different kind of failure
> Because one has only learnt to get the better of words
> For the thing one no longer has to say, or the way in which
> One is no longer disposed to say it. And so each venture
> Is a new beginning, a raid on the inarticulate.... [1]

And so I began my raid.

Many books and articles deal with new concepts of poverty and I read as many as I could find. I have listed some of them for you in the bibliography; they are excellent material. But still no significant insights came. What else could be said?

Then, the readings of the days before Ash Wednesday came around and I was forced to ask myself, "Is God kidding me?" and worse, "Am I kidding God?" Hear the voice of Jesus as I heard it in that week, focused on the vow of poverty as we are called as religious to live it:

> "How hard it is for those who have riches to enter the Kingdom of God" (Mk 10:23).

> "I tell you solemnly, there is no one who has left house, brothers, sisters, parents, children or land for my sake, and for the sake of the gospel, who will not be repaid a hundred times over—not without persecution ... " (Mk 10:29-31).

94

And to the rich young man:

> "One thing you still lack. Sell all that you have and distribute it to the poor, and you will have treasure in heaven; and come, follow me" (Lk 18:22-23).

To add to those statements, we know from our Bible that, from a very large group of men and women following Jesus from town to town, he called and chose a particular group and sent those disciples forth in his name to preach the good news. He even told them how to do it—with one coat, not a large purse, one pair of shoes—and he told them what to say: "The Reign of God is at hand—believe it!"

Jesus was not proposing a new idea. Hundreds of years earlier, when the Hebrews were enslaved by the rich and powerful Egyptians, Yahweh heard their cries and freed them from the oppression of slavery. He then entered into a covenant of intimacy and partnership with them and thereby called them to become a *people*—Yahweh's people. As Yahweh's people they would live together in peace and harmony with each other; they would not lord it over each other as the pagans did; they would be a people who had special care for the weak and powerless, the widow, the orphan and the alien. They would put their trust in Yahweh and not in material wealth or power.

And Yahweh would take special care of them and they would prosper as a people, living in a land flowing with milk and honey. Thus, as a people, they would be a visible sign to the nations of the wisdom of Yahweh, of the goodness and power of Yahweh. As Aloysius Pieris says, they would be a contrast society which would serve all generations as a memory of the future, a future to be realized by the whole of humankind. This was a vow, a covenant, a public agreement between God and the poor.[2] This was the vocation of Israel; this was why Israel was called into existence as a people: to be a witness people, to be a "contrast society," a memory of a future which is possible for the whole of humankind.

That first Jewish community that grew out of the confirmed relationship of God and a people tells us some very interesting things about poverty. By law they created barriers against the accumulation of riches, such as the periodic canceling of debts. Resources were shared and responsibility was distributed. The judges served the people in a way which made this possible. But time went on and in their human way the covenant people of Israel aped the ways of their pagan neighbors. The period culminated in Solomon's massive building program and militarization.

The *anawim*, the little people who once put their trust in Yahweh alone, now put their trust in material possessions and symbols of power common to their pagan neighbors. Worse yet, they became divided among themselves into "have's" and "have-not's." They took advantage of the widow and the orphan and the alien. See the complaints of the prophets Amos and Isaiah. The "contrast society" was assimilated and acculturated and the values of Egypt and Babylon won out; the people of Israel no longer gave witness to the glory, power and goodness of Yahweh. They worshiped false gods.

THE VOICE OF JESUS

A few centuries later, the Roman model of society became a new Babylon and the voices of the prophets were silent. But Jesus, the carpenter of Nazareth, heard the voice of God speaking in John the Baptist. God's call had again gone forth; the good news was heard in the land. Jesus responded with the totality of his life. He became God's word: "The poor have the good news preached to them." "The Spirit of the Lord is upon me because He has anointed me to preach the good news to the poor" (Mt 11:2-5).

And what is this good news? Blessed are the poor ... Blessed are the peacemakers ... Blessed are the merciful ... Blessed are they who follow the wisdom of Yahweh and not the wisdom of the "world"—for the kingdom of Heaven is theirs.

And now, today, make no mistake about it, we are living in Babylon, and in Rome, and here is the call to religious men and women today: Be the "contrast society." Our role is to be a witness society by preaching the good news by our words and our lives. We are the ones called now to be the "dangerous memory" in the church and society. We are called to be a society in which there are no poor—a society which shares with and cares for all members, especially for the weak, poor, helpless and defenseless.

This very brief look at some scriptural undergirding of the call to discipleship lived in poverty for the sake of the community, serves only to contextualize my remarks. I will look at four areas that affect and effect our living out of the vow of poverty in contemporary religious life, and then ask some questions which call for reflection. I will suggest some qualities essential for religious leadership and name three dimensions of the vow which will shape the future understanding of poverty.

ADAPTATION TO CULTURE

The first concept to look at is the challenge of adaptation to culture. Our context is the U.S. church. Catholics are middle class, mainstream, and upwardly mobile. We religious have followed our people up the socioeconomic ladder. As missioners, we at Maryknoll teach the virtue of adaptation to our members who work around the world, and even that is becoming a complex issue. One must, of course, adapt to language, to food, to climate, to customs about time, humor, and so forth. But, we have learned through hard experience that all cultures must be critiqued by the gospel; no culture or society is free of evil. So, too, a religious cannot both swallow the culture wholeheartedly and also be able to criticize its "other-than-gospel" values. As someone once said: "You cannot push a bus while you're sitting in it." Some distance and perspective is required.

Where have we religious adapted in the positive sense? We have learned the language of our people, be it Spanish or street talk or bureaucratic-ese; we have analyzed social issues and responded; we have assessed needs and acknowledged that huge schools for wealthy children do not always a Christian make. "There is," says Azevedo, "a radical difference between merely being with the rich and being a stimulating evangelizing presence among them."[3] We have made hard choices in this regard in the last two decades.

But our negative adaptation as religious is significant also. As groups, we can afford to live well, and so we do. We are "professional people," we say, and that calls for housing, clothing, constant updating and a measure of freedom to pursue our "work." We have adapted to a professional milieu. But what we must constantly recall is that our profession is not to be a teacher, a minister, a social worker, or administrator; it is to be a religious. That vocation calls us to another way of looking at life—from the stance of the poor. Azevedo also frames this question well. He says:

> With house, food, studies, clean clothing, car, entertainment, vacations and travel all assured, some of us speak of poverty in the abstract, but live completely at the margin of ordinary people. … Economic problems are something serious and cutting for the people with whom we claim to be in solidarity.[4]

Many of us even reject the notion that our personal lives should be at the disposal of our local religious community. "Religious have not been educated for the discipline of accountability—one of the great schools of poverty."[5] Adaptation of this sort needs to be examined. What do our lives mean if our religious profession, our vocation, is not as clearly witnessed to as our avocations?

Second, we religious have embraced the United States' value of Yankee independence and, in fact, have made an icon out of it. There is no need to repeat the stages of development in religious life as we moved from total dependence (child–parent) through to independence (isolated individuals providing for themselves). Sister Mary Jo Leddy's analysis, "Beyond the Liberal Model," addresses the latter issue well.[6] The gospel interdependence we seek can be achieved, if we understand it. Indeed, though we may appear self-sufficient, professional and well-educated, in reality we must recognize and name our weakness, our frailty, our radical dependence on God and our relative dependence on one another for challenge and encouragement, for correction and support. I have seen so-called religious people ostracize other religious persons and groups who challenged them to fidelity about gospel poverty. "See how they love one another." We live in community and rub elbows and hearts because we need the voices of others to call us to fidelity when we are unfaithful, and to the paths of holiness when we have lost the way.

The third concept that we need to look at briefly is the question some of us have heard at General Chapter after General Chapter: "Who are the poor?" There is no doubt in my mind that the poor in our society or in any society are those who are without the option of housing, food, education, health care; those who are squeezed out of decision-making at every level. If our vision statements speak of the poor and our personnel are committed to ministry to the middle class; if our religious lives are lived out among the non-poor, we fool no one but ourselves.

I have thought it might be refreshing to have a group come out and say, "We are in service to the really, really rich." I guess there are groups like that, say, *Forbes* and *Money* magazines, Rancho Mirage, those who make luxury cars and feel insulted that one's status symbol is not recognized for what it is. We may laugh at this, but are not the majority of our schools, health care facilities and parish plants in some ways geared to the upwardly mobile and the yuppie population? Haven't we moved out of poor areas because they are not "safe"? Haven't we ceased to model a "contrast society"? Haven't we resorted to lip service of the truly poor and in reality shut the door on their needs?

The public policy decisions of government do not attempt to address the needs or the cause of the poor. We criticize the government, but do we do any better? A few years ago a young religious in Indonesia said honestly: "Before I entered religious life, I was poor and worked among my neighbors and in village ministry. Now as a religious, I *talk* about the option for the poor."

A fourth concept that deserves our attention is particularly thorny right now, and that is institutional poverty. Is institutional poverty a goal, a mistake of mismanagement, or a concept we mouth without meaning? How do we balance the appropriate care of our members and the financial demands of the ministry? From the days of our early foundations in dire poverty, most of us gathered together to meet the needs of our people, usually of poor immigrant groups; our wealth was our personnel. The 1940s and 1950s brought substance to our people and to us, as well as large numbers of members. The late 1960s and 1970s brought fewer members, but we held on to our institutions as long as we could and also to the financial security they provided. Now, with aging members, a lessening financial base and (in some cases) an increasing number of lay associates or employees, we are faced with choices.

For me, this is a good moment. We need to make choices now with wisdom and gospel-rooted courage. Both Fr. Peter Henriot and Sr. Amata Miller dealt with these questions in addresses on the U.S. Bishops' Economic Pastoral. I share their views.[7] We do not have the luxury of inertia about this question. Leadership has a responsibility in this regard: We must engage our members in talking about expectations and implementing long-range decisions about health care and retirement. As we deal pragmatically with those fiscal and planning issues, we must keep in focus the fact that we are not supposed to retire from religious life or from our vow of poverty. We must be prepared to live out our commitments in hard choices.

We must look seriously at our investments and ask ourselves, "for what do we hold this money?" Do our mission and apostolic goals require it? What percentage of income can be allocated to care for members and what must serve mission support? How much do we need? How large should an investment be to care prudently for those entrusted to us? A ceiling should be set and guidelines for investment established which serve the causes of justice and the poor.

Can we say "No" to inappropriate models of life-style, fund raising and institutional management, or do we constantly back off because we do not probe the values behind them or because we are too lazy or too fearful to take a stand?

We cannot fail our members by our own faintheartedness or a fear that some may leave the community. Strong, clear leadership is required. A consultation that gathers the wisdom of the membership is the base of that leadership, and intense prayer and fidelity to the vision of the founder/foundress root our search for truth and direction. I propose with great candor that we should not be afraid to lead our members to fidelity.

Our role as religious leaders has undergone an immense change. Most of that change has been good; some of it, I believe, was not.

In public life we have a class of political leaders whose decisions are based largely on public opinion polls. I venture to say that some religious leadership has been similarly weakened. For too long, major superiors have neither clarified their expectations for the living of the vows nor demanded accountability from the members. In the pursuit of an understanding of poverty within religious life, I think three qualities needed for leadership in the next decade will be compassion, reconciliation and integrity.

We need to be compassionate—strong, loving and caring—in order to deal with ourselves and with our members as they experience the brokenness that has become a characteristic of our modern Western society. The weaknesses of our sisters and brothers are realities that we can all name, e.g., alcohol and chemical dependency and dysfunction rooted in an abusive past. Realities like this are the cross of Jesus in our time.

Our members need help in some areas, and it is good that we can provide it for them. But our compassion cannot allow us to be profligate with resources for endless courses in self-discovery and dilettante approaches to spirituality. That is not true compassion; it is an inability to face the real questions and a frustration at our own incapacity to respond. Courageous compassion must guide us as we walk with, weep with, and pray with our sisters and brothers.

We need reconciliation to bring together in a creative tension the struggles we are all having over the use or misuse of resources, the purposes of investments, and just compensation. Nothing makes provincial and regional discussions more conflictive and/or exciting than a discussion of stipends, retirement allotment, personal allowance, and so forth. True resolutions of these conflicts must call opposing sides to attention to the mission purpose, the raison d'être for our groups. Once that purpose is clearly in perspective, the discussion can become a source of unity. Leadership for reconciliation enables this to happen.

THE MANDATE IS INTEGRITY

Lastly, we ourselves need to be women and men of integrity. If we are not living lives of committed poverty, our calls to integrity will be foolish and empty. Some of us struggle with this vow, not having a charism for poverty in a personal sense. I myself find it extremely difficult, living here in the United States in an institutional setting, to be clear about what poverty means for me. In Indonesia, with little available to us, we lived a life-style in "harmony" with our Muslim neighbors; we were not "poor" as they are poor, but our lives were of a piece with those around us.

In this country, our Center House rests on a large site in Westchester county, our needs are provided for, our health care and retirement are assured. I think it is less than honest for us not to question, grapple with, and struggle with the issue of integrity with reference to poverty in this setting. Even more deeply, I wonder if the very mode of gathering religious together in large organizations creates an inbuilt hindrance to poverty.

Do we use the supports of the institution and fail as groups to take the risks inherent in commitment to the poor and the cause of the poor? One can never know ahead of time what such risks may mean in terms of a loss of lifetime security. We cannot conscientiously accept this kind of security if we are not struggling to risk mother, father, home, friends—yes, even our lives, for the sake of the gospel.

NEW DIMENSIONS OF POVERTY

The last area of the vow I want to touch on concerns new dimensions of the vow of poverty. You most likely have intuitions yourself about this topic and I encourage you to develop your own insights.

The first notion is regarding the theology of the environment. This consideration does not require an introduction or a rationale. As religious, we must begin to look at poverty within the context of our world; and the resources of that world are endangered. It would be both foolish and unfaithful for us to pretend that this newly-articulated call to poverty, to restraint and to sharing was not addressed to us. We own land, buildings, wetlands and the like. First question: What, if anything, as followers of Jesus, should we own and manage? Second, how do we do it in a threatened ecosystem? Third, what practical decisions can we make today to educate our members to this challenge to make do with less?

The second concept I see as needed is a new theology of work. I do not believe that the majority of religious are overworked. In fact, at the risk of argument, I agree with Azevedo when he says that: "The truth is that we have led many young religious to a genre of life that, working less than their peers, allows them to vegetate in our houses, often enjoying refined conditions of life."[8] He was referring to religious life in the third world; but if this is true for you or for any of your members, I have to ask why?

Is it a lack of clarity in purpose and expression of purpose? Is it a lack of faith? Is it common sloth? Is it because we find the gospel message too heavy to bear and so retreat into comfort? Whatever the reasons for its existence, indolence is not what we are called to. We must be faithful to the gospel and to the prophetic role of religious life, and this calls us to solidarity with those who struggle to make ends meet. True, many religious burn out. But why? We need to look at the root of the problem, not just its manifestations.

The third concept is a theology of wholeheartedness. I want you to take yourself back to your first experience of falling in love and savor it for a moment. See yourself in that marvelously vulnerable, anguishingly beautiful space. Did you sit down and count out the time you would spend on the beloved? Was it possible to measure the energy poured out on that other person? If you could parcel it out, you were not in love. Apply this now to your capacity for service in ministry, for time spent with God in prayer, for time "wasted" with the poor (our members included). Are we fooling ourselves that our lives are lives of love, poured out with joy and enthusiasm?

In conclusion, the real question is: poverty for what? A great measure of evangelical radicalism is required to live a vowed life in our times of gratuitous self-aggrandizement, of unearned profit boasted about in the public forum. We can languish in our inertia or, I believe, we can make choices:

- for poverty as a discipline against the weakened values of our time;
- for poverty as lived solidarity with those who cannot choose;
- for poverty as the external witness and manifestation of our utter dependence on God as persons and as groups; "Give us this day our daily bread";
- for poverty which alone engenders a freedom to risk our very lives for the sake of the gospel.

My last image, one that I have found stays with me, is that of a cat. A cat's nature in third-world homes is to catch mice with its claws and eat them; a healthy and integral life. The cat has a clear purpose and tools to accomplish the purpose! On the other hand, on TV now in the U.S., we are presented with a series of soft, obese, declawed cats sitting around a well-set table debating the relative merits of a variety of gourmet cat foods. My brothers and sisters—need I say more?

NOTES

This chapter was first presented as an address at the annual assembly of CMSM in Newport, R.I., in August, 1990.

1. T.S. Eliot, *Four Quartets* (New York and London: Harcourt Brace Jovanovich, 1971), "East Coker, V," 30–31.

2. Aloysius Pieris, "The Religious Vows and the Reign of God," *The Way (Supplement)* 65 (Summer, 1989), 3–15.

3. Marcello Azevedo, *Vocation for Mission* (Mahwah, N.J.: Paulist, 1988), 30.

4. *Ibid.*, 24.

5. *Ibid.*

6. Mary Jo Leddy, *Reweaving Religious Life: Beyond the Liberal Model* (Mystic Ct.: Twenty-Third Publications, 1990).

7. See, e.g., Amata Miller, "Implications of the Pastoral Letter, Economic Justice for All, for Congregations of Women Religious in the U.S.A." (unpublished address) LCWR National Assembly, August, 1987. Also, John Haughey, "God and Mammon: Mission and Maintenance," Presentation to National Meeting of the National Association of Treasurers of Religious Institutes, Oct., 1988.

8. Azevedo, *op. cit.,* 22. See also Mitch Snyder, "Homelessness," *New Theological Review* 1:4 (November, 1988); John O'Brien, "Theologians on the Side of the Poor," *Irish Theological Quarterly* 55:1 (1989).

Negotiating Loneliness in the Celibate Process

A. W. Richard Sipe

For thirty-three years I have listened to the celibate/sexual stories of American priests. The gift of their sharing has been an education in graced humanity. I have witnessed the triumph of idealism in the face of immense odds, the struggles of ambiguity, the joy of maturation and sustained growth, the failure of naiveté to foster development, the inadequacy of good intentions to overcome woundedness, and on occasion the sad victory of evil. My work was conducted in the spirit of "active listening" that Paul Philibert speaks of in his essay in this volume. My education has not left me unmarked or unmoved. I have wept with shared pain, held my breath as men struggled to integrate their instincts with their ideals, and stood awestruck before men whom Philibert describes as "icons of God's compassion."

Perhaps it is not surprising that I found both naiveté and wisdom, weakness and heroism among those pledged to celibacy. It is remarkable that so much growth in celibate identity is to be found in a system that demands celibacy but does not educate for it. The celibate/sexual system in which priests have to train and live does not favor sexual maturity. Celibacy as a lifelong process is not adequately dealt with in any seminary in the United States. Quite frankly, if we do not talk about and reflect together as a community on the realities of the celibate/sexual struggle and achievement, we cannot hope to foster them.

As will be clear in reading my essay, my data have been derived from the stories of men. Long ago I promised myself that I would not tell women what their experience was like. Yet I believe that much of what I have to offer here will be of value for religious of both sexes and of all types from monastic to apostolic.

The real story being told in these pages is the story of the human heart. When such a heart is convinced of a call from God to make itself available for total dedication to the following of Jesus, a certain kind of journey of faith and transformation begins. It is one element in that journey of transformation that I am about to describe.

Paul Philibert will address the theological context of celibate chastity in his essay and demonstrate the necessity of relational prayer in the development of celibacy. I will confine myself to an unavoidable reality of the growth process, loneliness.

I do not take lightly the responsibility to reflect on celibate convictions, existence, goals, struggles and achievements. Anyone who has read my book, *A Secret World,* knows that I am certainly *not* anti-celibacy.[1] Quite the contrary. My years of study of the celibate/sexual practice, process and achievement of priests in the United States have given me a deep respect for this tradition of religious practice. I also have some clear ideas of its difficulties and aberrations.

There is now a team of five scholars[2] working with me on the subject. I am almost overwhelmed by the multiplicity of aspects of the subject, hardly knowing where to begin speaking about an area that absorbs my time and interest. Rather than merely repeat what is already available elsewhere in print, I would like to go beyond what can be found in my book and address the painful problem of negotiating loneliness in the celibate process.

I invite readers to struggle with me in a difficult and not very pleasant exercise. I ask each one to enter for a time into a place accessible to no other human but oneself, a place incommunicable to any other human and only partially communicable to ourselves most of the time—their celibate/sexual experience—their celibate/sexual mind and heart.

First, let me make a statement I have not articulated previously. It is one of the discoveries made in our ongoing research on celibacy, and I am indebted to E. O. Wilson of Harvard for providing this clarification.[3]

Celibacy—that is, a non-reproductive, non-sexually active stance in the service of some group—is at base a natural phenomenon. The celibate state is not dependent on the Catholic Church. It exists in other cultures in relation to other religious beliefs—namely, Buddhist and Hindu; but it also exists independently of religious conviction or affiliation.

Celibacy also exists in other species, especially in the highly organized insect societies, ants and bees, and even among the larger mammals. For instance, among lions, some of the pride do not reproduce but devote their energies to the protection and care of their near kin.

We have so dichotomized flesh and spirit, divorced sex from spirituality and nature from supernature, that we have forgotten that somehow it is all of one piece. All life and existence is a unity. Each of us has our place.

Celibacy does not have to be defended as a valuable reality. It exists.

It is a valuable entity in the service of humanity and the formation of culture. It has always been and persists; and it will continue to be a reality quite independent of any determination of ecclesiastical law.

The first initial question each celibate must ask is: "Am I determined by nature to be celibate?" Even if one is predisposed by nature toward celibacy, this does not mean that celibate existence is easy. One who is predisposed by nature to sexual bonding, reproduction and parenthood does not find any of those adjustments easy simply because they are more natural for him or her. Celibacy is not unnatural in every case. Nor is marriage natural for all men and women.

Biologically celibacy and marriage have the same goal—the preservation and enhancement of the species. Spiritually the goal of marriage and celibacy for us Christians is also identical: the realization of the mind and heart of Jesus Christ in all of existence. *Life* is the goal: "That all may have life and have it more abundantly."

As a state, celibacy is not superior to marriage, nor is marriage superior to celibacy. But they are not identical ways of life or ways to life. Each has a distinct process and path to its goal. I think we Christians have lost our way in the area of celibacy/sexuality because we have obscured the uniqueness of celibacy and marriage behind assumptions about superiority and inferiority, and about the natural and supernatural with inadequate glib analogies. In the church and in society at large, we have paid and are paying a tremendous price for the ignorance and faulty assumptions about celibacy/sexuality among those who should know these areas best—its priests.

Personally, I will not be content until every major seminary training priests who wish to be celibate has a three-year, six-semester, sequence on celibacy/sexuality as a minimum requirement—a sequence based on integrative knowledge and transformational techniques.[4]

I said I would address loneliness and so I will in five points, describing steps toward the free appropriation and integration of the spiritual challenge of celibacy for the sake of the kingdom of God. Celibates should not feel sorry for themselves. Please remember that we could also address in a distinct but parallel way the loneliness of sexual encounter, marriage, and parenthood. Loneliness is part of the human condition, the price we pay for consciousness and self-consciousness. But here I wish to focus on the loneliness of the celibate process.

Dorothy Day, a willing celibate and an American saint, chose to characterize her life as the "long loneliness." She was inspired by that reflection of St. Augustine, "Our hearts are restless (lonely) until they rest in Thee."[5]

THE FIRST STEP

It is one's restless, lonely heart that gives impetus to the search for a relationship, and relationships that give meaning to life. When one confronts the possibility that "I may be called to celibacy," there is an inevitable and initial struggle with loneliness that marks that awareness. This is the first of five stages of the process of celibacy which have to be negotiated to achieve celibate integration.

I have interviewed hundreds of priests and have reviewed thousands of pages of biographical and autobiographical accounts of priests and their celibate/sexual lives. If I cannot find a trace of depression at the time of initial awareness of their celibate destiny, I know they will have more or less serious problems in their celibate practice. The ability to begin the celibate process is dependent on some awareness of loss and gain.

John Henry Cardinal Newman became aware of his celibate destiny at fifteen years of age. He comments on celibacy and its process relatively frequently and candidly in his *Apologia Pro Vita Sua* and his other autobiographical writing. Most tenderly he portrays the process in his novel *Loss and Gain*, where the protagonist knows he must leave his beloved Oxford to follow his conscience; he runs through the college woods embracing the trees he must leave to follow his vocation.

> [Charles Reading] crossed to the Meadow, and walked steadily down to the junction of the Cherwell with the Isis; he then turned back. What thoughts came upon him! for the last time! There was no one to see him; he threw his arms round the willows so dear to him, and kissed them; he tore off some of their black leaves and put them in his bosom.[6]

The whole passage echoes what he had written in a letter two years before about his farewell to Littlemore, the parish church he loved and served as an Anglican.

> I quite tore myself away—and could not help kissing my bed, and mantelpiece, and other parts of the house. I have been most happy there, though in a state of suspense. And there it has been, that I have both been taught my way and received an answer to my prayers.[7]

I have known bishops and priests ordained for many years who have evaded even the initial approach to the celibate process. They practice sexual abstinence with great difficulty if at all, and are deprived of the sense and security of any real celibate identity and satisfaction because they could not tolerate the pain of the sense of loss that awareness entails. Loneliness is like fear; it only gains power by avoidance. Until one can face the fact of the inevitable loneliness that celibate love involves, one cannot enter the celibate process.

This stage is frequently accompanied by physical distress or illness as are some of the subsequent phases of celibate crisis.[8] A person is lucky if he can experience the pangs of the process, as did Newman, before he enters formal training for a vocation that requires celibate practice for admittance. The reason is that training programs are designed to establish and encourage group identification, *esprit de corps*, and institutional loyalty—all important values. If one prematurely gains the benefit of these life supports prior to initial awareness, his celibate identity can actually be retarded by training programs as they currently exist. It is consoling to know that one can begin the celibate process even after years of evasion and pretense.

THE PAIN OF DIFFERENCE

The second phase of celibate process is generally experienced between two and five years after ordination. It is the awareness of separateness from most of the people one ministers to; I call it the crisis of "like me/not like me." The crisis is frequently precipitated in the exercise of one's ministry—hearing confessions, assisting in marriage ceremonies, teaching, preaching, and counseling.

One becomes aware that there are good Christian people whose lives may even surpass our own in virtue and goodness and meaning. Evidently their sexual love is not a hindrance to their spirituality or their Christian life. The crisis forces one to confront the celibate commitment more deeply or to endure temptations to sexual experimentation. At this time many priests, now free of seminary support, are often overwhelmed by the "dailiness" of celibate existence and become aware of companionship in ways that never struck them before. "I am not like other men" is the loneliness; the sense of isolation can be quite acute.

Listen to how Newman describes the reality and grasps the moment of it in his novel:

> [Charles Ready] went into a religious publisher's in Danvers Street..., and while engaged in a back part of the shop in looking over a pile of Catholic works, which, to the religious public, had inferior attractions to the glittering volumes, Evangelical

and Anglo-Catholic, which had possession of the windows and
principal table, he heard the shop-door open, and, on looking
round, saw a familiar face. It was that of a young clergyman, with
a very pretty girl on his arm, whom her dress pronounced to
be a bride. Love was in their eyes, joy in their voice, and afflu-
ence in their gait and bearing. Charles had a faintish feeling
come over him; somewhat such as might beset a man on hearing a call for pork-chops when he was seasick. He retreated behind a pile of ledgers and other stationery, but they could not
save him from the low, dulcet tones which from time to time
passed from one to the other.[9]

This is a period of time when many young priests leave the priesthood, if not physically, certainly spiritually. Many priests are not prepared
to be different—to be themselves. Some end up turning their restlessness
and loneliness into a search for love *from* others rather than *for* others.
Work can become a companion rather than a service.

Celibacy can be natural even as celibate intent and service is supernatural. But this is not the ordinary way of the majority of people. It
makes one different and it is lonely to embrace our differentness and
our uniqueness.

Yet religious and priests come to terms with their celibate differences.
They frequently find a renewed freedom for pastoral or priestly service.
A renewed peace of order and a certain self-confidence are the natural
reward for negotiating well this stage of loneliness. Would that that were
the last challenge.

ALONE AMONG MY OWN

Commonly an additional challenge to celibacy crystallizes between
thirteen and eighteen years of celibate practice. The focus at this time
is not upon those who are radically distinct in life-style and goals, viz., the
married; but upon the ecclesiastical system. Recently a number of inter-
views in Rome reminded me how many priests compromise their celibate
growth and become functionaries. The halls of power have some people
for whom "celibacy" is a badge, a card of admittance to the "club," a ticket
to advancement but not an inner reality. Sometimes the passage from external appearance or conformity to internal celibate alliance is almost
imperceptible. Sometimes it comes in a confrontation with authority or
the establishment. I characterize this crisis as one of interiorization, of
being "in control of or controlled by" the environment—the system.

If one is in control of one's celibate adjustment, it progresses to an internal level where it flourishes and deepens without regard for external approval. The former stage of loneliness came to terms with different-ness and the need to be understood; this level of resolution comes to terms with the need for approval. Much as adolescents need to transcend their family to "be their own person" and claim adult freedom and responsi-bility, celibates must transcend even their own institutions and their sup-ports to be their own person—to claim their celibacy at a mature level.

We should not kid ourselves. There is no way to claim a deep level of interiorization without a struggle within oneself. Even more aston-ishingly, sometimes the conflict comes from those from whom we have every right to expect support, approval and even reward. I refer again to the life of John Henry Newman who suffered greatly at the hands of those he sacrificed so much to join, his Catholic confrères, the Catholic bishops.[10]

This is the time we "buy into the Spirit" or "sell out" to the system. I'm not sure how much this natural process of growth is necessitated by the mystery of the cross, but I know it has to do with integrity, honesty and facing up to the temptation to sham. I know it has to do with reality versus appearances.

This is not an anti-institutional statement, by the way. It is merely the statement of reality. One cannot rely on any group, no matter how noble, to replace the need to internalize one's celibacy. One uses their help, but must do the lonely work alone.

When I was in Rome recently a professor from one of the Pontifical Colleges sought me out. He was delightful and diplomatic and for a long time I was not quite sure why he had asked to speak with me. Finally he came to the point. He had interviewed over twenty priests who had sexually abused women or children. They were, without exception, as he described them, congenial company men with fine working relation-ships in the system, productive and valuable assets to their bishops or com-munities. One factor common to all of them surprised him: not one of the men experienced any guilt for his behavior. Some experienced some discomfort and a few were embarrassed at being caught, but to a man there was no guilt. His specific question to me was this: How can this be?

I refuse to relegate this phenomenon simply to a psychiatric cate-gory. Celibacy can be claimed, celibacy can be feigned, celibacy can be postured; one cannot easily tell the genuine article from the imitation. Often it is only in the decade after celibates resign themselves to their lonely differentness that they consolidate their celibate identity or not. Frequently that decade determines their style: their relationship to work, to power, and to prayer. Their self-knowledge, quality of service, and awareness of others are all solidified in ways that indicate what is internalized. This is where they achieve either true integrity or just function so as to get through, to keep others happy, to receive their advancements, and get by.

Sometimes we don't know what is really our own or how deeply we hold the values we claim until we and they are challenged. Such a moment of crisis has come or will come to every person who searches for celibacy. Each knows its pain; each knows how unspeakably alone it feels in the face of the question: Is this celibacy mine? What of it is really me? No one but the individual can give the answer.

ALONE: THE OTHER SIDE OF PAIN

As the celibate seeker knows, the process does not end once we have met this crisis of self-control. We often get a rest. We reap the benefit of our progress but the dynamism continues. The reward for having negotiated celibate loneliness, as with loneliness within whatever love, will be further challenges. Very commonly between twenty-two and twenty-seven years of practicing celibacy, in one's late forties or fifties, just when we feel we deserve a rest, another level of loneliness assails us.

Has it all been worth it? That is the question. It's a bit like the dilemma of T. S. Eliot's J. Alfred Prufrock. Certainly Eliot captured the tone of the struggle, evoking the journey we have taken down "Streets that follow like a tedious argument of insidious intent/ To lead you to an overwhelming question."[11] I call this crisis the struggle between loneliness and aloneness.

There is a moving scene in the life of Pope John XXIII when he was envoy to France. He was returning to Paris on the train from his sister's funeral. She had been a devoted household servant in his service most of her life. Her life was single, confined, dedicated, celibate, given to the lonely tasks of household maintenance, and her prayers.[12] The future pope describes in his journal the frightening wave of loneliness that passed over him with the thought: "What if she had done it in vain? What if what she believed was not true? What if her sacrifices had not been worth it at all?" He was writing about his sister, but he was also speaking about himself; his own experiences exude from the reflection.[13]

I myself have been a privileged witness to the celibate stories and struggles of over two thousand priests. Does the loneliness of their stories frighten or discourage me? No, quite the contrary. I have been encouraged and inspired, because they have shown me the other side of the pain—that it is worth it all.

The dividends for their willingness to negotiate loneliness cannot be confined to themselves; their transformation glows in their service. We all benefit from their struggle with celibate existence and its meaning. Loneliness—the awareness of what we lack and what is absent from us —is resolved finally by aloneness—the awareness of what we have. The realization and acceptance of who we are, who others are, and who God is, is felt and savored in aloneness.

Why have I belabored the point of inevitable loneliness in the process of celibate identity and of identification with our heroes—Jesus, Paul, Benedict, Francis, Dominic, Ignatius, Vincent, Teresa, Ursula, Elizabeth Ann or others? My hope is that reflection on one's own celibate journey will profit by a review of the nature of the process. The recognition of the process of human integration of a call to celibate chastity will give encouragement to the striving celibate.

Nothing I can say or do can take away the inevitableness of loneliness in the celibate journey, just as nothing a parent can say can absolve a son or daughter, no matter how well loved, of the inevitable pains of life and learning. But your understanding that the process is natural can give you some comfort as you go through it yourselves. Also—and this is most important—you can understand and stand by others as they go through their progressive crisis of internalization. You can help them make celibacy their own. This is what community is all about: understanding and standing by. You cannot take the pain away, but you can make it more bearable, more efficient.

We Christians need each other. Celibate and married, we need each other. Too often we retreat from each other at exactly the wrong times. Too often we are silent in the face of exactly the things we should be talking about.

Celibacy and sexuality are crisis issues in our times within the present reform of the church. Somehow they are even connected with the tasks of evangelization and the challenges of peace and justice. If religious and priests refuse to take the lead, who will? The church is in as profound an endeavor of reform as at any time in her history. We should not be frightened or discouraged by that. One of the marks of authenticity is *ecclesia semper reformanda capite et in membris* (the church is always in need of reform in its leadership and members). The problem is that the reform now is being pushed by scandal rather than facilitated by leadership.[14]

The renewal of celibate energy will lead the church out of its present crisis. It will not be done without those willing to offer their loving, lonely service to their fellow humans and in concert with them.

When I was teaching at Woodstock Theological Center in Maryland,

John Courtney Murray told me about one of the former professors who taught an introductory course for all the incoming scholastics. He would begin each first class of the new school year by greeting these expectant and awestruck theologians thus: Spreading his arms wide, he would bellow "*Vos estis spes ecclesiae*" (you are the hope of the church) and then add "Freely translated that means: you're not much, but you're all we've got." That applies to us. We're it. We are all the church has.

INTEGRATION: ALL ONENESS

Quite simply what I have tried to say is this:

1. Be proud of celibacy. It is a natural and authentic form of service for the survival and enrichment of humankind. It is neither a better nor worse way than marriage. If it is "your" way, it is the best for you and others.

2. You have to be honest with yourself about your own sexuality. Celibacy is a mode of coming to terms with sexuality; it does not obliterate sexual desire. Celibacy has its own valuable and satisfying process of personal integration. Knowing your own sexuality will help you achieve celibate integration.

3. You need to be honest—completely honest—about your own celibate/sexual process and growth with at least one other human who understands and respects sex and celibacy. Lack of self-knowledge leaves you vulnerable to be blindsided by your own desires. Social isolation leaves you open to overidealization of the sexual. You can maintain fantasies that sexual activity can heal your loneliness. It can't. Fearless self-knowledge and reality-sharing are invaluable correctives to ignorance, naiveté and natural vulnerabilities.[15]

Eight years ago at the end of a workshop on celibacy to a group of religious, one of the 150 participants (they were all from the same community) asked, "How can we learn more about our celibacy?" I said that if I were in their situation, I would form a small group with confrères I trusted and meet regularly to study just that.

When I was in Rome I had supper with the person who was superior of that community at the time. I was really gratified to learn that some members of that community did exactly that, and some of the groups still continue to meet after eight years. That was a community of women. Religious men should realize that women, religious and married, have a great deal to teach male celibates.[16] We all have a lot of work to do to understand what celibacy is, how it works, and how best to achieve it. Let's help each other.

4. Don't run away from loneliness: embrace it, plunge into it. What will you find? Your true self, others, and God. Can you ask for more?

Remember that loneliness is like fear—the more you try to avoid it, the more force and power it gains. The more resolutely, directly, and honestly you confront it, the more certainly it gives way to the secrets that lie behind it—the place where there is peace and meaning.

Don't try to work, play, eat, drink, smoke, or socialize loneliness away. None of them will work. In the end, we must each confront our lonely selves. Sooner or later our isolated existence will have its way, and we have to face it.

What did successful celibates like the saints and your founders know? What do they have to teach you? Each of them plunged into their loneliness and embraced it as a gift of nature. Were they overcome by it? No. They accepted aloneness completely. What was the magic they found there that was so valuable to themselves and others, and so transforming of their life experiences? The mystery of aloneness.

Think about that word aloneness: one can parse that AL-ONE-NESS = *All one ness.*[17] This is what is on the other side of the pain, sacrifice and self-knowledge of loneliness—the reality that we are all one. At the core of St. Paul's excitement over celibacy, moving him to wish it for many, was that lived experience. "We are all one in Jesus Christ—there is no longer Jew nor Greek, slave nor free, male nor female." We are all one: rich and poor, homeless and sheltered, smart and dumb, sick and healthy, saint and sinner, powerful and powerless—we are all one. Only out of my oneness can I serve and bring the full weight of my talents to bear on the task at hand. The price I must pay is loneliness.

I venture to say that one will find, just as I have, this core experience in the life of any successful celibate one cares to study, living or dead. If one has not already found it, I pray that this is exactly what each religious vowed to celibacy will find on the other side of loneliness.

It is no secret that my wife and I have dedicated our experience, our energies, and our resources to passing on to others what we have learned from the generous gift of priests who have shared their celibate/sexual vulnerabilities, suffering, struggles and triumphs with us over the past three decades. We are convinced that many priests have to work too hard at the process of celibate integration because of unnecessary isolation and institutional avoidance of legitimate questions. For many it is these things, not the necessary challenges in the process, that make their lives so painful.

We Christians, celibate and married, are only "saints in the making." If only the ideal is presented to us, or articulated as if the ideal were real, we will suffer unnecessary alienation, not only from ourselves but also from our fellow travelers. If, on the other hand, we can maintain radical self-honesty, we can help others who follow us in the celibate/ sexual process as well as be encouraged and inspired by those who have negotiated the path before us.[18] Genuine investment in the process of learning celibacy for the sake of the kingdom of God will be a sign of grace to others even before the term of complete integration is reached.

We must endure the loneliness of patience with ourselves as we face our particular vulnerabilities, which are ever more clearly manifested as we move toward the integration of celibate reality into our unfinished selves. In the following essay Paul Philibert outlines some of the skills of celibate chastity and demonstrates that these are not achieved in isolation from God or from human relationships. Today we are all threatened by the isolation of self-absorption and violence. Today human society desperately needs the witness of those who can negotiate celibate love and loneliness. Lived celibacy and a genuine engagement in its process will always be a powerful curative force witnessing to peace and regeneration in a threatening and threatened environment.

We will all be the better and the richer for those having had the courage to face up to loneliness and grow through it. The church is sincerely indebted to those who give themselves to a genuine celibate life and ministry.

NOTES

This paper was originally delivered to the Vincentian Convocation of the Midwestern States, June, 1993.

1. A. W. Richard Sipe, *A Secret World: Sexuality and the Search for Celibacy* (New York: Brunner/Mazel, 1990).

2. B. C. Lamb, Ph.D., Notre Dame College, Baltimore; Harris Gruman, Ph.D., The University of Colorado, Boulder; Margarita Guri-Glass, Ph.D., and Marianne Benkert, M.D. are each chairing projects under the title: "Celibacy in Literature and Life." Novels of vocation as well as autobiographical accounts of celibacy are being analyzed along with the psychological studies of religious life. This ten-year project began in 1990.

3. Edward O. Wilson, *On Human Nature* (Cambridge: Harvard University Press, 1978). This is a classic in the exposition of evolution, instinct and culture. Also Professor Wilson has been most generous with his time in conversations both in Cambridge and by telephone.

4. Our research team has outlined a six-semester sequence addressing celibacy/sexuality precisely with these goals in mind. Training of the seminary staff in a transformational technique of bibliography and the

first sequence in this method is slated for use in 1994 at Collegeville, Minnesota.

5. Dorothy Day, *The Long Loneliness* (New York: Harper and Row, 1952) is a manifestation of the celibate heart and mind. Also of interest is Robert Cole's *Dorothy Day: A Radical Devotion* (New York: Addison-Wesley, 1987).

6. John Henry Newman, *Loss and Gain: The Story of a Convert* (Oxford: Oxford University Press, 1986), 256. This was first published anonymously in 1847. There is an extended discourse on celibacy (134-136) in which one character says, "I have a sneaking kindness for celibacy myself."

7. *Ibid.,* xvi (from Newman's Letters and Diaries, XI, 132-33).

8. Physical phenomena accompanying stages of spiritual growth are not to be considered pathological. The histories of spiritual development in both West and East are regularly marked by intense reactions that have pronounced physiological concomitants, for instance Jacob's lameness after a spiritual encounter.

9. Newman, *Loss and Gain,* 140-41.

10. Newman's life and celibate development are worth intense study. Ian Kerr's definitive biography, *John Henry Newman* (Oxford: Oxford University Press, 1988) merits attention.

11. T. S. Eliot, *The Complete Poems and Plays 1909-1950* (New York: Harcourt, Brace & World, 1950).

12. Peter Hebblethwaite, *Pope John XXIII: Shepherd of the Modern World* (Garden City, N.Y.: Doubleday, 1985).

13. Pope John XXIII, *Journal of a Soul* (New York: McGraw-Hill, 1964).

14. See A. W. Richard Sipe, "To Enable Healing: Professionals make recommendations to lift the church out of a sexual-trauma mire," *The National Catholic Reporter,* September 18, 1993.

15. Jarl Dyrud, M.D., a psychoanalyst from Chicago, spoke eloquently and in practical terms about the psychological possibilities and pitfalls of seminary education at the International Symposium on Celibacy, sponsored by the Vatican Congregation for the Clergy and held at the Gregorian University in Rome, May 26-28, 1993, under the direction of Giuseppe Pittau, S.J.

16. Sr. Joan Chittister, O.S.B., and her Benedictine Community of Erie, Pennsylvania have been leaders of several significant religious movements in the United States.

17. David Berenson, M.D., psychiatrist from San Francisco, uses this formula to explain emotional growth. It has features remarkably compatible with the process of *metanoia.*

18. Columba Stewart, "Radical honesty about the self: the practice of the desert fathers," *Sobornost/ECR* 12:1 (1990), 25-39 and 12:2 (1990). These

articles are excellent examples of the continuity of the celibate/sexual process from the earliest times. We have largely lost awareness of the essential structure of celibacy and its history as a process. The earliest monks knew that it was a process, discusssed it and therefore were able to live it. This is an awareness we need to recapture.

Celibate Chastity and Prayer

Paul J. Philibert, O.P.

The renewal of religious life is shaped by our understanding of the evangelical counsels known as poverty, chastity and obedience. These form the basis for the vowed life. Those called to consecrated life in an ecclesiastically approved institute are obliged by canon law to observe the values represented by these "counsels" and commit themselves to them by public vows or promises in the church. Quite often, ordinary Catholics imagine religious life to be a legal phenomenon—a form of institutional existence framed by the vows. It is also possible for religious themselves, once established in the routines of their institutes, to become forgetful of the gospel origins of the evangelical counsels. As Fr. Donald Senior's chapter on the biblical roots of religious life shows, the New Testament understands the counsels as a call to discipleship. The fundamental question is not the observance of a rule or the demands of the vows, but a new kind of freedom and joy which is the result of a personal response to the preaching of Jesus and a radical commitment to follow in his footsteps.

Therefore, all three of the vows can be seen in either a legal and institutional context or in a freedom and discipleship context. By this, I mean the following. All the vows have a pragmatic dimension of sacrifice to them. There is a "giving up" that is represented in each of the commitments: poverty is giving up property; obedience is giving up unilateral decision making; and chastity is giving up marital communion and sexual gratification. Unfortunately, this pragmatic and negative dimension is most commonly imagined to be the heart of the vowed commitment. Yet it would be a very unfortunate misunderstanding of religious life to allow the vows to be seen in that fashion alone.

There is a parallel understanding of the vows as empowering the freedom of the one committed to discipleship. The real meaning of religious life is a dedicated and radical following of Jesus. This loving discipleship is lived in gratitude to God, in friendship with Jesus, and in the power of the Holy Spirit. The negative dynamics mentioned above are certainly a part of the experience of living the vows. But the vows are neither for

118

the sake of sacrifice essentially nor a refusal of life. Unless they are seen as a joyful and free response to the love and liberation that one finds in the figure of Jesus Christ, they will never be able to enhance the humanity of the person as a foundation for genuine sanctification.

MULTIPLE DIMENSIONS OF CELIBATE CHASTITY

The phenomenon of chastity for the sake of discipleship is complex and confusing. This is because celibacy can have many possible meanings, each one of which is valid in a certain perspective. I want to list some meanings that occur to me as a way of indicating both the complexity of the religious phenomenon and possible conflicts of the meanings among themselves.

One meaning of celibacy is availability. The celibate person is not absorbed with the care of a family, as holy as that is, and so can become accessible, perhaps, to a wider range of families. St. Paul teaches that the unmarried person lives not for a wife, husband, or family, but for the Lord (1 Cor 7:32f). In part, this reality of availability is the disciple's witness to eschatological hope. The disciple is a person who has taken the perspective of trying to live now the mystery of the "end time." A life so lived makes one a challenge to others. Such a life of generosity, zeal, and charity must make others wonder what is the inspiration for so radical a generosity.

Celibacy is in this sense a special form of apostolic commitment as well. Such commitments as missionary activities, intense involvement in social justice and action for the poor, and parallel expressions of a life of asceticism and prayer are rarely easy for married persons. Each of these roles represents a more than typical investment of human energies in a religious project. Such an investment would not normally be possible without the celibate state.

Celibate chastity also represents the discipline of impulse control. Even married people, if they are to live a clearly Christian life must learn the discipline of marital chastity. All persons who grow into moral maturity are obliged to learn how to control their passions. For the religious who has vowed chastity for the sake of the kingdom of God, this discipline means much more than controlling the rampant urges for gratification that all are prone to from time to time. Celibate chastity is the discipline of transforming our powerful sexual drives into equally powerful zeal for promoting the well-being of others and sharing affection with those who have none. The love of Jesus for little ones—widows, orphans, marginalized persons—becomes the model for the celibate disciple whose discipline of control becomes as well an energy for mercy and compassion.

Celibate love is also a totalization of self-offering. It does involve a sacrificial dimension. But the point of the sacrifice is not the renunciation of one's humanity, but rather the total oblation of the self in a response of loving gratitude for life itself. This "yoga" of gratitude is at the very heart of celibacy's meaning. As life goes on, the motives for this gratitude become more profound and more personal. As God's goodness unfolds within the providence of a life lived in faith, the spirit of reciprocal generosity becomes more obvious.

Celibacy is also the expression of a positive attachment. In one way, it is a loyalty to the church and to the church's discipline. In another way, it is a loyalty to a particular community. For young religious who take on the discipline of chastity, it is in its initial stages a way of being bonded profoundly to the community. It is an affiliative gesture, linking them to the customs, attitudes, and values of a new "family" of religious confrères and sisters. Usually in the early years of religious life young religious experience celibate chastity less as a struggle for self-control and more as an *esprit de corps* with their new religious family.

Celibacy is, finally, a positive expression of love, devotion, and absorption into God. The disciple has met the Master. Mark's gospel gives us the touching description of Jesus' outreach to a young idealist: "Jesus looked steadily at him and he was filled with love for him, and he said … come, follow me" (Mk 10:20f).[1] Every woman and man whose life is finalized by the generous gift of self in religious service in a public institute of the church is (or ought to be) someone whose life can never be the same, simply because they were touched by grace. Like St. Anthony of the Desert who was moved by the gospel saying, "what good is it for persons to gain the whole world, yet forfeit their soul?" (Mark 8:36), the religious brother or sister is someone whose life has taken a new direction because they were touched by the words of the savior.

Frequently discussions of celibate chastity become bogged down in complaints about the repressiveness of religious formation or of the abnormality of the gospel's claim on the whole of the disciple's life. Sometimes this is done without a clear understanding of the mystery that celibate chastity finds its integrity in a spontaneous gratitude for life and for the call to discipleship. If, indeed, the discipline of chastity is not rooted in such a spontaneous gratitude, it will in all likelihood become more bad news than good news for the individual religious.

In his remarkable volume, *A Secret World*, Richard Sipe concludes his study by making three remarks very pertinent to our interest here.[2] His view is that seminaries have been negligent in teaching seminarians how to appropriate positively the discipline of celibate chastity. Seminaries commonly clarify the institutional demand. But then the seminary presumes that living the life itself will be adequate to lead the seminarian into living celibate chastity with integrity. (In my view, much the same problem has existed for religious in this country.)

Secondly, Sipe says that in his experience of working for fifteen years with seminarians and priests, prayer is essential to the successful appropriation of celibate chastity.[3] (This is the major point that I will explore in the following pages of this present chapter.) Finally, he indicates that one can only gradually grow into the full realization of celibate chastity.[4] The sense of this claim is clearly spelled out in the preceding article by Dr. Sipe himself. For this reason, I would like to devote the remaining pages of this reflection to the specific relationship of prayer and celibacy.

PRAYER AND CELIBATE CHASTITY

Both prayer and celibacy are highly elusive realities. Both make profound demands upon the person, while both have as their object a divine "Other" who cannot be touched or heard or embraced directly in ordinary day-to-day reality.

In celibacy, as I have suggested above, a dedicated religious person enters into a path of transformation that is motivated by gratitude and aimed at a loving union of friendship with the divine Beloved. This path of transformation can be filled with illusion. Without being bonded with a physical other in a living dialogue of ordinary human language, we can find that our relationship to Christ and to God can be loaded with fantasy. It is almost inevitable that young religious go through a romantic phase of their vocation in which they imagine their call to be a form of heroism which obliges them to enter an existence that is marginal to ordinary human development. Yet, as with all other loving relationships, celibate love must lead one to express the power of that love within all that is ordinary and to incorporate it as part of one's real existence. Clearly, authentic celibacy requires much social and psychological growth.

The psychologist Erik Erikson can be very helpful here. In talking about the sixth stage of his Life Cycle, he indicates that the challenge of "intimacy" is the challenge to love the other as the other is, not making the beloved a fantasy of one's own imagining, but respecting the unrepeatable originality of others in their uniqueness.[5] This is a struggle in every human friendship. It is equally a struggle in prayer.

Learning to respect God as God is, involves learning how to live on God's terms. As we grow more deeply attuned to the mystery of God, we realize that we may often see God more profoundly in darkness and hear God more profoundly in silence than in any tangible evidences of the world around us. We must come to respect the transcendence of God.

We must attune ourselves to the subtle reality of God's presence and recognize that we are unable to control the ways in which God touches our minds and hearts. We must, in other words, be stripped of our desire to control the relationship and surrender to the subtlety of a God who is so transcendent as to be beyond the reach of our manipulation.

The theology and psychology of "providence" are engaged in this phenomenon of prayer and celibate love. Put in the terms of a somewhat mythical popular understanding, God weans us away, through the prayer of silence and waiting, from the dispensation of our own providence and teaches us the ethos of God's subtle providence. Put more theologically, as we become less obsessive about manipulating our lives according to the illusions and desires that fill our self-preoccupied fantasies, we are able to become more aware of and sensitive to the "giftedness" of our lives. Our "existence" is pure gift. Further, the circumstances, conditions, and destiny within which we receive "existence" from God are likewise gifts. This is the shape of a providence whose mystery and complexity is never adequately translatable into either thoughts or words. So surrender is required—a surrender that is both gratitude for and cooperation with God's hidden action.

THE SKILLS OF CELIBATE CHASTITY

There is a skill dimension to living honestly the life-style of a religious vowed to chastity. Just as in friendship persons must learn to accommodate themselves to the personality, interests, and spirit of their partners, so in the vertical relation to God of a Christian at prayer, there is similar need for personal learning. One skill needed here can be called "active listening." This is a theme in clinical psychology—particularly in the American school of psychology of Carl Rogers.[6] Rogers was convinced that people only gradually learn to listen with all their minds and hearts to the full meaning not only of the words but also of the feelings of those who speak to them. A clinical psychologist in a counseling setting tries to draw out from patients the fuller understanding of feelings (many of them hidden or even repressed) that are the source of conflict and psychological pain in their lives. Little by little, a link of trust grows so that the therapist and the patient come to understand one another with a deep sympathy, and then there is a resonance of feeling and subtle understanding that is much greater than the grammatical and logical signification of the words used in therapeutic conversation.

In a metaphorical sense, something comparable happens in prayer, I think. I believe that someone who is patient enough to wait lovingly and attentively in silence begins to understand the power of God's presence in the act of loving attention that is contemplative prayer. A spiritual energy erupts from the hidden meaning of the words of scripture, liturgy, and Christian conversation that occur in the life of a religious in a typical day. The scriptures are dense words: words whose fuller meaning is never arrived at in disjointed moments of speaking, preaching, or study; words whose fullness can only be grasped in contemplative savoring, surrender, and worship.[7]

Part of the skill of active listening is knowing how to enhance the silent waiting with nourishing esthetic, musical, and spiritual enrichment. Many people find that a candle lighted in front of an icon of the Christ figure can offer spiritual focus. Others find that a stripped-down environment of spareness and peace invites them into trusting silence. All kinds of assistance are available from various traditional Christian devotions, e.g., chanting, incense, rhythmical breathing, journaling and the like. Obviously, each of these demands a serious discipline for a deeper growth in openness in meeting God, as well as an honest sensitivity to the gifts and needs of one's particular personality.

Another skill touches how to become honest with oneself about one's search for human wholeness in generative love. Erikson again is helpful, telling us that the mature adult stage of Life Cycle growth is "generativity."[8] This is a capacity to go beyond self-interest to loving interest in the well-being of others. Generativity is the development of an instinct to reach out and sponsor the liberation and maturation of the gifts of those with whom we live and whom we serve. So dramatic is the need for this quality of generativity in Erikson's eyes, that he tells us that its absence leads to "stagnation." There is a real possibility that religious might arrive at that frequently seen dead end of finding little meaning in their lives, little energy for their activities and little inspiration for their ongoing commitments. I believe that this is exactly the challenge for senior religious: generative prayer or stagnation in prayer!

A skill that is helpful for many people is openness to guidance in the process which we commonly call "spiritual direction." Here in the United States, at least, the word "direction" is not really appropriate. What most commonly takes place in the process of spiritual guidance is "accompaniment." We are not really looking for someone else to tell us what to do with our lives or to take on a dogmatic role of speaking in the name of God. Rather, this kind of spiritual friendship offers the possibility of listening with another to the echo of God's voice and God's will within our own testimony to what we sense is the grace and the mercy of God in our lives.

Without someone to share these dimensions in faith and prayer as we concretely spell out our experience of God's presence in our lives, we will very likely tend to forget or ignore the reality of God's mercies in our lives. It is hard to imagine how someone can continuously renew the commitment of celibate love without some process similar to this spiritual accompaniment.

There is another skill as well in growing through loneliness to solitude. Richard Sipe's article in this volume expresses the stages typical for movement through this loneliness. This is an important dimension of the reality of the celibate life. At one and the same time we can really and truly believe ourselves called by God and enter into a genuine relationship of gratitude and responsiveness to the grace of God's mercy and yet still find ourselves feeling a certain emptiness in the social dynamics of our days.

I will speak in a moment of the importance of healthy social relationships in the life of a religious. Celibate chastity does not ask for or even condone loneliness as a form of self-punishment for the sake of pleasing God. God is not pleased by unhappiness. But, in fact, loneliness is a dimension of every life. Most married persons in successful relationships find themselves lonely at times because there are dimensions of their lives where their partner is unable to meet them at the same level of intensity or understanding as they themselves have reached. All the skills discussed here will be factors in the outcome of success or failure, peace or anxiety, joy or depression in a dedicated life of celibate love for the sake of God's kingdom on earth.

GROWTH IN PRAYER

Prayer is "God's time." In many self-help books about relationships, we hear that it is important for people in relation to share quality time with one another if the relation is to become or remain real. This is true as well in our relation to God and in our support system for celibate chastity. What is quality time with God? It has something to do, I think, with the power of the symbols which mediate God's love to us. Let me spell out a few ideas that express some sense of the symbolic relation of growth in celibate love.

In the traditional customs of religious life (as handed down to most religious—even of active congregations) there were many signs of one's dedication to the religious state and one's seeking to live in the presence of God. For example, the full and abundant robes of the classical religious habit were a sign of one's being set apart and one's attachment to the role of total dedication to the gospel in discipleship.

The ample garment of the tunic, which formed the basis of most religious habits for both women and men, was traditionally understood to be a sign of one's being completely vested in charity. I am not advocating a return to the continual use of such vesture in contemporary religious life, but rather pointing out that most religious have laid aside this powerful symbol without seriously reflecting upon what it meant in the past and what might replace it in our present social context. In a certain sense, the ancient garb of religious also symbolized God's embrace of the religious. Clothing rites often expressed a command: "Receive the garment of salvation, given to you as a sign of mercy and grace."

The rhythm of religious community life was filled with many symbols of God's presence and God's call. Examples include the saying of the Angelus three times a day, the common recitation of the De Profundis for the dead, the prominence of religious *objets d'art*, and the general spareness of environment of the religious house. In older days the cell of a religious would typically be an austere environment, stripped of many comforts. While again I do not recommend our living in such austerity necessarily, we need to ask ourselves how this functioned symbolically to evoke a sense of God's providence and God's presence, and how we now might functionally replace the symbolic value of these elements in a very different culture. Ignoring the way symbols functioned in religious life in the past is overlooking a strong factor in the spiritual formation of a disciple.

The goal of all of these skills is to produce a man or woman confident and joyful in an experience of total dedication to disciple of the gospel. We do see people who have the traits of conviction, luminosity, simplicity, availability, and loving generosity. This is the positive image of celibacy. This is the reason for the vow. This is the shape of chastity embraced for discipleship. There are such people living today in renewal communities who have found ways to nourish their faith and their generosity in a style very different from that of the classic monastic context. But I would be willing to insist that in no case is this kind of result possible without some structuring of skills and symbols to challenge, support, and enable the miracle of freedom that is chaste, generative love for the sake of the gospel.

PARALLEL CONSIDERATIONS

It would be misleading to leave out of account a consideration of the way in which many religious and priests experience the mercy and tenderness of God in their exercise of ministry. In my judgment, the majority of Christian ministers experience a more intense sense of the presence of God during their moments of helping others than they do in their times of silent prayer and watching. This means that they are nourished by an often profound awareness of God's compassion in their own lives as they extend their own pastoral care to others. The importance of this

dynamic of spiritual growth through pastoral care is anything but neg-
ligible. Yet it is a mistake, I believe, to imagine that this active approach
to growth in relation to God suffices to lay a stable enough foundation for
celibate discipleship.

Obviously, pastoral care offers human gratification of a kind unavailable in silent prayer and meditation. Except for those like cloistered monastics whose form of life precludes such ministry, these times
of nourishing pastoral care are vitally important for growth in apostolic
love and for the confirmation of one's call to dedicated discipleship.
Most apostolic religious are confirmed in their call to this form of life
by the positive reinforcement which they receive in their pastoral relationships.

But American pastoral care is shadowed by the problem of activism.
Virtuously, we can become overwhelmed by the enormity of the need for
our ministry and find ourselves driven beyond reasonable limits of
exertion and commitment. Less virtuously, we can find the waiting and
surrender that characterize so much of contemplative prayer a frightening emptiness that scares us away from the exercise of deep prayer.
There is little in the mainstream popular culture to reinforce or support
the quest for interiority. It is quite easy for an active religious to survive
(or even thrive) on a regime of apostolic workaholism. The test is what
happens when one has come to an end of one's reserve energies or when
one must deal with loss, depression, or failure.

The theme of *kenosis*—the emptying out of self in order to become
a vessel of God-life—is so central to the gospel that it is a wonder that we
do not more commonly seek to understand its practical embodiment in
our experience. "Take up your cross and follow me...." "Unless the grain
of wheat fall into the ground and die..." "Jesus emptied himself..."—these
are the common coinage of our preaching and our pastoral reassurances.
Yet in our own lives, the most evident place for this emptying-*kenosis*
dynamic is in our stripping ourselves of words, of willfulness, of control,
even of understanding, and submitting to the tutelage of the Holy Spirit
in prayer.

I submit that this strange new language of silent loving of God is
never easy, but always a struggle and a surrender. Yet as with any worthy
discipline that entails the learning of skills, little by little one becomes
more practiced and more sure. Ultimately the tide turns and one is made
aware that prayer is not our trying to persuade God or even entertain God;
rather prayer is an opening of oneself to God's secret initiatives. A Japan-
ese spiritual master has said that "prayer has no other end than to beg the
Lord to make himself irresistible."[9] A religious who has utterly lost interest in this haunting mystery of prayer or who has given up on it risks

either living in cynicism or leaving the life. Perhaps more important, those who pray but have lost hope of growing in intimacy with God fail to realize the joy and generativity of a fulfilled human life.

The structures of the past helped to foster attitudes that prepared religious for the encounter with contemplative prayer. But my point is not to recommend a return to the solutions and structures of a former age. Rather, my point is that there are symbolic dynamics that are necessary to support the transformation of a human personality made for relation, love, community, and generativity into a witness to the reality of God's compassion, love, and friendship. Prayer is at the heart of any success in this transformation.

CELIBACY AND CULTURE

It would be unreal to leave aside all reference to some very serious additional considerations. While it goes beyond the objectives of this chapter to attempt to develop any of these considerations in depth, they must be remarked upon if this essay is to have any claim to plausibility. I refer to the following matters: the evidently graced ministry of ordained ministers in the reformed churches who are married; the moot character of the Roman church's disciplinary norm of mandatory celibacy as a condition for priestly ordination; and the social and spiritual wounding of the church by numerous incidents of the sexual abuse of minors by priests and religious. To completely ignore these factors would risk placing both the author and the reader in a fantasy of wishful thinking.

Relative to married ordained ministers in the Protestant churches, the fundamental issue is the fact that their successful exercise of gospel ministry and sacramental administration is admirable. Aquinas occasionally used the dictum "*de esse ad posse valet illatio*": *the existence of something proves its continuing possibility*. In our pluralistic, ecumenical religious-cultural environment, it is no longer credible to argue that celibacy is a necessary condition for generous, spiritual, and dedicated service as a pastor.[10] The evidence to the contrary is too patent. Therefore, my argument about the tight relation between celibate chastity and deep prayer should not be read as a claim that celibacy is an irreplaceable condition for either ordained ministry or for a profound spiritual life. Rather, my argument should be focused as stated, namely, that generative celibate chastity is so closely linked to a generous personal response in discipleship to Christ, that its success is most unlikely without a culture of contemplative prayer.

In addition, even though Pope John Paul II has repeatedly insisted on the discipline of celibacy as a condition for ordination, there continues to be a stream of resistance that asserts that sacramental ministry has often been exercised through the ages by married priests, and that it is difficult to understand how the Roman church will maintain a requisite number of priests unless its current discipline is changed. Again, my argument in this chapter does not intend to take a position with respect to celibacy as a mandatory discipline required by the church for ordination.[11]

My argument concerns the meaning of celibate chastity and the means that effectively support the personal appropriation of this element of religious life in the church as a form of dedicated discipleship. Unlike candidates for priesthood whose focus may be spiritual ministry to God's people without a call to radicalize their response to the counsels, candidates for religious life know that the form of life which they are entering is structured precisely as a radical embodiment of the values of poverty, chastity, and obedience.

With respect to the matter of sexual abuse cases involving priests and religious, it is extremely difficult to generalize. Most likely, there are proportionally no more sexual abusers among priests and religious than among other comparable population groupings in our society. This is not an excuse, just an important contextual observation. What the present crisis of abuse does suggest, however, is that vocation directors and superiors need to make sure that in accepting candidates they are dealing with persons with a clear understanding of the demands of the form of life which religious live and a specific desire and probable capacity to live that life. Sometimes we can encourage as candidates for religious life individuals who experience a positive attraction to religious ministry but who are unsure of the demands of the vows or half-hearted in their intention to embrace the vowed life.

A further thought about clerical sexual abuse touches the central interest of this chapter. Celibate chastity is not sexual neutrality or indifference. The chastity of the disciple requires the elaboration of a culture of chaste loving—an enthusiastic generativity such as I tried to evoke earlier. The chastity of the disciple is meant to be joyful, free, and attractive, as the gospels portray the chaste ministry of Jesus. Jesus in the gospels is portrayed as a man alive with love and compassion. His sexuality, lived in spirit-filled generativity, was expressed in outgoing, joyful, compassionate initiatives to awaken deeper life and joy in others.

As with any complex culture, the life-shaping power of celibate chastity will depend upon reinforcing rituals which provide support and coherence for its special vision of life. Unquestionably many religious find the daily routine of prayer as a supportive ritual for the culture of celibate chastity difficult and elusive. Further, the issues of loneliness and the self-pity which loneliness can engender are apt concerns as well. In the context of religious life, at least, the problem of sexual abuse by priests and other religious underlines the cohesiveness of the complex factors which contribute to a successful life of discipleship. The neglect of community, common prayer, meditation and contemplative prayer, and conversation about religious goals can break a link in the chain of social, theological and personal growth whose elements mutually sustain the development of the culture of celibate chastity.

GROWING IN SKILLS OF FRIENDSHIP

A part of the romanticism that sometimes afflicts young religious beginning their journey of discipleship is the fantasy that imagines that an individual can become deeply responsive to grace while disdaining to become involved in the lives of living, breathing persons who rub elbows with them day by day. It is interesting to note the text of 1 John 4:20 which says that those who do not love their neighbors, whom they see, cannot love God, whom they do not see. Romanticism often waxes enthusiastic about ideas of the good without ever getting around to enacting the imagined good. As Peanuts' Lucy sometimes says, "I love humanity—it's people I can't stand."

Put another way, a celibacy that is supposedly a radical response of friendship for God is sheer fantasy if it is disconnected from the ordinary toil of horizontal human friendships. It frequently happens that young religious are in part prematurely foreclosing the difficult developmental task of working out their identity with honesty and authenticity by entering a religious institute. Assuming a prefabricated role in a complex society offers definition and status to the individual. In fact, both the definition and the status that a young religious supposes will be provided by entry into religious life are often less clearly shaped than one might have imagined. If one drifts into self-glorification and escapist piety as a compensation, the result is risky business indeed.

In past years, out of fear of sexual temptation, young religious were warned away from "particular friendships." As best I have been able to understand, this term appears to mean those exclusive, closed-in friendships that can tend to lead to genital expression. The parallel problem of mutual self-absorption occurs as well when young people are infatuated with friends; this can be disruptive of the common life of a community.

Oddly, as a novice or a young religious in formation, I never received any encouragement to develop positive relationships with either male or female friends. I observed older Dominicans enjoying special relationships—usually with people they met in pastoral work. But the notion that either my human authenticity or my capacity to love God more deeply

might be linked to what I would learn and what I would become in friendships was never raised.

While it remains true that those who have pledged celibate chastity
for the sake of discipleship must guard against occasions of overwhelming temptation, it is likewise true to say that they must guard against
human stagnation as well. Realism and openness with God normally arise
out of our experiences of learning realism and openness with others. By
realism, I mean the give and take that characterizes growth in human
relationships, the ability to respect and cherish others even with clear-
sighted awareness of their limitations, the "active listening" mentioned
above, and the ability both to genuinely love another for his or her beauty
of body, mind and spirit and simultaneously to draw the line that sets
inappropriate expressions of physical love off bounds.

Religious learn a great deal about openness in the interactions of
community living. Today it is truer than years ago that community life
offers greater possibilities for genuine friendship beyond the structured
encounters of prescribed rituals and community business. But it is also
important for religious to have real friendships with both men and
women.[12] The spiritual likeness that is a consequence of growth in friendship is not only a pastoral benefit rendering a person more able to assist
others, but a human benefit as well—making a person more whole and
more interesting.

The observations that I have made in this chapter are an effort to
point up the similarities of growth necessary in both chastity and prayer.
I do not believe that either contemplative prayer or a devoted chastity can
be present without significant growth occurring. I believe that both are
extremely difficult endeavors. I believe that both chastity and contemplative prayer represent a profound and generous response to a powerful
sense of the love of God in one's life. Both call persons to become icons
of God's compassion. Both represent in a certain way an unusually rich
experience of human fulfillment and the attainment of life-giving generativity capable of challenging, supporting and inspiring others on their
Christian journey.

THE DIFFICULT, JOYFUL JOURNEY

Frankly I have some misgivings about whether I have done justice
to my topic in this essay. Discussion of the celibate vocation of the religious is so complex that it is hard to maintain a healthy balance. The core
reality is that God does call some women and men to make their lives a
radical sign of discipleship, demanding a totalizing generosity that invites

the gift of one's whole being in love. But this very God is a gentle, under-standing God, who pardons as well as calls; who trains by the ironic graces of failure, exile, and captivity (if the Bible's account of God's people can serve as a model). Our response will always be chastened and purified by God's mysterious invitation to enter into a divinely anointed silence and waiting. But God's tenderness will also be manifest in countless ways—most generously in the graces of ministry. We will be asked to place God's love above every other love. But we will also find that friendship will become the alphabet of God's caring within our own secret journey of searching, responding, and surrender.

All of this happens at the same time. All of it is equally real. Our problem is either losing perspective or losing heart. But perhaps this small effort to evoke the strange ensemble of love, discipline, and hope that is celibate chastity will serve some purpose. All of us will have to search until our journey is complete to know just how God is calling us to be generous and alive. All of us will continue to make the zigzag journey of growth in honesty and growth in generativity. As we learn to speak more readily to one another about this mystery, may God bless us on our way.

NOTES

1. In his apostolic letter to youth in 1986, Pope John Paul II used this text as part of his exhortation to youth urging them to understand that they are beloved by God. A similar reflection on a parallel text in Matthew 19 forms the opening meditation in the same pope's encyclical letter *Splendor Veritatis.* The sense of the powerful impact of a "call" from God and its interpretation as a sign of God's love is at the heart of both of these texts.

2. A.W. Richard Sipe, *A Secret World: Sexuality and the Search for Celibacy* (New York: Brunner/Mazel, 1990). See especially Part III: "The Process and the Attainment," 237-295.

3. *Ibid.,* 268: "I have never interviewed a man who has attained celi-bacy without finding in him a rich and active prayer life. . . . A celibate's prayer life will reveal the capacity, quality, and nature of his relationships not just with transcendent reality but also with other significant human beings and his self-concept as well." Parallel studies of the celibate jour-ney of religious women would be most worthwhile, since one would an-ticipate different images of growth in generativity, if not necessarily different mechanisms of psychological appropriation.

4. See Sean D. Sammon, F.M.S., *An Undivided Heart: Making Sense of Celibate Chastity* (New York: Alba House, 1993). Sammon patiently ex-

plains the dynamics of gradual growth in sexual self-understanding and warns against absolutizing understandings of sexuality as dangerous taboos. His book is an excellent resource for formation in this area.

5. See Erik H. Erikson, *Insight and Responsibility* (New York: Norton, 1964), 127-130; cf. J. Eugene Wright, Jr., *Erikson: Identity & Religion* (New York: Seabury, 1982), 90-95. See also Patricia H. Livingston, "Intimacy and Priestly Life" in Donald J. Goergen, ed., *Being a Priest Today* (Collegeville, Mn.: Liturgical Press, 1992), 124-150.

6. Carl Rogers, *On Becoming a Person* (Boston: Houghton Mifflin, 1961), esp. Chapter Six, "What It Means to Become a Person," 107-124.

7. See Paul J. Philibert, "Elements for a Catechesis of Silence," *American Ecclesiastical Review* CLXIV:1 (Jan., 1971), 16-24.

8. Erik H. Erikson, *Childhood and Society* (New York: Norton, 1950), 266-268; also *Insight and Responsibility, op. cit.*, 130-132 and 152-157.

9. Paul J. Philibert, "Zen Spirit in Christian Contemplation," *Spirituality Today* 33:2 (June, 1981), 161. The words are those of Fr. Shigeto Oshida, O.P.

10. Note that the Vatican has approved the ministry of married priests who are converts from Anglicanism in the U.S. One presumes that their bishops find their service to be valid and valuable.

11. For a recent study that questions the wisdom of celibacy as a condition for ordination, see Heinz-J. Vogels, *Celibacy: Gift or Law?* (Kansas City: Sheed & Ward, 1993). Also interesting as a study of celibacy in the context of diocesan priesthood is: Matthew Clark, "The Priesthood and Celibacy," D. Goergen, ed., *Being a Priest Today, op. cit.*, 151-168.

12. The American bishops new *Program for Priestly Formation* indicates that an ability to relate meaningfully to women must be considered a condition of readiness for priestly ordination.

The Conference of Major Superiors of Men has produced a series of videocassette learning programs entitled "Men: Vowed and Celibate," which provides excellent discussion about key areas of formation in celibate chastity. These programs are particularly valuable because they feature many different voices of persons who are appropriating the charism of celibate chastity in ways distinctive to varying age groups and a range of temperaments.

Retrieving, Reclaiming and Reappropriating Monasticism

Mary Margaret Funk, O.S.B.

When I became a Benedictine prioress in 1985, I was not sure it was possible to name, claim and work toward a future in religious life. Monasticism especially was suspect among women religious in the United States.

Among my questions were the following: Can today's mature women be obedient to an abbess figure? Does celibacy stunt personal growth? Can institutions make a difference in a broken world that is in need of front line, hands-on help? Who is called to a life of living with the herd? Are not holiness and prophetic witness precisely beyond the interests of any group? Is the church so laced with self-interest that it no longer mediates the holy?

During a time when all institutions are failing, can religious life expect to press on without being oppressed by the weight of infrastructures? Being a religious superior felt like being tangled up in a bale of steel wool. Only this mesh of wire is wound by layers of piety and pride.

More troublesome than all of the above was the fact that no monastery seemed to be refounded from within. There may be new foundations which send members back to the old ones. There may be reform efforts aimed at groups of monasteries such as those of the great St. Teresa.

Nonetheless, here is the story of a monastery that has set about refounding its common life out of the shared concerns of its own members. We sought and received help from the Lilly Endowment and we remain deeply indebted to them for the possibilities that this support opened up for us.[1] I would like to summarize the findings of our efforts in these pages.

THE REFOUNDING PROJECT

This is a first glance. Not even ten years have elapsed since we began. I hope to take a deeper look in a few more years to see what will develop.

Also, this is the point of view of just one monastic woman who was prioress for eight years (1985–93).

As a monastery of Benedictine women religious, we tried to attend to three areas of concern: poverty, divine office and *lectio divina*. We also shifted our image of ourselves with our public by changing our name from convent to monastery. When I wrote the grant proposal, it was a concoction of bits and pieces. Now I see the design to have been in three parts: (1) to retrieve the tradition, (2) to reclaim the parts that are desirable, and (3) to reappropriate the tradition as a living reality. Let me explain.[2] Although some of our practices are new, most things have been done before and will be done again. To go forward, one must make sure one is mining the best of the past, because there simply are not time or resources to rediscover everything important in each lifetime of an individual or a group. Much wisdom gets lost and hence every few generations there is the need to retrieve the past.

In monasticism the best wisdom seems to be found in the practices and attitudes touching material things, common living, common praying, individual asceticism, shared authority, meditation, hospitality, wholehearted service and selfless charity. Most aspects of monastic life reflect the tradition.

There is debate about which past should be retrieved: the moment of origin or the expression of one's culture? In monasticism this debate makes a big difference. If we take the desert fathers/mothers as the point of origin and refound our monastery based on that, that will be radically different than the point of foundation within the American culture. The latter is definitely an apostolic and missionary perspective. The earlier point of reference requires traditional stable community to safeguard cloister for the sake of contemplation.

I preferred the focal point to be the culture out of which arose the Rule of Benedict. That is reached through the study of scripture, Cassian, Pachomius, Augustine, Basil, the Rule of the Master, and Athanasius (especially his great tale of Saint Anthony) and other mothers and fathers of late antiquity. This is for more than just to understand the sources. Benedict was a fine editor. He shaped monasticism by what he didn't include as well as by what he did say and how he said it.

I used the Rule as a referent, not a constraint.[3] The other referents were scripture and tradition, the teachings of the prioress (one interpretation for a particular community), and the lived experience of a particular community. These four references seemed to carry the burden of retrieving (and reclaiming) a tradition. I studied the Rule of Benedict and taught it to as many sisters as would come to classes. The sisters in formation memorized it like we did in the old days. Committing the 72 Chapters of the Rule to memory gives access to the word at will.

With a foundation in the four referents (scripture/tradition, Rule of Benedict, teachings of the prioress, and the lived experience of the community), we were ready for the refounding process of retrieving, reclaiming and reappropriating the tradition of monasticism.

FROM THE SIMPLE VOW OF POVERTY
TO TOTAL RENUNCIATION

We started with poverty. In popular culture, poverty is not a value; it is a human problem with human solutions. However, it was in the vow of poverty that I found the tradition that contained the wisdom about things. In Benedict's Rule, what we call the vow of poverty is total renunciation of things. There was meant to be a total dependence on the abbot and the monastery for everything necessary.

We began with the Rule of Benedict, studying the commentaries and various other texts to arrive at not only an understanding, but an interpretative method. We tried to use the best available scholarship. Then we studied history, recent interpretations of the vow of poverty and finally the 1983 revised canon law provisions. In this country we were previously classified as sisters, and therefore fell under the canonical norms of taking the simple vow of poverty. Then in the 1983 code the historical distinction between solemn and simple vows was abrogated. The new situation made possible a retrieval of the monastic promise of total renunciation.

This was the retrieving part. We also stepped outside of the monastic tradition and looked into the best traditional forms of institutional leadership. From contemporary management we brought to our institutional life collaborative budgeting, planning, computerized communications and data functions, and public relations and development to fund not-for-profit organizations such as our St. Paul Hermitage and Beech Grove Benedictine Center. Development fits in well as a mechanism for total renunciation. It manages the human tendency to give and receive gifts. In development work all gifts are received and given in the name of the monastery.

RECLAIMING

To retrieve is only one third of the process. Reclaiming is the second step. To reclaim means to sort out in a discerning manner what part of the theory makes sense and how those ideas can be practiced today.

For this part a civil lawyer (Brian Hewitt) and a canon lawyer (Daniel Ward, O.S.B.) aided us in finding the actual mechanism to express the vow of poverty. The prioress (me) and council (elected and appointed members) selected four levels of poverty and norms for their implementation. The chapter discerned the steps necessary for the community to adopt policies and procedures that captured the spirit of total renunciation.

Some practices were not reclaimed because they were not able to be implemented—not fitting our times or not functional for our group's particular history. This process took about eighteen months.

All the practices reclaimed awakened a sense that "this was what I came to the convent to do in the first place!" I designed a planning process that fit the monastic structures that are hallowed in the Rule. The monastic strategic planning model took the structures found in the Rule and fit them into a contemporary planning process to implement the reclaimed practices and continue the search for other monastic themes, so that we could continue in the direction of being more of a monastic community. This was our first strategic goal. The reclaiming was accepted by a chapter decision and placed in our book of Monastery Norms.[4]

REAPPROPRIATION

Here starts the long journey of reappropriation. Reclaimed norms touching the monastic spirit of total renunciation were given concrete forms of implementation. There were several possibilities and some members chose a less taxing form. Only the prioress knew which form each member subscribed to. All members were expected to work toward the spirit of total renunciation, which means giving the monastery all rights of ownership present, past, and future.

Things needed were sought for from the monastery, symbolized in the permission and/or blessing of the prioress. The common library swelled with books from individual bedrooms. The community closets took on a new importance. Material goods were for one's use but owned by the monastery. The value was the common life. The asceticism was to relinquish the unilateral disposition of goods, the point being to seek God through the medium of things.

So we signed forms, redoing our vow of poverty, new legal wills, medical releases, living wills, personal budgets, gift giving and receiving, etc. Each sister[5] was interviewed by the lawyer and seen by the prioress in a one-to-one conference. The lawyer witnessed the signing of the civil forms. The prioress witnessed the canonical documents. The community treasurer was involved in every step. Patiently and competently she listened to each sister's needs and made sure all was done with due respect to individuals' needs in compliance with all the complexities of the civil and church law.

Dialogue was needed to accommodate those living alone or away from the monastery. To the extent that such persons were the exception and not the rule, it seemed to work. We need to find more apostolic expressions of poverty. The traditional permission system can be revised to allow more adult dialogue, but living in common seems to be essential to the cenobitic life-style. If one lives alone and desires total autonomy for her adult life-style, there can be bureaucratic methods of accountability, but no spirituality of total renunciation.

ONGOING EFFORTS

The reappropriating continues today. I taught classes on Wednesday afternoons, working through the Rule and other classic texts, such as Evagrius, Cassian, Pachomius, the Rule of the Master, Augustine, Basil, Francis, Mother Teresa, and Thomas Merton, to name a few. About thirty to forty percent of the community came on a regular basis for about five years.

For reclaiming, a group process time outside of chapter was necessary. The membership was divided into small groups to discuss how the appropriation process was going in their lives. Groups maintained the same membership for three years. For small group exchange, we needed a model that fell between intense therapeutic groups and work/action groups and that fell somewhere between celebrations and chitchat appropriate for table and recreation[6]

APPROPRIATION

The task of appropriation is the most difficult stage. It requires study. Each one must know the tradition and identify with the values at stake (or at risk). Also, each member must be willing to accept the consequences of the decision process. In other words, each one has to accept the observance with a willingness to internalize the value that it expresses. Total renunciation must be an expression of faith and a commitment to the monastic way of life or it becomes merely a group contract respecting good order.

The most difficult part of the stage of reappropriation is for the individual and the group to relinquish the behaviors and attitudes that prevailed before the task of reclaiming. At this stage, some folks dropped out.

For example, we tried to make our community retreat an opportunity for group learning. We had Joan Chittister, Terence Kardong, Ambrose

Wathen, Ron Fogarty and Thomas Keating. Each time about sixty percent of the community would ask out of part or the whole of the retreat for some exceptional reason. Remember, these topics were ones that the entire membership agreed to address in chapter meetings. (The percentage of agreement was usually ninety-eight percent.) The attitude of many was that our culture is full of multiple options and everyone is doing the best they can with all their responsibilities.

It was difficult to sustain attention for group learning. There was not much open resistance, just a lack of attention to the importance of what we were trying to do. Resistance wasn't limited to the young or the older sisters. The middle-aged group was simply stretched beyond their ability to take on another major initiative beyond their personal and professional lives. Nonetheless, at each chapter meeting we got the nod to continue the monastic recovery process.

In addition we selected to have a feminine, context-sensitive breviary for Divine Office, adult practices of obedience, and *lectio divina*. A fourth action was to change our name from Our Lady of Grace Convent to Our Lady of Grace Monastery. This did not take much energy and seemed self-evident. Our Board and constituents accepted our explanation and wished us blessing on our direction. They promised their support. The need for a monastery in Beech Grove is strongly supported by our public.

RETRIEVE, RECLAIM, REAPPROPRIATE
THE MONASTIC DAILY OFFICE

The council appointed twelve sisters to the Breviary Committee. They were our best musicians, artists, writers and poets. Four years later we had a four-volume set of office books weighing twenty-five pounds! The Psalter included one hundred chants and scripture selections taken from the Hebrew and Christian scriptures. Contemporary women and men were used as authors in place of the traditional canticles. Original drawings, songs, versicles, and antiphons were lined up side by side with the classical texts.

Most monasteries have done this since the Directory of Abbots and the Vatican II documents recommended that each monastery compose its own book of common prayer using the classic lines of morning, noon and evening office, vigils and feasts in parallel with the Roman calendar. So we took our three-pronged approach: retrieve the tradition, reclaim what we needed for our times, and reappropriate individually and collectively the living of that tradition in our daily practice.

Some key dimensions of our reappropriation of the monastic office are these: We restored the liturgy of silence and worked hard on selecting scriptural reading of continuous or connecting themes. Each year we examine our horarium to see that it is as beneficial as possible for as many sisters as there are at the monastery. Today we number seventy-two living at Beech Grove.

We had to determine how the office fit with eucharist liturgy (and/or communion services). We chose inclusive language, yet we tried to remain as scholarly as possible in our translations of psalms, scriptures, petitions, and song texts. We reclaimed some of the Latin hymns and texts when they expressed what no other language has accomplished to date. We crafted our own ordo, lifting up saints (or putting them down gently) as appeared coherent with our need for meaningful models. We set out to retrieve Ordinary Time as well as a quiet Advent, a single-minded Lent, a festive Christmas and a solemn Easter/Pentecost. We made sure guests were welcomed and included with us in our worship. The twelve-sister committee had a sister assigned to the project as a full-time staff member. She worked with another sister who was gifted in art, graphics and re-sourcing. The community had provided these two sisters with master's degrees in music, library science, education, art history and theology.

In the retrieving stage, the entire community studied *Time Made Holy* under the direction of Sister Mary Collins, O.S.B. We studied the history of the divine office and brought to the table all the options while remaining faithful to the monastic tradition. The musicians sorted through musical texts, tones and translations. Some parts of the office went through three and four drafts before being set into our final (yet three-ring binder-provisional) form.

The reclaiming stage was the dialogue with the community on each book as they tried it out in choir. We set in motion a way to keep up the standard of the books, but to add new or delete old materials on an annual basis.

The reappropriating stage is still in process. Since it is a "practice,"[7] we are just now experiencing the benefit of praying season after season, and not just deliberating about the content and form of prayers. As a result, there is a quorum at prayer and an attentiveness and silence as eloquent as the music. While the product is neither ascetically severe nor esthetically sublime, guests can recognize that the assembly is praying from the heart.

There are sisters "on missions," not living at the monastery, that use the office books in part or whole. When the missions were little monasteries, it was more appropriate to pray common prayer. This is an area that I think needs more work in reappropriating. If the sister is in an apostolic work, she should pray with people she serves whenever possible. Some sisters have been able to form a stable group in the parish that would do morning and evening prayer.

Sisters can be "on mission" for fifty of their seventy years as a religious. While the divine office works within the monastery, it doesn't seem to work where there are too many variables of people, time, space and place. It works in medium-sized monasteries like Our Lady of Grace, because there are always fifty or so there to carry on, even when sisters must be absent for this or that hour of office in choir. Critical mass is important for implementability. Divine office is a prayer form for a group.

We sorted through the timeless questions: How much time should we be giving to prayer? How many hours should we be working (including apostolic work)? How much time does each sister need for individual study and personal prayer? How much time should be allotted for leisure, that is, undesignated time at the person's discretion? Is all time mine, and then the community claims certain times? Or is all time the community's, and I have permission to bracket some for personal use? Should our professional life take precedence over monastic practices? Or personal growth and development?

We eventually saw that these questions were divisive and meaningless in the light of faith. The language of faith asks a different set of questions. Faith asks how I can serve. Where can I both really and symbolically express my commitment and zeal? Since I have completely surrendered to the monastic way of life, what is God's will for me and how is it mediated? We will come back to these themes, but you can see that a mystical life of faith is essential to make any sense of this monastic way of life.

The best way to look at the spiritual side of monasticism is through the traditions which speak about personal prayer. The prayer form that is prescribed in the Rule is *lectio divina.*

LECTIO DIVINA

In Benedict's Rule, the monastic is asked to spend four to six hours a day in *lectio.* This tradition has been lost. The current practice seems to be some form of spiritual reading, journaling, guided meditations or even tapes and music.

As part of the Lilly Grant, I obtained a mentor. Sister Mary Collins agreed to work with me for a few years. I read, studied, listened and dialogued with her. Sometimes we met at Atchison and other times we met in Washington, D.C. I will never forget going into Newman bookstore with her and selecting books that were pertinent. She thought I should look into the work that Abbot Thomas Keating was doing out of Snowmass, Colorado. Bob Funk, a first cousin of mine who is a lay seeker, had made a retreat there in 1985 and also recommended the Snowmass Trappist Abbey. So I went through an intensive retreat in January, 1986, after reading *Open Mind and Open Heart* and practicing the method as I understood it. One fundamental choice I made was to let go of all my previous methods of meditation and surrender to this new practice, before I made a judgment as to its merits or demerits.

Trappist Thomas Keating's method is called "Centering Prayer." He has put together an organization called *Contemplative Outreach* for extending this prayer practice.[8] Thomas, a former abbot, put together a new way to do the *lectio divina* component of the monastic way of life. The method could be used by a monk, a nun or a lay seeker. I was excited by the theory and the practice of centering prayer. This divine therapy combines the best of spiritual, psychological, and anthropological insights. It seemed like a perfect match for reclaiming *lectio divina* for our times.

Thomas came to Beech Grove several times and taught both the nuns as well as lay seekers at the Beech Grove Benedictine Center. Our practice has had lasting effects on me and my community. The combination of monastic office and *lectio divina* has had the effect of rekindling a life of faith. The scriptures were heard with new depth, and substantive and lively conversations were renewed at the common table. As retrieval, we studied the Rule and read about *lectio divina*. We found several contemporary forms of *lectio:* centering prayer, John Main's meditation practice, and an applied lectio—the Jesuit Exercises.

As reclaiming, we entered into a group practice of centering prayer through retreats, classes, practice sessions, reading books, tapes, etc. Everyone was expected to do some form of *lectio divina*. Whether or not a sister did centering prayer as the fourth step of *lectio* was left to the individual, but silence and contemplative practice became an expectation for each sister's daily schedule.

At times we set up opportunities for common *lectio,* to support the individual practices. This meant doing in common the *lectio,* meditation, oratio and sitting in silence. Sitting occasionally includes faith-sharing by the participants. The difficulty with this in a monastic community is the blurring of lines between the two prayer forms: monastic office is for prayer in common, while *lectio divina* is for prayer as an individual. There seemed to be a need for informal prayer. But over time all this got entangled.

So *lectio divina* was retrieved as a particular prayer form. We searched for contemporary expressions to reclaim *lectio;* we found centering prayer to be especially fitting. We appropriated the practice individually according to grace and nature.

It seems that the combination of working on the divine office and *lectio divina* moved us closer to naming our experience as monastic women. We needed the tradition and its mystical power. Faith was the only language to name why, what and who we were on this journey. And then, as in any journey, new questions emerged.

When you live, pray, eat, share things and do the work of an intentional, in common group, some of the usual structures take care of some of the agenda. The chapter and house meeting governed the large decisions. The prayer practices and apostolic assignments became routine. But life issues emerged. In short, is there another referent beyond scripture/tradition, the Rule, and the lived experience of the community?

The missing link in communication was some form of human contact that was beyond ordinary conversation and beyond decisions formalized in writing. This is the role of obedience to the prioress and mutual obedience among the membership.

OBEDIENCE

RETRIEVING OBEDIENCE

We went back through all the literature on the role of the abbot and the role of mutual obedience in community. We read and studied history. We sorted through some of the contemporary "experts," examining the ideas of the Whiteheads, Chittister, Fiand, and Schneiders.[9] I had individual conferences with each sister, asking them what they thought of when we vowed obedience. When did they feel like they were being obedient? What would they recognize as fulfilling the idea of obedience today? We had a retreat on obedience given by Ronald Fogarty from Australia. We taped his sessions and discussed the fourteen conferences in small groups over two years. Each sister had outlines of the fourteen sessions that ranged in topics from scriptural warrants, to psychological stages, to theological dissent and case studies of dilemmas from real life situations.

RECLAIMING OBEDIENCE

As prioress I reclaimed some of the prerogatives of the prioress figure at prayer. These included blessings and domestic rituals as well as official prayers and gestures in funerals and professions. I entered the role mindful of chapter two of the Rule which urges the abbot or prioress to mediate Christ to the sisters, both in the liturgical settings and as far as possible in ordinary daily activities. For me this meant to love without return and do selfless service and less service of the self. Once I had internalized this, I had more energy, because my ego was not on the line so much. This is probably the best part of being prioress. I had never really "surrendered" in this way before.[10]

About this time, the refounding process met its limit. At this time, the community decided not to give me a third term.[11] This was difficult for me, but I think the group simply reached the end of its comfort zone for the time being. The biggest issue was that the process of retrieving, reclaiming and reappropriating was not intelligible to the group as a whole. The community wanted a change. While they liked the direction, they did not like the consequences that were beginning to emerge.

If the group had seen that their autonomy would have been safeguarded by particularizing the "reappropriation" and if they had known that the community would not inappropriately claim earlier traditions or retrieve uncritically from the past, then maybe there would have been less resistance.

Let me share some fears about this process. Anxiety about fundamentalism is our biggest enemy. Many a group has taken something out of the past, lifted it up, given it the weight of authority, and passed it on to the members of the group with heavy sanctions. As leadership persons formulate planning and prepare chapters, fears of this kind must be shared and steps must be taken to prevent such misunderstanding.

There are at least three ways this process can go wrong: retrieve the wrong tradition, reclaim the wrong parts of the tradition, or reappropriate the tradition in a manner inappropriate for our culture or particular situation. Some sisters did difficult things in the spirit and practice of obedience. Obedience seems to thrive when there is a lively mystical sense of putting on Christ. In human terms, without the eyes of faith reform can be reduced to a gridlock of wills. This project on obedience raised the real issue touching what we had lost. This is a tradition of asceticism.

ASCETICISM

The other half of the mystical life-style is the virtue of humility that shows itself in ascetical practices. I never got the chance to work with our community on this, but I can sketch out an agenda that may save some group a few chapter meetings and papers about the prerequisites for a culture of monastic obedience.

There is little a group can do once it sets its goals and goes about its collective practices, if it doesn't acknowledge the need to undo previous behaviors, thoughts and attitudes. This is what asceticism achieves. It is only negative in the sense that an "undoing" is required before any layering of "should's" upon the community.

Monastic asceticism finds its origins in the work of humility. Chapters 7 and 73 of the Rule of Benedict are key texts for wisdom about humility.[12] I found pertinent assistance in Evagrius and in Cassian's *Eight Thoughts* which came over into the West as the *Eight Capital Sins.*[13]

Surrender of the self is at the heart of asceticism, but what are healthy ways to do that? What would a contemporary community of monastic ascetics look like? Here is where apostolic spiritualities pitch in and show how disciples extend their faith in imitation of Christ and in giving, especially to the poor. The monastic setting is supposed to be an exemplar of church as well as to contribute to the transformation of the world by work and hospitality.

In this particular American culture, there needs to be a discipline of asceticism to train thoughts, desires and passions to move toward God and the other, and away from the self and the ego. That "turn" of conversion is found in the tradition of asceticism. This kind of work is the real work of the monastery. Other works are integral but not essential. We do them because it makes sense to serve others. Our ministry flows from the impulse of our own interior work, motivated by our desire to serve God who has become the center of our thoughts and hopes.

While asceticism is not an optional part of any spirituality, it is the most difficult to bring forward. It must take into consideration the best insights of psychology and anthropology. This is an ongoing agenda. There must be some language that feminist, adult seekers would recognize as helpful. The single most effective practice to promote an ascetical life-style is meditation. That seems to be consistent in all the major religions.

A SUMMATION OF THE REFOUNDING PROCESS

Our refounding process started with a spirituality of things and shifting from the vow of poverty to the monastic theme of total renunciation. The practices of divine office and *lectio divina* were substantially and meaningfully renewed. The mystical tradition had to be interpreted for any of the traditional monastic ideas to become practical for women today. Finally, obedience was dead in the water without an ascetical practice to unlearn ego-centered motivations and attitudes.

Let me go back to my opening questions. If I were to start again I would now have a different set of questions. Nonetheless, I trust that the findings of this project can still be helpful beyond my own monastic community.

Is Monasticism suspect? Is it like the Royal Family in London that has lived out its relevance? The values of monasticism are classic. There is a monk or nun in everyone. There will always be a few who will make that the center of their being and the shape of their life-style. The structure of a monastery works to the extent that there is faith and a complementary discipline. A vocation seems to be the inclination to receive those graces.

Monastic living has only a few essentials: Rule, and scripture, believing community, prioress, and tradition. These four elements always refer to each other and cannot be appropriated in isolation. There is a tension in the structure of the monastic way of life. If the prioress doesn't succeed in the role, the energy becomes flat. If the membership is not in dialogue with the tradition, then the intelligibility is lost and meaninglessness ensues.

Can today's adult women be obedient to a prioress figure? With faith, this works. The superior mediates Christ. The community is where believers treat each member, especially the least, as Christ. The gestures of monastic community are a constant liturgy. The "altar" is extended to the dining room, the kitchen, the chapter room, and wherever the community is gathered. The symbolic is the real. That's why faith is the only thing that makes the difference; also why without faith there is nothing.

So back to the superior figure. It is like a liturgical role. In the traditional role, the prioress is both an administrator and a teacher. She administers the institution and teaches the tradition. It is appropriate that the prioress should interpret the tradition for the community and discern how to live it. Yet the prioress is not the sole interpreter of the tradition. The lived experience of the community, and the whole of the scriptures/tradition of the church informs the institution. The prioress is not a parent nor a friend, but a pastor.

Of all the human institutions available to women, monasticism is the most sensitive to the feminist perspective. The relationship between the prioress and the woman monastic should not be one of domination. While the prioress is not Christ, we are willing to let her mediate Christ. We are willing to enter into the liturgical rituals that are hallowed by that mediated presence.

Should celibate chastity continue to be the norm for monastics? Yes. The fullest expression of monasticism is possible only when the community is celibate. Functionally, community doesn't last when there are children. Oblates and so-called lay communities live the Rule proportionately. If the community is always making choices as to its stand on celibacy, there is no way to get on with the agenda of the monastic life.

Maybe someday there will be celibate couples in our midst. This question is sometimes linked with the gay and lesbian life-style issue. We cannot be blind to the fact that these questions are being raised. In my opinion, traditional monastic groups are fragile enough at this time. Without judging one way or the other about multiple life-styles, it seems reasonable for traditional monastic communities to stabilize for the sake of the future and limit members to celibate, single-sex members.

Can someone be celibate and also personally healthy? Yes. But that question presumes that the goal of the monastic life is personal health. In fact, the goal is to seek God. Health follows, but it is not the goal. If health doesn't follow, then discernment might be more appropriate than medical attention or more friendships.

Who is called to live a life with the herd? Are not holiness and prophetic witness beyond the capacity of a communal response? Must I leave the monastery, if I see the dark side of self-centered religious? No. Monasteries have a responsibility to be communities of consequence. If a monastery is to matter, the intent for conversion must prevail. So, my question is a good one. But if the monastery is not seeking God, then it is not a monastery. There is nothing to leave. If it is a place where faith moves one toward charity, then the very difficulty of its institutional life can be instructive and helpful.

Is the church so laced with self-interest that it no longer mediates the holy? The church is meant to mediate God's reign. Yet the human condition is inescapable. Older traditions have difficulty staying faithful, but the richness of a long tradition more easily corrects itself over time. Centuries of witnessing to the gospel's call to holiness make the monastic life a privileged structure of the church in any age.

During a time when all institutions are failing, can religious life expect to press on without being oppressed by the weight of infrastructures? Some monasteries will not make it through this period. The forces of diminishment are intense. Some members think that decline is inevitable. Comfort seems to be the agenda in the interim. Corporate planning usually fails. Ideas generated in a group setting are often too optimistic. It is easy to accept good ideas in a meeting. Follow-through is more difficult. Leadership becomes more timid after repeated failures.

The personal problems of members and of extended dependents on the monastery can sap energy. The serious study needed to ground discussion and responsible decisions is usually neglected by the majority of members. Members prefer to go to workshops where they are entertained, rather than undertake a discipline of careful study and prolonged reflection. There is little follow-up or follow-through done by individuals.

Do our structures mediate the holy? Some members center their religious fervor more in popular religious movements than the wisdom of the monastic life. My guess is that most monasteries have a lot of facing-up and sorting-out to do. The point, though, is that the work of the transformation is worth the effort.

Who can lead us through this steel wool tangled in piety and pride? Mystics can, who have found appropriate ways to also unlearn the cultural conditioning of our times so that God can work through them.

Finally, can monasteries be refounded from within? I have not seen it yet, but hope is in the unseen. I am confident that there is a future for monasticism today. I also think apostolic orders can be refounded according to their original charism, if that charism is still a compelling value for the church today. In the meantime, I continue on the journey of emptying the false self through a practice of living the monastic life. If I, as an individual, find that difficult, then why should a group find it any easier? Only by the grace of God!

CONCLUSION

To refound a monastery or any other religious institution, there must be a process of retrieving, reclaiming and reappropriating the tradition. Practical spirituality must retrieve the mystical and the ascetical. Too often today mysticism is associated with "individual" interest and devotional life is thought optional. Asceticism may be mistakenly viewed as meaningless or even harmful to personal growth. Yet there must be appropriate ways of being a mystic today. For persons giving the whole of their life to seek God, piety isn't enough. Do we have the energy to address the contradictions which entangle religious life and fashion a new people of the Way?[14] That is what refounding is all about.

NOTES

1. Two Lilly grants were provided to support strategic planning for a feminine monastic community and to research the renewal of the monastery's spirituality. These programs were executed between 1987 and 1991. I appreciate the dialogue with the Lilly staff and consultants who were informed, concerned, and helpful.

2. These categories have been commonly used in catechetics as well as in studies of inculturation. After eight years of working on refounding, I have seen these sequential operations at work. The first is research and study, the second is group discernment, and the third is group and individual conversion. Planning usually accomplishes the retrieving and reclaiming, but doesn't touch the aspects of conversion.

3. This is a post-modern hermeneutical method. To read the Rule as a referent, you must understand it as the backdrop for all the reality

under study: the imagination plays more fully in intuiting the sense of the text. Cf. Sandra M. Schneiders, *The Revelatory Text* (San Francisco: Harper, 1991).

4. Many women are put off by voting. We still vote at the end of much discernment for the sake of good order. No other method comes close to providing the clarity that voting does.

5. It was in these one-on-one sessions that I got a first-hand look at "vocation." I met sisters who took to the reappropriation phase with zeal and ease. Others had difficulty understanding why we would even want to do these things. Thomas Merton once remarked that for those who understand, no explanation is necessary; and for those who don't no explanation is possible.

6. Groups were initially divided according to age groups. Persons were able to move in and out of a group. The group leaders were trained. Group behaviors and dynamics are quite difficult in settings where the expectation is to live closely for many years in succession. Some chose not to be a part of a group. In the election of the new prioress, many cited that they wanted to keep the structures of these small groups for continued dialogue about things that matter.

7. "Practice" supposes that an observance becomes part of your way of life. A "practice" has a training effect only after years of observance. Monastic practices suffered in the past because the intention and meaning behind the practice got disconnected from the observance. Today we are experiencing a "practice" deficit, because when the practice gets difficult (just at the moment of its maximum benefit), some advisor may counsel moving to another observance.

8. For further information, write or call the National Office of Contemplative Outreach, P.O. Box 737, Butler, N.J. 07405: (201) 838-3384

9. See Evelyn and James Whitehead, *The Promise of Partnership: Leadership Ministry in an Adult Church* (San Francisco: Harper, 1991); Joan Chittister, *The Rule of Benedict: Insights for the Ages* (New York: Crossroad, 1992); Barbara Fiand, *Living the Vision: Religious Vows in an Age of Change* (New York: Crossroad, 1990); and Sandra M. Schneiders, *New Wineskins: Re-Imagining Religious Life Today* (New York: Paulist, 1986).

10. At the recent World Parliament of Religions in Chicago (Sept., 1993), members of the Monastic Interreligious Dialogue Board had a session with the Dalai Lama on Sunyata and Kenosis. We have much to learn from the Buddhists on the matter of emptying the ego or the false self. In preparation, I read Don Mitchell's *Spirituality of Emptiness* (Paulist, 1992). This book introduced me to a theological conversation that named my experience of being prioress.

11. The vote was decisive. Only seven voted for a third term. Another interpretation would be that other sisters were ready and eager to take leadership at the time.

12. Timothy Fry, O.S.B., ed., *The Rule of Benedict* (Collegeville, MN.: Liturgical Press, 1980). This is an invaluable book, with commentaries, indices for scripture and ancient writings, etc. Its lack of inclusive language almost put me off. But until a better text is ready, there is no more comprehensive study of the Rule. We turned the language liability into an asset by looking up variant translations.

13. See John Cassian in *Nicene and Post-Nicene Fathers of the Christian Church*, Second Series, Vol. XI (Grand Rapids, MI.: Eerdmans, 1986).

14. The Lilly Endowment has temporarily cut back funding for projects such as this because of market changes. But for a project like this, maybe we should continue to fund research of this kind from our ordinary income.

PART THREE:

Facing the Signs of the Times

Transforming Life:
The Charism of Religious Life

Margaret Brennan, I.H.M.

Religious life will survive the challenges of this period of cultural change. Despite various obstacles to the simple continuation or expansion of our religious communities as we have known them in the past, our form of dedicated Christian life will flourish again. We are slowly becoming more aware of a fundamental reality at the heart of all of our religious lives and apostolic ministries—the reality that we hold in common as the charism of religious life itself. The conviction that there is a common charism shaping our responses as religious to the opportunities of a society in transformation is growing stronger among us here in North America. In my view, our future as religious will develop out of our ability to embody this charism in our lives and works.

I will try to grapple in a new way with this concept of charism that was given as a framework for renewal and adaptation in response to the challenge of Vatican II. I now believe that the Spirit of God is inviting us to expand our understanding and to enter into a deeper theological reflection about how we are called to be a charismatic reality in the church as we stand at the threshold of the twenty-first century and of an emerging new worldview.

Two sets of images come to mind which speak about charism as something developing and unfolding. The first comes from the paintings and reflections of Meinrad Craighead in her book titled *The Litany of the Great River*. Craighead's river is both the river of memory and the river of life. It holds and connects us to the stories and the dreams of one another mingling past and present as we travel in the river of life that continues to flow and to nourish our spirit with the Spirit of God, the fountainhead from which we flow.[1] This says something to me of the way in which charism is memory and the power that comes from keeping the story alive and moving in our deepest desires and our future hopes.

I found a second image reflected in a hymn sung at a convocation in one of the theological schools of the Toronto School of Theology. In the opening stanza the faculty and students were invited to praise God as the source of faith and learning who has sparked and stoked our minds with a passion for discerning the truth, while maintaining a sense of wonder for the mysteries which we cannot fully fathom. The struggle to bring faith and learning together was pictured as two currents in a river that struggle against each other's undertow until they at last converge into one coherent flow. That metaphor spoke to me of the unavoidable tension that exists as we try in the church to bring the authority of hierarchy and that of our charism together in a common commitment to the liberating mission of Jesus. In the end, hopefully, the intensity of our turmoil will serve to carve out a clear course as we seek to move the church forward in its service to God's reign.

In reflecting on this swirling current in the church which is religious life, I will first review the biblical understanding of charism and how it has been interpreted in church documents as a particular gift of the Holy Spirit to assist the church in carrying out its life and its mission. Second, I will offer some further thoughts on what I believe is a new impetus or charismatic invitation that is summoning all of religious life in its many forms as it moves into the future. Finally, I will make some concluding remarks and suggest some further implications.

RELIGIOUS LIFE AS A PARTICULAR CHARISM

The Greek words *charis* and *charisma* are found frequently in the letters of Paul. *Charis*, literally meaning "grace," appears often as a salutation and final greeting in the epistles. It is usually combined with "peace" and became a kind of slogan in the early Christian communities expressing the atmosphere of the early church, the blessing which Christians wished for one another and which we continue to invoke today—"the grace and peace of our Lord Jesus Christ be with you." This grace that Christians wish to one another is in reality the grace of God that appeared in the incarnation of Jesus. It is given to us in Christ and received with the Spirit. It is a participation in God's life, dynamic and life-giving, never withdrawn or repented of (Rom 11:20)—a reality that the followers of Jesus must communicate and share.

Charisma, as distinguished from *charis*, represents the favor granted by God rather than the will of God by which it is granted. It describes and designates a particular kind of spiritual gift of God which enables the recipient to perform some office or function in the church (Rom 12:16; Eph 4:11). Such gifts are received, not for the benefit of the individual, but for the good of the community.[2] They represent something new and fresh.

The extraordinary outpouring of gifts in the early church was a sign that a new force, a new spirit, was at work in the Christian community. Among the variety of charismatic functions listed by Paul (1 Cor 12:8–11), none surpasses that of love (1 Cor 13), and prophecy is considered as superior to the rest.

Although religious life has had a long and esteemed place in the life of the church, it was not until the Second Vatican Council that it was understood as a charism. Pope Paul VI later described it specifically as a charism, a gift of the Spirit to the church. *Lumen Gentium* stated that it was under the inspiration of the Holy Spirit that religious life has been acknowledged as a divine gift which the church has received from her Lord (§43) and, as such, belongs inseparably to its life and holiness rather than to its hierarchical structure (§44). But it was in *Evangelica Testificatio* that the actual biblical vocabulary of *charism* was applied to the reality of religious life.

In this apostolic exhortation of Pope Paul VI published July 1, 1971, we were encouraged in our renewal and adaptation to the modern world to be faithful to the charisms and evangelical intentions of our founders and foundresses, who were raised up by God within the church. The pope described religious life as a charism and fruit of the Holy Spirit, who is always at work in our midst (§11).

It was with this mandate and challenge that we sought to return to the Spirit and origins of our beginnings, seeking in them for sources of revitalization in our life and ministry that would find expression in new ways. In the early 1970s a great deal of time and effort went into the study of congregational charisms and the intentions of founding persons as we entered into new ministries in response to the compelling question of Paul VI: "How will the cry of the poor find an echo in you?" (*Evangelica Testificatio*, §18).

As apostolic religious congregations, most of us had come into existence in the early decades of the modern era when the industrial and scientific revolutions left large segments of the urban European population struggling with new expressions of poverty and deprivation without adequate education, health care and social services. In the Second Vatican Council, as the church took its stand in the modern world, the pope reminded religious once again that we were obliged by our very commitment to Christ "to awaken consciences to the drama of misery and to demands of social justice made by the Gospel and the church" (*Evangelica Testificatio*, §18).

The decade of the 1970s also witnessed our attempts to rewrite our basic congregational documents in a manner that would separate the legal aspects of canonical legislation from those which expressed our rootedness in the gospel, the charisms of founders and foundresses, and the manner in which we interpreted their spirit for our times. In the last decade Pope John Paul II, when writing to religious or to bishops about their relationship to them, has continued to use the language of charism and to speak of the distinctive character that marks the difference among religious congregations.

Most recently, the *Lineamenta* document, written to prepare for the synod on consecrated life, continues to make use of this terminology. In addition to affirming the charismatic nature of religious life, the writers are particularly mindful of the tension that can exist between religious and bishops when a certain boldness in responding to new initiatives can appear to be "manifestations of dissent in both theory and practice in relation to authority and the magisterium of the Apostolic See" (§28).

Religious congregations, in exercising their freedom to explore new initiatives in accord with their charism, have resisted a kind of parochialization of ministries in the light of clergy shortages. The language of charisms as applied to religious congregations has not always been understood by bishops. This can be particularly problematic in the light of the bishops' role to exercise a responsibility of discernment in authenticating the charisms of religious that can appear to be unseasonable because unforeseen.

In 1983 Pope John Paul II asked the American bishops to conduct a study of American religious life. When they came together to do some corporate reflection two years later in the spring of 1985, they were addressed by Michael Buckley, S.J., who offered some provocative thoughts on the meaning of the charismatic nature of religious life. Quoting *Mutuae Relationes*, a document drawn up by the Congregation for Bishops which deals explicitly with relationships between bishops and religious, Buckley asked the gathering of bishops to recall the statement that "every authentic charism implies a certain element of 1) genuine originality and of 2) special initiative for the spiritual life of the church. In its surroundings, it may appear troublesome and may even cause difficulties, since it is not always and immediately easy to recognize it as coming from the Spirit" (§12).

Drawing out the implications, Buckley observed that once religious life is understood as charism then it has already been said that "the church expects to be continually challenged in many ways, and the hierarchy is bound by God to the difficult and nuanced discernment of the authenticity of these challenges."[3] He noted further that the Congregation for Religious in "Religious and Human Promotion" encouraged religious to be enterprising in their undertakings and initiatives because this is in keeping with the charismatic and prophetic nature of religious life itself (§27; see §4a and §24).

Engagement in unpopular issues of social justice was interpreted as something that the church may rightly expect from religious women and men. Discerning the authenticity of such engagements, rather than repressing them, is a grave responsibility of the bishops as well as that of the religious congregations themselves.

Three criteria for such discernment are enumerated in *Mutuae Relationes*: 1) the expectation that the signs of the Spirit enumerated in Paul's letter to the Galatians are present: charity, joy, peace, patience, kindness, goodness, faithfulness, gentleness and self-control (Gal 5:22-23); 2) a costly and inescapable element of the cross; and 3) a constitutive love of the church in spite of almost inevitable conflict.[4]

In conclusion, Buckley notes in referring to writings of both Paul VI and John Paul II, that what is "most profoundly at issue—demanding prayer and discernment and those sufferings which go with any struggle to recognize the Spirit of God—is the radical identity of religious life as developing charism" (p. 662). It is this point that I wish to pursue and develop further.

RELIGIOUS LIFE IN THE FUTURE

Within the last few years a number of books about religious life have been published after many years of silence. The silence, I believe, was not because there was nothing to say, but because the thoughts that would produce the words were struggling to come to birth as we sought to name ourselves in the post-Vatican II church, which was also on the threshold of the postmodern world. The volumes which have come forward have offered theological, sociological, psychological, cultural and feminist research and reflection on where we have come from, where we are, and where we hope to be going.

All of these books have had something to say about the charism of religious life in general and about the fostering of particular charisms that belong to individual congregations as well. Following their analysis, we have discovered a similarity of experience and future direction articulated in general chapters and assemblies, even though described with the particular "family differences" that are found among us. Growing collaboration and communion among religious in terms of shared ministries as well as shared formation and retirement programs have established stronger links between us.

This is not to say that religious congregations do not have their own particular charisms. But it is more important today for us to reflect not so much on what is distinct to each of us as on the radical identity of religious life as a developing charism in a church that finds itself at the crossroads. The church faces an emerging worldview which calls for a shifting of ways in which we have understood the cosmos and our place in it. What was unique about the spirit of our founders was their ability to see into the needs of their time in new and creative ways.

In *Gaudium et Spes* the church reflected on its role in the modern world in terms of its service not only to those who invoke the name of Christ, but to the whole of humanity. Seeing itself in solidarity with the entire human family, the church believes that the human person deserves to be preserved and that human society deserves to be renewed. The church, in "carrying forward the work of Christ under the lead of the befriending Spirit, understood that mission as giving witness to the truth ... scrutinizing the signs of the times and interpreting them in the light of the Gospel" (§3).

This meant, in the words of the council, that we must "understand the world in which we live, its expectations and longings" and "respond to the perennial questions which women and men ask about this present life and the life to come" (*Gaudium et Spes*, §4).

ECOLOGY, FEMINISM AND RELIGIOUS LIFE

As we move toward the twenty-first century, we seek to interpret the words of *Gaudium et Spes* in a world that has changed dramatically. We are entering into a new period of time which calls for a revision of the ways in which we have understood the world and our place in it. Growing numbers of non-governmental citizen organizations all over the world have become conscious of the global crisis provoked by unprecedented poverty, environmental destruction and social disintegration that have disrupted whole communities and threatened the well-being of countless human persons.

One of the most pressing challenges today is the need to regenerate, protect and liberate life wherever and however it is being threatened. As we try to discern the authentic signs of God's presence and purpose in these times, we need to look for those endeavors and movements that are most at the service of life in all its dimensions. Life itself is God's greatest gift to us.

The winds of the Holy Spirit blow where they will and often at unexpected times and in unlikely places. I believe that a particular invitation of this befriending Spirit of God for both the healing and the hope of humankind and of the planet is present within the commitment of ecological and feminist movements to sustaining and enhancing life. To assert that the creative and renewing Spirit of God is present in the deepest aspirations of these movements is not to be unaware of the need for discernment of other spirits operative within them nor of the need for the wisdom to know how to live with patience, composure and forbearance before the ambiguity present in their plurality of views.

The issues involved in these movements are basically about creating an alternate vision of reality. This vision includes all peoples of the Earth, is mindful of the rediscovery of our interconnectedness and of the spiritual energy that joins all living things. It is committed to bringing about healing relationships between genders, classes, races and, in a special way, between humans and the Earth itself. Such an alternate vision has serious implications for exploring Earth-centered spiritualities that reverence all creation, engaging in ecumenical dialogue, which encourages us to seek to listen, to search for and to find the *holy* in the wisdom of other faith traditions while remaining committed to our own. This vision is also a summons to a simplification of life-styles, to living within our means and responding to the call to transform global economic structures which have ignored the interconnections in the web of life which makes up our ecosystem.

Our disregard for the living organisms of the cosmos is in great part responsible for soil erosion, deforestation, toxic waste and the pollution of our air and water that keep so many of our brothers and sisters living lives of desperation, displacement, oppression and marginalization.

In keeping with the prophetic and charismatic nature of religious life, I believe that we are called and challenged in a particular way to be committed to these issues, to reevaluate our mission as apostolic religious and ask how our way of life, our particular charisms and the diversity of our ministries can respond to these needs in new and perhaps nontraditional ways. The particular charisms of our congregations that gave cohesion and spirit to our commitments, to our long history and experience in community life, and to the sharing of goods which enabled us to extend our ministry and resources in ways not possible to isolated individuals, have something to offer to non-governmental agencies and other networks about solidarity and shared enterprise in the service of others. Our commitment to the urgent issues of our day can bring the church to play a major role, as it did in the past, in initiating educational institutions, health care facilities and projects focused on community development.

WOMEN RELIGIOUS AND THE FEMINIST MOVEMENT

Religious faithful to the ongoing development of the charism of religious life have met a very specific challenge as they have opened themselves to the feminist movement and tried to find their way amid the many voices of feminist theory. Because feminists have a vision and know that the world can be different, we find ourselves allied to them in desiring the transformation of structures that have oppressed and brutalized women through national politics, through poverty, unemployment, racism and violence. The marginalization that women have experienced is symbolic and symptomatic of similar expressions of domination aimed at races and classes of people as well.

Women religious have found these feminist perspectives true and urgently needed, not only because we have found a new vision of Christian truth expressed in feminism's basic commitment to equality and mutuality, but also because feminism brings something new to the church in its acknowledgment and understanding of the giftedness that women contribute to its liberating mission. This prophetic element of the charism of feminist religious often meets with reluctance and resistance. Nowhere has this been more evident than in the commitment of women to overcome the dualisms that have taken root in the structures and symbol systems of the church itself.

The discernment of what we as Christian feminists have perceived as a gift of the Holy Spirit to the church has and continues to be a difficult and painful reality. While church documents and papal exhortations continue to acknowledge and honor what are called the special and unique gifts of women, our basic inequality remains. The *Lineamenta* document prepared for the upcoming synod cautions that "in some cases a mistaken idea of feminism has laid claim to the right to participate in the life of the church in ways which are not in keeping with the hierarchical structure willed by Christ" (§29). This is an example of a failure of the Vatican authors to grasp the fundamental perspective of Christian feminism.

It is particularly painful as well as paradoxical when the church champions and praises the promotion of human rights and acknowledges the Spirit of God in secular movements but fails to do so within its own structures. My reflection on this has put me in touch once again with an experience that remains a poignant memory, even though it happened more than twenty years ago.

In June of 1972 I was in Rome with the officers of the Leadership Conference of Women Religious at a meeting with the Congregation for Religious. From the earliest years of the Vatican II renewal we had been seeking an audience with the Holy Father to bring him the greetings of American sisters and to carry back a blessing to our conference.

Our inability to obtain an audience that year was particularly painful because it seemed related somehow to what the Congregation for Religious had named as the independent spirit with which we had undertaken the restructuring of conference bylaws and to our criticism of the Vatican's imposition of "essential elements" of religious life that imposed directives about our way of life without any kind of consultation.

One morning, during these days of deliberations while perusing the Vatican newspaper, *L'Osservatore Romano,* we noted that the pope had granted a private audience to Betty Friedan on the previous day. Among other things, he praised her for "her indefatigable zeal for women's rights." In recounting this incident I do not mean to criticize Paul VI for acknowledging the emergent women's movement as a positive sign of the times, but rather to lament his inability to name and to honor this same movement within the life of the church itself.

The women's movement in the church does not aim to overthrow the church's rich tradition, but rather to propose a revisiting of the church's theology, preaching, patterns of pastoral care and liturgical and institutional life. We need a pastoral life that not only reflects women's experience, but also offers a corrective to all that continues to denigrate women and deny the exercise of their gifts.

The theme of the 1993 International Union of Superiors General meeting in Rome was "apostolic women religious at the service of life in all its dimensions." One of the major speakers was Dr. Maria Teresa Porcile Santiso from Uruguay. Prescinding from Pauline vocabulary to describe charism, she reflected on life itself as the most extraordinary gift of God. In particular, she spoke of the giftedness and specificity of a woman's life, which is alive in a cycle linked to nature—her own human nature as well as that of creation.

For Santiso, to accept the symbol/meaning of a woman's body is to accept life as a place of growth, of birth and of transformation, all of which she believes are essential tasks for today's society.[5] Do not women have an "innate" capacity for allowing the church "to be more visibly a space of life, of receptivity, of acceptance of the other, of open doors?" she asked.

Today we are challenged as never before to live interdependently and in relation with persons of diverse cultures and religious traditions and to offer one another a habitable and hospitable space. In this context, too, the voices of women have offered a diversity of responses. Can we hear a summons of the Spirit within the global and local voices of ecofeminists? They not only argue the inextricable connection of racial, classist and gender oppressions with the domination and destruction of natural environments, but call for systemic change as well.

FURTHER IMPLICATIONS

The charism of religious life that all religious share in common concerns the transformation of life. Motivated by Jesus' declaration that he had come "that others may have life and have it to the full" (Jn 10:10), our own founders and foundresses responded to spiritual and temporal needs that were not being answered either by the church or by society. Their solidarity with those in need, which gave drive and dynamism to their vision, derived from their belief that the reign of God was not only a transcendent reality but also a visible one that fosters peace, justice and right relationships. Diarmuid O'Murchu maintains that religious are intended to be kingdom-spotters, belonging to both church and world, to the here and hereafter, responding to the supreme prophetic task of the re-creation of life and living at the intersection between the kingdom and the world.[6]

Our founders were able to comprehend pressing needs and to respond to them in innovative ways. These needs were made known to them within the social context in which they lived. For us to return to the spirit of our founders today, to come in touch once more with the charism that gave us life and existence, requires deep attention to the significance of our congregations' originating impulse within the cultural context of the world in which we live. This may mean that what we will be doing in the twenty-first century may not resemble what we did in the days of our beginnings. But, hopefully, we will continue with the same dynamism.

New forms and adaptations of religious life have always emerged to interface with significant changes in culture. I believe that religious life will continue, not only because God does not take back the gifts once given (Rom 11:29), but because we will continue to stand at the intersections between the world and the reign of God and to hear the voice of the Spirit. The revitalization of religious life will come about as we respond to invitations to be about the preservation, enhancement, and transformation of life wherever that is happening.

I make my own this challenge from Diarmuid O'Murchu speaking about what it means to set free the charisms of our founding persons as we stand at the edge of the twenty-first century:

Above all, religious need to take renewed responsibility for their charismatic identity. Religious are a global movement, not just a religious phenomenon; they have a message and mission from and for the world and not merely an agenda from or for any one church; they have a sacred history which does not justify a nostalgia for the past but never ceases to point to the future. Finally, religious are about the creation of a new world (the transformation of the kingdom), which often demands a readiness to part with the institutions sanctioned by time and tradition.[7]

NOTES

This chapter was originally a presentation to the annual assembly of the Leadership Conference of Women Religious in Dallas, Texas, in August of 1993. It appeared in slightly different form in *Origins* 23:12 (Sept. 2, 1993), 207–211.

1. Meinrad Craighead, *The Litany of the Great River* (New York: Paulist Press, 1991).
2. John D. McKenzie, S.J., *Dictionary of the Bible* (New York: MacMillan, 1965), 324–326.
3. Michael J. Buckley, S.J., "The Charism of Religious Life," *Review for Religious* 44:4 (October 1985), 658–659.
4. *Ibid.*, 660–661
5. Dr. Maria Teresa Porcile Santiso, "The New Enthusiasm: A Gift and a Power of the Spirit" (address to International Union of Superiors General in Rome, Spring, 1993).
6. Diarmuid O'Murchu, M.S.C., *Religious Life: A Prophetic Vision* (Ave Maria Press: Notre Dame, Ind., 1991), 9.
7. *Ibid.*, 243.

Communities of Hope

Donna Markham, O.P.

Metaphor is a window into the realm of human desire and longing. It reveals the human spirit by fusing our deepest-held beliefs with our lived experience. Metaphor expresses the kernel of what has been forgotten or lost in the whirlwind of our distracted lives. Metaphor has the power to break through obstacles that stand in the way of the truth.

Metaphor is the power of the mystic, the therapist or the artist to bring forth healing and change at the core of the human spirit. Because it touches the core of reality, an interpreted metaphor provokes change. Consequently, metaphors can be disturbing both to the speaker and to the listener.

A metaphor disturbs because it cannot be pursued very far without leading to the boundaries of the sacred. It cannot be grasped by the intellect alone—it is an empathic resonance of the the spirit, an affective expression of what is true. Like a parable, metaphor uses ordinary language to express the extraordinary truth of what it means to be human.

Community, as metaphor, expresses the human longing for relationship, the best expression of our humanness. Community inspires awe and wonder as it webs hearts together in a world where individualism, separatism and nationalism conspire to keep us isolated and disempowered. Strategic to the birthing of an alternative world grounded in compassion and justice, community threatens the prevailing culture by conspiring with the transformative power of God. Thus, a genuine community of hope can disturb and disquiet when it disrupts the social drift toward autonomy and self-sufficiency. It can disturb those of us who aspire to live it and unsettle the environment in which it is situated. It can threaten change on every level and demonstrate that conversion and healing are, indeed, painful processes. Community is a healing metaphor for a fragmented world.

Human community is not optional. It is an obligation essential for the survival of the planet. It is our obligation as religious women and men who have committed our lives to working for the reign of God in our world to understand, foster, and share authentic community.

THE PREVAILING MOOD

Profound longings of the human spirit are identified in the language of critics, scholars, theologians, poets, and even of ordinary folks who are capable of verbalizing their inner pain. Repeatedly our society's cultural products witness to persons feeling alone and orphaned, to individuals searching for meaning.

Not too long ago, a 31 year-old mother of two sat with me in tears as she said, "I don't feel like I belong anywhere or to anyone. I just feel unwanted and not connected to anybody. I keep looking for things to make me feel better, but nothing is working". She went on to tell me how she had bought a high resolution TV and a new VCR and, most recently, had gotten a stationary bike. In spite of her new acquisitions, she continued, "I feel like I'm on the verge of dropping out, giving up. I can't sustain a lasting friendship or belong to a group for any length of time. Nothing lasts. The pain is horrible. I am trapped, cold and alone. I can't get out. Nothing makes sense anymore."

Her feelings approximate those of a prisoner in self-enforced solitary confinement. "I am trapped, cold and alone. I can't get out." The deepest truth of her experience was expressed in this analytic metaphor. In the act of expressing her truth, accompanied by the response of someone interpreting her excruciating pain of helplessness and isolation, she begins her journey toward freedom.

Similar experiences of disengaged subjectivity and alienation have led others to escape into materialism and consumerism in a desperate effort to find some solace and comfort. In a rather disturbing analysis of contemporary experience, Robert Bellah notes that one of the most prized and non-expendable commodities for Americans is a microwave oven—the antithesis to the sacrament of the family meal.[1] A family's shared preparation of, participation in, and cleaning up after Sunday dinner, is replaced all too frequently by each member "zapping" his or her own favorite micro-ready food and rushing off to the next scheduled event.

Daily news commentaries reveal the progressive fragmentation of family units and a parallel political separatism. Separatism, often disguised and justified under the rubric of American "pluralism," promotes division and deterioration in every corner of our social experience. American religious sometimes feel a comparable sense of disconnectedness from other religious, from the church's hierarchy, or from groups of

laity who were for years our supporters or the clients of our pastoral services. We know from personal experience that competitive private agendas
during this period of divergent understandings of ecclesial renewal have
led us to crises of meaning and belonging. In a similar way, in the larger
secular world, our poets, ecologists, sociologists and even business analysts
warn us of the dangers and numbing effects of individualism, separatism
and the disregard for unity and the good in common.

COMMUNITIES OF HOPE

Entwined in these commentaries on our times is a longing for connection, meaning and belonging. Community is the deliberate, human,
metaphoric expression of a profound yearning for intimacy and purpose.
I am convinced that genuine community is our final hope for establishing reconciling communication in a pained world. It holds hope as well
for building the future of religious life despite the dynamics of exclusion,
competition and confrontation that affect both the culture at large and
our religious institutes. Communities of hope become organic bridges
connecting islands of the spirit where compassion, friendship and commitment to the mission of the gospel still flourish.

Vibrant communities of hope have the power to proclaim the truth
that we are profoundly interconnected with God and with all creation.
We are part of a living system which is our home. Communities of hope
witness to our being embedded in the whole of God's creation and, as
living parts of this system, they can become catalysts for the conversion
of those who remain committed to little else than their own individual
survival.

What are the demands and consequences of living at the heart of the
metaphor of community? What does it mean for us, women and men
religious at a precarious moment in history, to commit and entrust ourselves to ultimate belonging—to the creation of communities of hope
which attest to the truthfulness of God's relationship with us and with
our world?

This question has occupied many provincial and general chapters.
The candor and self-critique with which we are addressing this question attest to the maturity of American religious life. We respond by calling ourselves to the profound communal transformation of contemporary
religious life. We acknowledge that norms and life-styles which were
sufficient and effective yesterday are painfully inadequate to address the
crises of today. Yet, in spite of uncertainty and despite misunderstanding and criticism from those upon whom we have counted, we entrust
ourselves to our faithful God and move on. We have been faithful through

the great changes which Paul Philibert describes in his introductory essay. We cannot be less faithful now as a new moment arrives.

We are taking the charism of religious life extremely seriously. We are now risking new ways of being communities of celebration that radiate coherence and hope into society. More and more, we are immersing ourselves among the marginalized and most vulnerable.

Here are some examples. In the blighted core of an inner city, a group of religious engaged in various ministries opens its home to neighbors as a place for prayer, respite and hospitality. This becomes a contradiction in an environment charged with violence and suspicion. In a border town, young adults and religious respond to the needs of Central American refugees by establishing a center for illegal aliens. Theological reflection, common prayer, radical simplicity and advocacy form the non-negotiable basis of their communal life. Surrounded by affluent retirement communities, a growing enclave of destitute migrant workers is aided and empowered by altruistic college students, religious brothers and some committed couples who live and pray with them as they work on behalf of this neighborhood of previously ignored people.

These communities of hope are growing in strength and numbers across the country. Increasingly, we religious are embedding ourselves in uncomfortable places where we are committed to challenge the dominant norms of our society and our church. Counting on God's friendship, we are venturing into places where many—and, indeed, where we—may not wish to go. Nevertheless, with all the metaphoric power of being part of a greater whole—a part which contains and is contained by every other part—we are conspiring in and committed to the healing and unifying transformation of the earth. We are becoming a metaphor for "covenant," God's covenant. While we have reason to be encouraged, we realize we have a longer, deeper journey to make.

The growing commitment of religious to be communities of hope is inspired by God's own covenant with us. God has bound us to the divine reality; in response we bind ourselves to God's will for mercy, justice and peace. This intimacy and the continued conversion to which it calls us destabilizes the status quo. It may be perceived as subversive by those who feel more at home in an environment of separatism and elitism. But we are not surprised to see that the metaphor of liberating community is always fiercely resisted by the dominant reality.

THE COST OF COMMITMENT

There are obligations which follow from taking responsibility to live at the core of this metaphor. To begin with, communities of hope relinquish the security of the rigid constructs and protective routines that once defined religious community life. They must be resilient and responsive to the ebb and flow of the needs of those among whom they live, while still claiming time set apart for contemplative space.

Participation in these transformative communities calls us to let go of our own accommodation to personal comfort and possessions, to lay aside rugged autonomy and private agendas in order to respond in solidarity to the most urgent needs. Those who live in the metaphor strive to represent the covenant of God's compassion. For many of us, this will call us away from the more comfortable environments that we have known in the past.

Communities of hope call for the ability to remain a marginalized *anawim* while, at the same time, being surrounded by the dominant culture. We are being called to make a home with the dispossessed and vulnerable in the midst of a culture that rejects them. We are committing ourselves to live in the midst of the prevailing social norms while maintaining a distinct identity as outsiders who refuse to be co-opted. We are committing ourselves to articulate responsible criticism of the prevailing culture as we search for and proclaim the truth of transformative communities of hope. We sustain this posture through the rigorous practice of a shared faith, non-defensive and honest interaction with those who oppose us, uncompromising commitment to contemplation and common prayer and, most important, reconciling compassion.

Communities of hope have the capacity to grieve together as they recognize what has been forgotten about social integrity and feel the shared pain of being outsiders. The catharsis of grieving leads to the celebration of a faithful God who is friend and companion, who has called us together to be an organic conspiracy for the healing of our world. The inability of persons to feel and admit sadness reveals the dulling of their responsiveness to reality. One of the more disturbing symptoms an individual or a group can exhibit is the absence of the human emotion of sadness. Those who are unable to grieve have closed themselves to the transformative power of empathic love and compassion. They have sealed themselves in smug detachment.

As members of transformative communities, we must have the hope and the stamina to sustain rejection, misunderstanding, unfair judgment and even ridicule from the dominant secular and political majority. Walter Brueggemann addresses this in saying that exiles "must hold and practice faith in an empire that is deeply hostile ... to our most precious social vision."[2] He continues, "The empire has a plan for the exiles: that they should be forever displaced, homeless, at risk, restless, administrated."[3] "The empire will never understand. In the end however, it will yield."[4]

STAYING FAITHFUL

Danger always lurks in the shadow of metaphor. By their nature, metaphors are rooted in concrete reality. They threaten to tell the truth about what is happening and they strain to upset the way things are working. Dominant social reality may try to deflect the metaphoric message and render it passive, incomprehensible and meaningless. But the real power of metaphor is to break through the constrictions of the conventional order and provide a vision of greater wholeness and deeper freedom.

Communities of hope risk becoming sidetracked from their dynamic function of bringing forth new structures of life based on collaboration, mutuality and respect. The dominant system will try to entice us to set aside our agenda and replace it with its own. It will untiringly try to seduce us into spending time and energy in reaction to it, rather than in being about the task of proclaiming truth, justice and compassion. It may even attempt to entrap, freeze out and isolate us, in the hope that we might feel just as imprisoned as that 31 year-old mother. But as long as communities remain faithful expressions of the human desire for healing and solidarity with the suffering and vulnerable and of longing for communion with God and with creation, we will continue to agitate and disturb society and address the conventional inequities of racism, patriarchy, and materialism. This is our agenda of healing.

The prevailing culture attempts to undermine communities of hope by co-opting individual members to sell out to a more comfortable existence, allowing escape from the stringent demands of proclaiming what is true and just. The dominant system cleverly realizes that solitary persons will not survive long as outsiders in its midst. They are ripe to be picked off and assimilated, thereby diminishing the power of the metaphor to convert and transform. Nowhere is the evil of the dominant system more apparent than when it works to devalue and fragment those who are bound together to work for the common good. The more hostile, intransigent and wily the environment, the greater the need for the community to gather hope, strengthen desire and realize vision.

LEADERSHIP AT THE HEART OF TRUTH

Good leaders have the courage and wisdom to interpret the metaphor. They know that powerful social meaning is hidden in the heart of the metaphor. Leaders risk telling the truth. They realize that left uninterpreted, the metaphor is bereft of the fullness of its power to bring about change. But this metaphor can be interpreted only from a posture of deep love. If there is any element of judgment or reprisal, the interpretation will be powerless.

To prepare ourselves for the act of interpretation, we must love with a passion that transforms our whole being and that is rooted in and nourished by contemplative relationship with God. We pray for a love that is so transparent and pervasive that it gives us the greatness to accept our own failings and those of our sisters and brothers, the courage to proclaim the vision of an alternative world ruled by the common good, and the wisdom to challenge any acquiescence to the status quo. This is the foundation of interpretation.

What might interpretation entail for leaders today?

- Recalling the memory, the charism and the values of the covenant which God has made with our institutes and their membership;
- Acknowledging, supporting and celebrating examples of the deepening communities of hope which are emerging;
- Sharing the sorrow of the community of "outsiders" as they struggle to maintain integrity and unity in the face of misunderstanding, stereotyping or ridicule;
- Challenging those who are being tempted toward assimilation by the prevailing values of individualism and materialism;
- Asking difficult questions when the purpose and engagement of our prophetic calling are compromised.

The honesty of the interpretive act reveals the truth and promotes continued conversion. The interpretive act of communities of hope is a commitment to radical solidarity, a refusal to allow our attention and our compassion to be incarcerated within rigidified structures, and an exercise of hospitality that makes our resources and our friendship a power for the powerless and a support for the despairing.

When we take on the responsibility to interpret the metaphor of community, we must know that we will be called to profound experiences of inner conversion and suffering that emerge from loving the community so very deeply. In this act of interpretation we are led with our communities to the edge of what is, simultaneously, overwhelming and most sacred.

Our call is to promote the coming of the reign of God. We bind ourselves in communion, united in a vision of religious life that is unafraid to live truthfully in the face of criticism from the dominant secular and sacred systems. We pray in the words of the prophet that we will continue to "seek God with all our heart, with a single loyalty, with a centered hope" (Jer 29:13).

NOTES

This chapter was presented initially as an address to the joint assembly of LCWR and CMSM in Greensboro, N.C., in August of 1992. It appeared in *Origins* 22:14 (Sept. 17, 1992), 247–249 and in *Review for Religious* 51:6 (Nov.-Dec., 1992), 815–822.

1. Robert N. Bellah, Richard Madsen, William M. Sullivan, Ann Swidler, and Steven M. Tipton, *The Good Society* (New York: Knopf, 1991), 93.

2. Walter Brueggemann, *Interpretation and Obedience: From Faithful Reading to Faithful Living* (Minneapolis: Fortress Press, 1991), 206.

3. *Ibid.*, 223.

4. *Ibid.*, 232.

Setting Free the Charism

Paul Hennessy, C.F.C.

As the title of this collection of addresses would indicate, the concept of *transformation* has replaced the notion of *transition* in writings and talks on religious life. As Sean Sammon, F.M.S., has noted, *transition* is a very personal, psychological experience. It leads to confusion, a temporary loss of identity and fear. In the manner in which it is now being used, however, *transformation* is a deeply religious and theological term. True transformation depends principally upon God.

I constantly return to the resurrection narratives for wisdom and sensitivity about transformation. It mystifies me how so many of those closest to Jesus did not at first recognize him. Mary of Magdala, with whom he was so intimate, thought at first that he was a gardener (Jn 20:15). When he appears to the disciples in the upper room in Jerusalem, "they were startled and terrified and thought that they were seeing a ghost" (Lk 24:37). In the context of contemplation, however, it has become clear to me that transformation is at the very heart of the paschal mystery. Forms will change. The substance will remain. What the new form will be, however, we can only very generally anticipate because it is not brought into being by our power.

Many assemblies of leaders of religious communities have gathered over the past years to listen, to dialogue, to pray, and to anticipate what a transformed religious life might look like. Those thrust into leadership at a time of great transition and change want to integrate all the resources at their disposal to provide effective guidance to their membership. They recognize the agony of many of their sisters and brothers with the dying form of contemporary religious life and they cannot fully describe the new form. This causes frustration and even bitterness. Some religious just separate themselves from the struggle for transformation and enter into forms of denial.

Our founders and foundresses were people of exceptional faith. Deep in their hearts, they recognized a call from Jesus and they were moved to some generous action on behalf of the gospel. Generally they met with opposition, but in some marvelous way they were allowed to enter into the paschal mystery of death and rebirth in a manner that went beyond the ordinary. They received a grace to co-create a new form of gospel life and ministry. This grace we now refer to as "charism."

The Second Vatican Council called communities of consecrated women and men to fearlessly set free the originating charisms of their founders and foundresses. In many cases, we have found that these charisms became so institutionalized and so identified with a singular mode of activity that it is a real struggle to set them free. But who is called to lead the struggle?

At times we can become immobilized by reminders to be faithful to traditions which were never in the originating charism but which developed as certain ways of fulfilling the founder's intentions. Certainly we have to consult widely in order to discern the signs of the times before taking action; but having completed the discernment process we must then act. Leaders must see themselves as part of a much greater assembly which we call church. We cannot isolate ourselves within our own community. Associating with others called to a similar ministry, who are also going through discernment processes in their respective communities, can give us a wonderful support as well as a clear *sensus fidelium* (awareness of shared understanding) about authentic renewal of religious or consecrated life.

As background for what I would like to develop here, I call to your attention the fifth transformative element developed at the joint Conference of Major Superiors of Men/Leadership Conference of Women Religious assembly in Louisville in 1989. There the leadership of U.S. men and women religious said:

> By the year 2010, religious groups will have reexamined, reclaimed and set free the charisms of their foundresses/founders. Corporate ownership of a focused vision gives meaning and expression to mission and ministry. Some groups who share similar vision/charisms have already joined together.

Our founders and foundresses were outstanding leaders. Renewal following the vision of these men and women has been a central feature in the post-Vatican II refounding of both congregations of consecrated life and societies of apostolic life. But note the three tasks articulated in Louisville: "reexamine, reclaim and set free." All three must be achieved for proper refounding. Preserving the founding charism cannot mean encircling it in lucite. A restorationist thrust which would merely return to practices and customs of the past is not fidelity.

My own thoughts on renewal are inspired by the journey of one whose thought has been frequently characterized as a primary influence at the Second Vatican Council and that is John Henry Newman. With the Louisville transformative elements and Cardinal John Newman as inspirational backdrops, I would like to reflect upon three contemporary challenges: a) setting free our founding charisms; b) true consultation as a vehicle for corporate ownership; and c) a proper understanding of authority and obedience in the church. The first two are clearly enunciated in the Louisville "transformative elements"; the third, I believe, underlies all effective renewal.

SETTING FREE OUR CHARISMS

Not long after having converted to Catholicism in 1845, John Henry Newman made a pilgrimage to Rome with the intention of being ordained in the Roman church. During this sojourn in Italy, Newman studied various ways by which he might lead his priestly life as a Roman Catholic. His attention came to rest on an independent society of priests founded by St. Philip Neri, known as the Congregation of the Oratory.

It seems Newman may have become acquainted with the Oratorians years earlier through Nicholas Wiseman, his mentor (and future bishop), but it was not until his time in Rome that Newman seriously considered this society of diocesan clergy who live in community as a way of life for himself. Having returned to England in 1847, Newman decided to found an oratory according to the principles of St. Philip Neri, but adapted to the British mentality. In 1849 the Birmingham oratory was established. Newman would live thirty-three years as an Oratorian.

To appreciate how a nineteenth-century Catholic neophyte could accommodate a sixteenth-century Italian model of consecrated life to a community of fellow converts from the Oxford movement, one has to study Newman's whole thought on development of doctrine. He is very consistent, I believe, in applying the same criteria for authentic doctrinal development to authentic change and renewal in religious life.

These three criteria are: there must be 1) a logical sequence, 2) a preservation of type, and 3) a continuity of principles. One of his many biographers, Dom Placid Murray, O.S.B., in his work on *Newman the Oratorian* says: "Only Newman's deep docility to the spirit and bold freedom with the letter of the Oratorian rule could have harmoniously effected a successful transplanting of the Italian shoot to English soil."[1] It is clear from the so-called "Santa Croce Papers," which present Newman's thinking about the Roman Oratory in the Fall of 1847 that he was meticulous about examining every detail of the practices of the Oratorians in Rome and Naples to discern what was essential to their charism and what was not.

Dom Murray says that, from the first, it was Newman's intention to return to the original inspiration of St. Philip Neri. "The need for adaptation of the Oratory to English conditions," writes Murray, "appeared imperative to Newman from the first, and he carried out this adaptation in the spirit of what we now call *aggiornamento,* i.e., not the mere transmission—even the faithful transmission—of an existing religious tradition, but a return in spirit to the founder's life and ideal, and applying them in a fresh and bold way to modern conditions."[2]

In a celebrated dispute between the Birmingham Oratory, led by Newman, and the subsequently founded London Oratory, with Frederick Faber as its head, we see Newman's principles at work. St. Philip Neri had stressed the need for the intellectual development of the members. They were to be men of training and intelligence. Similar to other founders, it is unlikely that St. Philip had a vision of a series of oratories. On the contrary, he was intent on addressing a particular need in the Rome of his time.

We now know that others, including Newman, saw the possibility of establishing oratories in places apart from Rome. In a letter written before he left Rome for England, Newman made it quite clear that he wanted to establish an oratory according to the inspiration of St. Philip. He says, "Certain it is, we shall do our best to import a tradition, not to set up something for ourselves."[3] Newman understood his mission as being the continuation of an existing tradition. His work was to assure that the adaptation was faithful and a logical sequence. Hence his charge, as he saw it, was to preserve the type, which for him was that modeled by St. Philip in sixteenth-century Rome but now adaptable to nineteenth-century Birmingham.

Faber and the members of the London Oratory felt that the sole purpose of training the intellect was to perform pastoral works. Newman develops at great length his understanding that the type of work that he and the others in Birmingham were doing, by researching and writing, was truly Oratorian and merely an adaptation, to English soil, of St. Philip's original intention.

Another aspect of the Oratorian tradition that was central to Newman's thinking was an emphasis on community charity as the principle which bound the members together. They took no vows, yet they were committed to living in community. For both St. Philip and John Newman the glue which bound the enterprise together was charity. This concept appears in many of his Oratorian sermons. For him this is a principle of the Oratorian way of life without which the life would be impossible.

A leader's task is to foster the reexamining, reclaiming and setting free of the founder's charism. We can be guided in this by Newman's principle that there must be some logical sequence between the original and the actual. This means that we must search for those practices and devotions which gave life to the founder and to his or her contemporaries. How are those same traditions embodied today? We recognize that culture has changed through time and location; nevertheless, we would be endangering the reclaiming of charism if we did not perceive how the devotions and customs of the founder illuminated his or her spirituality.

For example, to ignore the great Marian devotions in communities founded in post-revolutionary France or in Ireland would be seriously misguided. In my own province it became the custom in the 1970s and 1980s for those men professing perpetual vows to design the vow ceremony. The Magnificat had been a traditional part of the ceremony from the founder's time. In some of the contemporary ceremonies neither it nor any reference to Mary was included. It took a number of years and some misunderstandings to establish the fact that these ceremonies were congregational in nature and individuals could only be given limited freedom to change them lest something very significant be lost. The manner in which we celebrate Mary's part in the paschal mystery might be different now, but Marian devotion is essential to understanding our way of life.

On the other hand, there were practices foisted upon communities over the years which may have had nothing to do with the founder's intentions or perhaps were even contrary to them. For example, there were apostolic communities of non-ordained men who adopted clerical garb for wear outside their houses because men who were regulars did so when they were in public. The examples of active women religious who had a cloister imposed on them, contrary to their foundresses' original inspiration, are familiar to all of us. In none of these was there a logical sequence, a preservation of type, or a continuity of principles. For some congregations, living together in a community is clearly a logical sequence of the founders' and foundresses' vision; for others that may not be true. A congregational leader must not only be alert to the signs of the times, but able to articulate the founding inspiration with ease.

TRUE CONSULTATION AS A VEHICLE
FOR CORPORATE OWNERSHIP

Most Newman students would agree that the *Grammar of Assent* and the *Development of Christian Doctrine* are his key theological works. I would like, nevertheless, to dwell a bit on some of his thinking expounded in the essay *On Consulting the Faithful in Matters of Christian Doctrine.* I do this for two reasons: first, because I think it underlies all of Newman's thinking about the development of doctrine; and second, I consider it a good guide for leaders in matters of consultation to assure ownership of a vision.

The essay was first published by Newman in the *Rambler* of July, 1859. Note that this is after the dogmatic declaration of the Immaculate Conception in 1854 and prior to the convocation of the First Vatican Council. Newman reprinted part of it, with some additions and emendations in 1871, which is after the conclusion of Vatican I. This essay is fundamental because it gives us an insight into the importance that Newman places on the laity in his theology. Newman was one of the great champions of the role of the *sensus fidelium* in dogmatic development, an element conspicuously missing in much of our contemporary church teaching.

In varied forums and on numerous occasions, it has been pointed out that the church is not simply a democracy. Nevertheless, members of religious communities frequently reach decisions after much consultation and discernment. This is not necessarily the way in which other corporate entities, including the hierarchical church, may reach conclusions. While methods of consultation and decision making have varied over the centuries, the "chapter," in some form, has been rather basic. Since the Second Vatican Council there has been a concerted effort in most religious communities to involve the whole body in the reaching of decisions which affect everyone. I believe two reasons have inspired this: the wider the dialogue, the greater opportunity there is for the activity of the Holy Spirit; and greater involvement in the process should lead to firmer ownership of the outcome.

Wide consultation is part of a discernment process which attempts to understand the will of God and then act upon it. Our purpose, of course, is to achieve ownership of a vision, so that we might move in unity to be open to the transforming movement of the Spirit. First of all, when I use the expression "wide consultation," I suggest that we must go beyond traditional boundaries. For many centuries, representative chapters were seen as sufficient. In more recent times, assemblies and "open" chapters have become common. Now I think that it is time for us to go beyond our own membership in our consultations.

We frequently articulate that consecrated life is meant to be "counter-cultural." We also use the verb *to witness.* While witnessing is an active process, the receiving of the message must be just as active. Hence, if we seriously expect the people of God to understand our witness, should we not consult with them about the forms it takes?

While religious men and women may be quite certain about a

number of paths they are taking, others may be very confused. Through processes of internal discernment, for example, religious may have come to the conclusion that traditional garb was anachronistic, elitist, clerical or reflective of a monastic rather than an active spirituality. Hence, they began to dress in a manner similar to other members of the people of God, except perhaps when performing some liturgical function. Nevertheless, that effort toward what was perceived internally as legitimate renewal could be perceived by others as secularization, buying into middle-class culture, losing "religious" identity and so forth.

In the thinking of Newman, "consultation" with the faithful is both historical and contemporary. There must be both a preservation of type and a reflection of the contemporary reality. I do believe that we would serve ourselves and our church better if we were to open our "chapters" beyond our own membership to true representatives of the people we serve. We must avoid the pitfall, however, of selecting only those whose thinking is already conditioned to agree with ours. I titled this section "true" consultation because we all have the tendency to be close-minded when those who see things differently from us are involved.

During a visit to Rome of the LCWR/CMSM leadership, a few years ago, Cardinal Pironio, former Prefect of the Congregation of Religious, and now President of the Pontifical Commission on the Laity, remarked that most of the lay movements throughout the church have developed as a result of the direct influence of religious orders and congregations. He went on to remind us that the charisms of religious founders and foundresses were gifts given to them for the good of the whole church and not for the religious communities alone.

The focus of our processes of renewal has been principally internal, neglecting the wisdom of the Holy Spirit in those people with whom we collaborate in ministry and whom we serve. The cardinal also warned against the tendency of some religious to want to turn lay people into religious. The two forms of consecrated life—religious and lay—are distinct.

A consequence of any discernment process must be action. Once a religious body through consultation of its members has chosen a path, it is the task of leadership to provide for the implementation. It is important from the beginning to make sure that even those who disagreed with the conclusion realize their obligation to the corporate body. This is not an easy task at times. The charge is made, probably correctly so, that in some of our rhetoric about charism, we put an individual's gifts and needs on the same level as the corporate mission. While each person is graced with his or her own gifts and abilities, she or he has voluntarily entered into a body which believes that corporate action is more fruitful than individual action.

Many leaders have had the experience of having reached conclusions at gatherings where everyone was invited to participate and then shortly afterward heard an individual say that he or she is called to something quite different. What does the leader do? Our responses may vary, but we do have to examine honestly the impact that "lone rangers" may have on the corporate vision. We also neglect to reflect adequately on the meaning of the vow or the promise of obedience and its importance in community solidarity when we allow significant exceptions from the corporate will.

A true discernment process is one which involves openness and prayer, wide consultation, dialogue, more prayer, decision making and still more prayer. We believe that the Holy Spirit truly works through the process. This has been the history of how religious orders have made decisions. I think the word *charism,* when applied to a small group, is misused; but I am going to do just that now for a purpose.

Let's say, for example, that the congregation determines that the charism of the community calls for living the common life in communities of three or more, or that the ministry of the society is retreat work rather than parish work, or that the common good is better achieved when there is a local director, prior or superior. These are just some examples of decisions that might be reached through legitimate discernment processes. But one of the members disagrees. "I am happy in what I'm doing and where I'm living," he says, and then adds, "and I believe that God wants me to do this." How much weight can we truly give to that?

Is it not the role of the leader to call people to live what the community expects? I know from personal experience that the call may be difficult and may cause friction, but I also know that we cannot justify a course of action different from the expressed will of the community simply because a person desires to do it. It may be the path of least resistance, but it is not faithful to the meaning of community discernment or to the vow of obedience.

A PROPER UNDERSTANDING OF LOYALTY IN THE CHURCH

Our communities were brought into existence to be at the service of the church, the people of God. We struggle to remain faithful to that. In doing this we must listen to many voices. It is not unusual, at times, to hear the allegation that in their renewal religious ignore their obligation to be "faithful to the magisterium." Certainly one of the reasons for the establishment of a special pontifical commission to examine religious life in the United States was a fear that religious life was "out of control" in its renewal. No one can deny that in the activities surrounding the re-

examination, reclamation and setting free of charisms misunderstandings and mistakes took place. The realization of *charism* is not tidy.

Unfortunately, however, the expression "faithful to the magisterium"
has become a question about loyalty to the church. Once again, if our
call is to "set free" the charisms of our founders and foundresses, we must
do it in the context of church membership. I have never heard this denied.
There is a tendency, however, to use the litmus test of "loyalty" in such a
sweeping manner that it really springs from a restorationist mentality,
because of what Philibert in his introduction refers to as "the grip of
nostalgia." Once again, I think we can find much in the thought of Newman to aid us in distinguishing that which is true loyalty.

At the time of the convening of the First Vatican Council on December
8, 1869, Newman sided with the "inopportunists" regarding any declaration on the infallibility of the papal magisterium. In England he was
pitted against such outspoken "infallibilists" as Henry Edward Manning
and W.G. Ward, who saw a strong papacy with unlimited authority as a
need in a disturbed Europe.

An interested observer of the Roman Catholic scene was William E.
Gladstone, who had a deep admiration for Newman from their Anglican
days. By the time the dogmatic decree *Pastor Aeternus* was promulgated
in June of 1870, Newman had carefully followed the discussions and recognized all the limitations placed on the infallibility of the Roman pontiff
by the conciliar decree. The decree clearly linked the notion of infallibility
to revelation. Nevertheless, the infallibilists, who considered that they
had won the day, were the dominant Catholic stream in English society,
and they were inclined to stretch the limits far beyond the conciliar
definition. Manning was the head of the hierarchy. Their rhetoric caused
Gladstone, who was now the Prime Minister, to write an essay in 1874
titled *Vatican Decrees in Their Bearing on Civil Allegiance: A Political
Exposition.*

Newman responded the following year in his *A Letter Addressed to
His Grace the Duke of Norfolk on the Occasion of Mr Gladstone's Recent
Expostulation.*[4] The duke was the leading Catholic member of the aris-
tocracy. From Newman's point of view it was a very difficult letter to write
because he had already been accused by the right-wing party in the
church of minimalizing the authority of the pope and of disloyalty to
Pius IX.

The "Vatican Decrees" in Gladstone's title referred as much to the
encyclical *Quanta Cura* with its accompanying Syllabus of Errors as it did
to these decrees of the Vatican Council. W.G. Ward had already made it
clear that he considered the encyclical and the syllabus as infallible

utterances. This was the context in which Newman demonstrated his true loyalty.

Newman was in a position not unlike many religious leaders on the contemporary scene. In the past few years the Leadership Conferences of both men and women religious have taken a strong position objecting to the process used in the formation of a new Council for Women Religious Superiors. It was precisely because this was seen as divisive and opposed to true and open dialogue about the fundamental nature of religious life. The process also lacked any previous consultation with the NCCB, CMSM or LCWR. CMSM also issued a statement questioning the wisdom of the declaration from the Congregation for the Doctrine of the Faith titled "Responding to Legislative Proposals on Discrimination Against Homosexuals."[5] We did not see it as a constructive evangelical statement and feared that it would also exacerbate the growing gulf between gay and lesbian people and the message of Jesus and the sacramental life of the church. In the past we have expressed disagreement with the decree of the Congregation for Divine Worship and Sacraments which requires a promise of celibacy in the ordination rite, even for religious with a perpetual vow of chastity. We believe that this demeans the very nature of religious vows. Are these acts of disloyalty? There are those who would answer in the affirmative. For some, the expression "faithful to the magisterium" has been stretched beyond credible boundaries.

Newman was in an even more difficult bind. The key item raised in Gladstone's expostulation was the question as to whether converts to the Catholic Church could be loyal citizens of England, since they seemed to forfeit mental and moral freedom. Newman was expected to defend the loyalty of the English citizen by showing that misinterpretations of *Pastor Aeternus* were prevalent and that Gladstone had been misinformed. He had to do this without naming those promoting the confusion, since some were members of the hierarchy, including Cardinal Manning. He vigorously defended and even supported the notion that differences of thought on matters of discipline or theological opinion can exist in the church, whereas there can be no differences on matters of faith. He says, in part:

> If a matter of faith is in question I grant there ought to be absolute agreement, or rather I maintain that there is; I mean to say that only one out of the statements put forth can be true, and that the other statements will be at once withdrawn by their authors, by virtue of their being Catholics, as soon as they learn on good authority that they are erroneous. But if the differences

which I supposed are only in theological opinion, they do but show that after all private judgment is not so utterly unknown among Catholics and in Catholic schools, as Protestants are desirous to establish.[6]

In an article in *Commonweal* of June 18, 1993, Bishop Kenneth Untener addressed the issue of the credibility of church teaching when a significant number of devout church members disagree with a teaching. He quoted from an intervention he made on the floor of the November, 1990, meeting of the National Conference of Catholic Bishops when he said:

> The *sensus fidelium* is, of course, more than an opinion poll. But when people disagree with us, we cannot simply assume that it is mere opinion. The *sensus fidelium* is more than a head count, [... this] belief in the heads and hearts of our people must count for something."[7]

I truly believe that there is nothing wrong with different theological opinions on non-defined issues of faith. Similarly, I believe that it is not disloyal to take a position that certain processes or documents are dysfunctional or harmful. There are those who would hold that to disagree with the document "Essential Elements in the Church's Teaching on Religious Life as Applied to Institutes Dedicated to Works of the Apostolate" (1983), which accompanied the establishment of the Quinn Commission, is to be disloyal. Like the Syllabus of Errors, that document was merely a compilation of statements made in diverse places and contexts.

The unfortunate thing is that while the word *magisterium* refers to the teaching of the church and is more appropriately used for statements about truth or orthodoxy, it has been widened to refer to discipline. There are various theologies of religious life because there are varieties of faith experiences in our search for understanding the mystery of God. Discipline can be codified in law; faith cannot be.

Let me return to the Louisville "transformative elements." In order for religious orders to recapture and renew the spirit of both the gospels and the originating charismatic call of our founders and foundresses, freedom is necessary. To stifle the Spirit under the charge of disloyalty or heterodoxy in discipline is inappropriate.

Both CMSM's and LCWR's national boards have already published their initial reflections on the *Lineamenta* prepared for the Synod of Bishops in 1994, and we are continuing to dialogue about it in our regional meetings.[8] Together with many brother and sister religious, we question the overemphasis in church descriptions of religious life on *communion* and consecration. This questioning comes from our lived experience of discerning what our founders and foundresses wanted and applying this to our times and culture. The *Lineamenta* document appears to presume a uniformity in religious charisms that does not match our experience.

I heard a story earlier this year about a prominent church leader at a meeting of the International Union of Superiors General of women's institutes. On seeing so many African women religious dressed in their native garb, he stated how impressed he was by their fidelity to their culture. Meanwhile, American women religious who are being equally faithful to their foundresses' intentions within the U.S. culture are lectured on "Essential Elements." Refounding means truly to begin anew now. Not just in Africa or Eastern Europe but here in our culture.

There are those in our society and church who describe religious life as dead or finished. We can all agree that a phase, perhaps I should say *another* phase, is certainly finished. In that phase it seemed possible to lump all orders or congregations of women and men under a generic term *religious* or *consecrated* life, including in this undifferentiated mass societies of apostolic life such as the Oratorians and even the newly developed Secular Institutes. The Synod of 1994, it should be noted, still intends to cover all these quite diverse forms under a common rubric.

As I stressed at the beginning of this essay, true transformation requires a dying. There can be no renewed life without it. My conviction, as one who has been active among religious and others on the national as well as international scene for a number of years, is that many communities of men and women have moved to address the consequences of returning to the original inspiration of their founders and foundresses. Leaders are called to facilitate this return, even though the outcomes might be disturbing. Above all, leadership cannot settle for the lowest common denominator where no one's life is challenged.

Jesus fully understood that there were those who would disagree with his message. He listened to them and respected them—even when exhibiting what has come to be called "tough love." But he was clearly not paralyzed by them.

In the recently published research report, entitled *Future of Religious Orders in the United States,* completed under the direction of David Nygren, C.M. and Miriam Ukeritis, C.S.J., in remarking on the qualities of outstanding leaders, the aspect which is most relevant in our ministries is that these people are men and women of deep faith.[9] They are true contemplatives; people who look at reality from the perspective of an intense and loving relation to God. They fully recognize that they have no lasting city here. They understand and believe that they will see God, be rewarded by God, enjoy the loving embrace of God as they complete this life. They are entirely open to new forms for the continuing substance of the founding vision which brought their religious communities into existence. The adage, "No farmer ever plowed a field in his mind," suggests that "setting free" our founders' and foundresses' charisms will be heavy. But setting our charisms free will also be a time of very wonderful and graced moments for the church.

NOTES

This chapter was prepared initially as the author's presidential address to the Conference of Major Superiors of Men at its annual assembly in Buffalo, N.Y., in August of 1993. It was published in *Origins* 23:10, 169-73.

1. Dublin, Gill & Macmillan Ltd., 1969, p.xiii.

2. *Ibid*, 9.

3. Letter to Cardinal Franzoni in *The Letters and Diaries of John Henry Newman,* edited at the Birmingham Oratory by C.S. Dessain, 1960-68, Vol. Xll, p. 45.

4. *A Letter Addressed to His Grace the Duke of Norfolk on the Occasion of Mr Gladstone's Recent Expostulation* (London, B.M. Pickering, 1875), cited in *Newman and Gladstone: The Vatican Decree* (Notre Dame, IN.: University of Notre Dame Press, 1962).

5. *Origins,* Vol. 22, No. 10, pp. 173-177.

6. Newman and Gladstone, op. cit., pp. 201-2.

7. "*Humanae Vitae:* What Has It Done to Us? And What Is to Be Done Now?", *Commonweal,* June 18, 1993, 14.

8. *Origins,* 22:42, 724-727.

9. "Research Executive Summary: Future of Religious Orders in the U.S.," *Origins,* 22:15, 257-272.

Is the Eucharist Still a Source of Meaning for Women?

Mary Collins, O.S.B.

It simply is not possible to deal honestly with issues concerning the transformation of religious life at this time and avoid the question of the impediments to communion that many women religious experience as they approach the celebration of the eucharist. We were raised on a sacramental theology that told us that this sacrament is the source and center of our lives. But too often our experience is that the eucharist is celebrated as discounting or repudiating our life energies. Let us look squarely at the problem. Who are women religious today within the ecclesial institution?

We are women who manage church institutions. We provide leadership for other women who live within and work with or within church institutions. We have accepted public office within church institutions. We have obligated ourselves to accountability within church institutions; we are prepared to give an account of ourselves and to call our sisters to do so.

We meet with bishops, vicars, chancellors, secretaries—to have lunch, to make plans, to take counsel, to contend with them when we decide that their judgments are harmful or unjust. The bishops' conference, under each of its banners, the National Conference of Catholic Bishops and the U.S. Catholic Conference, considers us an important resource.

We have working relationships of participation and collaboration with clergy in our dioceses and regions that are based on mutual regard. Many of us are extraordinarily skilled in what we do, and the Catholic Church has benefited enormously from our institutional leadership in the past three decades.

Yet there is an issue that needs to be addressed, which none of the professional contacts sketched above would suggest to be an urgent matter. Nonetheless the crux of our problem has to do with coordinating specified roles that we play in an institutional church and personal needs we have as individuals growing in faith.

The phrase *institutional church* reveals a core problem within the matter we need to address here. Of course the church is an institution, one of the oldest and most complex of religious and cultural institutions. One becomes a member through the ecclesial institution of baptism and over a lifetime is formed and transformed by its dense network of institutions: symbols, creeds, a canon of scripture, a canonization process for identifying saints, traditions of public prayer, of contemplation and of piety, traditions of service, music, art and architecture.

In recent years feminist historians, theologians, and anthropologists have exposed the androcentric character of all the institutions of Christianity. But many Christian women, women religious among them, are already actively contributing to the reinterpretation and reappropriation of the church's androcentric heritage in ways that remember and celebrate women's active presence. We are already responding creatively and constructively within a religious institution that has minimized and even negated the significance of its women members.

Institutional church currently names something much more precise among women whose lives are intimately associated with the shaping of ecclesial institutions. *Institutional church* designates that controlled and controlling exercise of power and the symbols of power which feminists have helped us to identify as "patriarchal." But even after we shatter the institutional church euphemism like a clay pot, what do we find? We are face-to-face with something already familiar, like a threatening pit bull in the family room.

As leaders in our own institutions we have seen coercive ecclesiastical power at work; it has forced us to make compromises against our own better judgment. We may have found ourselves, as leaders in our congregations, becoming mediators of this coercive power, compromised by appeals to maintain unity. At other times we have taken the risk of refusing to coerce others with patriarchal power or to be coerced by it ourselves. And we have prevailed.

But there is a problem troubling women religious nonetheless. In my judgment as a student of liturgical performance, the crux of the troubled relationship American women religious have with the Roman Catholic Church is clear. It is centered in contemporary Catholic eucharistic praxis.

So here is an examination of the eucharist, the central symbol of Catholic Christianity, the central symbol also of clerical power and the dominant symbol for the self-understanding of women religious. It is in the clash of eucharistic horizons that the conflictual relationship lies.

THE EXPERIENCE OF EUCHARIST

The testimony of many women religious converges. Is this also your experience? However subtly balanced the collaborative working relationships and the friendships any of you have established with bishops and with other churchmen in the service of the gospel, however much trust and mutual regard you have built up, these strong, personal, social and ecclesial relationships are reconfigured when you move into eucharistic assembly. There, the hard-won mutuality is destabilized.

Entrance into ritual space separates you physically from the churchmen who are your friends and collaborators. Much ingenuity has been expended on many occasions to minimize spatial arrangements that would set you over against one another. But even when the liturgical space has been successfully reconfigured, the very entrance into ritual performance of the eucharist of the Roman rite activates a set of religious meanings which negates the positive meanings of everyday ecclesial experience. For the churchmen who want women to celebrate with them the mystery of Christ as the bond of the world's unity, peace and salvation, claim to find in the eucharist a warrant for legitimating male dominance in the community and their own clerical hold on institutional power. Such theological claims about male superiority and clerical power have begun to hang over eucharistic assemblies like storm systems. In the electrically charged atmosphere, no one knows at what moment something said or left unsaid, done or not done, will strike at the heart of the assembly, destroying the fragile unity we seek in Christ's name.

Writing about the social impact of Corpus Christi processions in fourteenth-century England, Oxford University historian Miri Rubin notes that everyday social relations, which were by their nature fluid—the relations for example between a master craftsman and a journeyman—were disrupted by the new processional arrangement for the eucharistic festival that separated people who normally lived and worked together. Their place in the procession defined them, asserting higher status for one and lower status for another.[1]

As I read Rubin, I recognized that our situation was analogous. The potential for social and ecclesial volatility associated with defining and limiting status in terms of one's place in eucharistic liturgy is what we know. The gains women and men have made in ecclesial collaboration at the level of ministry have only made ritual separation more poisonous.

Yes, the matter of women in relation to the institutional church has as its symbolic center in the 1990s the matter of women in relation to eucharist praxis—our ecclesial performance and our theological claims about God's saving design. We all know that. Now we need to face it together. Our purpose is analysis of our situation. As we will see, the question of an appropriate response to our situation is less clear.

WOMEN RELIGIOUS: EUCHARISTICALLY DEFINED

My focus will center on the way contemporary Catholic eucharistic praxis strains the relations between women religious and church office-holders, bishops, priests and deacons. Much of what I say will also speak to the experience of laywomen, especially those who are employed in church institutions. But women religious differ from laywomen in the centrality that ecclesiastical tradition has given to the eucharist as the normative center of their spirituality. Canonically established institutes for women have long had as one of their constitutive norms the members' participation in daily mass.[2]

Many laywomen may have embraced the norm voluntarily. (The Beguine movement of the Lowlands in the late Middle Ages was defined by its eucharistic spirituality;[3] our mothers and grandmothers slipped off to early morning mass whenever they could.) But a spirituality grounded in eucharistic liturgy was neither expected of laywomen nor was specific ecclesiastical provision made for it. By contrast, it is commonly understood that religious superiors have as one of their official responsibilities making provision for the observance of this norm by all the sisters of a congregation.

When conversations about constitutions were being conducted in the 1970s and 1980s, the Roman See was insistent that the norm of daily mass be stated explicitly prior to approval of each congregation's constitution. If all other congregational customs of common prayer were up for reconsideration, even up for grabs, it was assumed that the eucharistic center of congregational life would hold. But the ambivalent responses of general chapters to this institutionalization of eucharistic observance signaled a new situation emerging in women's congregations.

Many women religious had already moved into patterns of less-than-daily celebration of the eucharistic liturgy. In some locales communities were already experiencing the consequences of dwindling numbers of priests. In other places, the communion service presided over by community members was emerging as an attractive alternative to a mass said by an appointed priest chaplain with whom the community members had little or no rapport. As ministries diversified, so did living arrangements; daily work schedules collided with local liturgical schedules.

Most congregations navigated the rocky shoals of constitutional approval by making compromises to write a text that affirmed histori-

cal continuity and canonical identity in terms of specific eucharistic observance. Those relatively few institutes that maintained monastic identity
also included common celebration of the hours of prayer as part of their
self-definition and have subsequently found in the hours some buffer
against wholly clericalized public prayer.

The approved constitution on your bookshelf is now being interpreted
in daily living. Even the best efforts to make operative that declared eucharistic liturgical center for congregational and personal spirituality have
been aggravated by circumstances few of us anticipated. As we pass
through this decade of the 1990s, matters related to women and the eucharist promise only to become more publicly conflicted.

Abundant anecdotal evidence supports that judgment. Who does not
know of sisters who have arranged non-eucharistic liturgies for jubilees
and for rites of final profession, causing at least comment and heartache
if not acrimony and dissension within the congregation and among its
clergy associates? Perhaps you yourself made such a choice.

Who has not been asked to explain when sisters demand that a woman co-preside with a priest at the eucharistic liturgy of a congregational
assembly or retreat, while ruling out the possibility of presbyterial concele-
bration? Perhaps you yourself made the demand or were the co-presider.

Who dares dismiss the testimony of community members when they
report how they were renewed in faith because they participated in a
women's seder celebrated as an alternative to a clericalized eucharist of
the Lord's Supper on Holy Thursday? Perhaps you were the one who
testified.

Who among you sees as insignificant the alienation of the sisters who
chose to remain members of your communities but who no longer participate in any eucharistic liturgy? "I am no longer part of the institutional
church," they say. And they identify eucharistic liturgy as part of the
system of power and privilege they reject. Perhaps your office carries with
it your own private struggle with alienation.

It is tempting to say that what we all know amounts to many individual spiritual crises and nothing more. But one of the consequences of
the rising feminist consciousness among us forces us to avoid such easy
explanations. The personal is the political—so goes the feminist axiom.
Persons live within social and political and religious systems, and it is the
system of institutionalized eucharistic spirituality that must be examined.
Only then can we hope to understand both the emergent resistance among
some women religious to joining in celebrations of the eucharist of the
Roman rite and also the inherent ambiguity of that resistance. For the
eucharistic mystery is greater than every reductionist effort to control
it for human purposes.

THE EUCHARIST: CLERICALIZED, DECLERICALIZED, NEOCLERICALIZED

In her study of the eucharist in late medieval culture, Miri Rubin speaks of an intentional "designing" of the eucharist that took place from the eleventh to the fifteenth centuries, the collaborative work of theologians who were clerics and prelates and who were consolidating their power in a new world order. Rubin does not look at the depth and density of eucharistic faith that was central to Christian self-understanding from the beginning. What was of interest to her was how eucharistic celebration was "refigured" in the eleventh and twelfth centuries to create a new structure of power-laden relationships.[4]

The outcome of this ritual reconfiguration of ecclesiastical relationships, clerical and lay, was a eucharistic cult that became the central symbol of the emergent medieval culture. The "new" eucharistic performance successfully announced to a fragmented feudal world a universal order and a universal salvation in Jesus Christ directed from Rome. Changes were made in the design of eucharistic bread and in its handling; changes were made in the church building and the arrangement of its interior space. The daily offering of the eucharistic sacrifice by each priest became an obligation. Laity were encouraged to view the host often but were expected to consume it just once a year. Lay drinking from the eucharistic cup was eliminated altogether.

The eucharistic liturgy as a symbolic center of both temporal and spiritual power relationships has persisted—not without challenge—up to the present. The Council of Trent emphatically rejected efforts of Protestant reformers who hoped to reform the clericalized system of power relationships by redesigning the liturgical performance of the mass. After Trent, the eucharist of the Roman church became even more firmly the eucharist of the clergy under the authority of the Roman See.

The Vatican II reform of the eucharistic liturgy was a move in the direction of a declericalization of the liturgy. The council reclaimed two principles from the ancient eucharistic tradition that had been suspended by the fully clericalized medieval/Tridentine performance: 1) that the eucharist was the action of the whole church,[5] and 2) that lay and ordained ministers collaborated in leading the assembly in the eucharistic action.[6] Once again, the redesigning of relationships in the church was being manifested symbolically, which is to say really, in the redesigning of relationships within the eucharistic assembly.

Latent in the "new mass" was a design for the emergence of a new ecclesial community. What I would call an "ecclesial eucharist" in contrast to a "clericalized eucharist" held promises about relationships that waited to be actualized.

The place of women in that new liturgy and new church taking shape in the 1960s and 1970s was highly ambiguous. Some assumed that the inferior status of women was a given, to be maintained in the eucharistic liturgy and in ecclesial life. Others assumed the opposite. For over twenty-five years, the matter of women's place has been negotiated in liturgical performance; it is being resolved issue by issue. The surface questions were about liturgy. The deeper question was about identity.

May women be lectors? Cantors? Any women, or are sisters preferable? If women read and sing, do they stand inside the sanctuary or out? May women take communion to the sick in their home? Any women or just sisters? Can they give communion at Sunday mass?

If women can be communion ministers, can they serve at the preparation of gifts? If adult women can serve at the altar, can there be girl altar servers? If adult women can set the altar table, break the bread, prepare the communion cups, read the scripture, announce the intentions for the general intercessions, can they preside at communion services?

If women can preside at prayer in some eucharistic services, can they preside over the life of the parish?[7] If ecclesial and liturgical ministries have become publicly inclusive, can we make the language of our liturgy inclusive?

If women can preside in ecclesial and liturgical communities, then leadership among the people of God is not gender marked as we once thought, so why not affirm the fullness of God's holy being through images of God male and female? Inclusive language can emancipate both the church and God! And why not ordain women to confirm their full ecclesial and spiritual identities?

Women religious, whose spirituality and whose ecclesial identity had been defined for them in eucharistic performance, have waited since the 1960s for judgments to be pronounced in favor of their full human and ecclesial identity. But as authoritative judgments have been pronounced about women's place in the liturgical assembly and about women's ecclesial identity, many women religious have been shocked into unexpected recognition of an unpleasant truth: the institutional church has a problem with them.

It did not take secular feminist theory to bring Catholic sisters to this realization. A quarter-century of planning and taking part in festive eucharistic liturgies has been enough to destabilize the trust of women religious in institutionalized eucharistic spirituality.

Slowly it is becoming clear that the "ecclesial design" for a declericalized eucharist latent in early documents of Vatican II's liturgical reform lacks support among current officeholders. Many ecclesial and eucharistic possibilities have gone unrealized because of active interventions[8] by officeholders whose vision and interests remain clerical. But this is the twentieth century, not the twelfth, and this is the New World and not the Old, so what is emerging is a clerical liturgy and church order with a difference. For purposes of identification, let us call it *neoclerical*.

In the North American expression of neoclerical praxis, the cultural model for women's ministries, liturgical and pastoral, is World War II's woman defense worker, "Rosie the Riveter." Women workers supply: wherever there is a dearth of churchmen to fill available positions, women are being invited to step in. In the neoclerical doctrine that articulates this praxis, God did not make women inferior, but neither did God make them equal. Women can be whatever clerics want them to be.

The going gets difficult when the dynamic is recognized and named. Catholic women wisely refuse to internalize this incoherent identity, even though it keeps surfacing in ecclesiastical documents and in the gathering of the church around the eucharistic altar table.

It is easy to stop reading the documents. But do women religious wisely refuse to celebrate the eucharist? Will our doing so make neoclerical Catholicism more self-critical and more authentically ecclesial? Do we wisely take it upon ourselves to redesign the eucharistic liturgy for our comfort, apart from the larger, often comfortably neoclerical Catholic community? I think we do not know the full answer to any of these questions, although they are worth asking. But I think we know answers to some other equally important questions about the eucharist.

EUCHARISTIC BELIEF: THROUGH THICK AND THIN

What does the eucharist celebrate? Power relations in the church are a facet of the eucharist's meaning. Circumstances have recently conspired to suggest that this is the central meaning, perhaps the only relevant one. But to enter into eucharistic liturgy, to give praise and thanks, to take and eat, to take and drink with controlling ideological commitments is reductionist, no matter which ideology prevails. Symbolic reductionism destroys religious mystery. Symbolic reductionism settles on the thin surfaces of things. Symbolic reductionism equates the historical church with the reign of God and identifies Jesus Christ with the one who presides in Jesus' name. Symbolic reductionism denies the reality of the transforming Spirit who effects more than we can hope for or imagine. Symbolic reductionism finds it unbelievable that what is humanly incoherent coheres in God who is a crucible of dark concealment and blinding light.

What are we missing when we make maintaining or dethroning gender-marked pretensions of spiritual power the only operative meaning in eucharistic liturgy? The strong sign of the assembly of outcasts and strangers—people so unlike that they would never choose one another's company—being invited to welcome and to forgive one another in Jesus' name, to be at peace, to sin no more. This is suppressed when we reject ambiguity and demand clarity and coherence in our ecclesial relationships before we can celebrate eucharist.

What I desire, what you desire, what church officeholders desire, what the poor women of the world desire might well cancel each other out if we attend only to the words of our asking and the present poverty of our imaginations. The well of the church's memories dries up, imaginations atrophy and hopes shrink when we celebrate sacramental liturgy with prevailing over others on our minds. Eucharist is only fully real when we are all one—equal—in Christ.

When our own experiences of eucharist become occasions for lament and our own best stories are tales of hopes unfulfilled, we need to listen to the voices of other believers telling tales of the power of the eucharist for personal and social transformation. Two reports, one from the fourteenth century and one from the sixteenth, have recently alerted me again to the deadening narrowness of our own current preoccupation with an admittedly neoclerical eucharist, understood only in the normative terms mediated by official teaching. That teaching has long been preoccupied with clerical identity. But we do not have to be.

Enrique Dussel has written about the spiritual and ecclesial journey of the Spanish Dominican Bartolomé de las Casas during the colonizing of the Americas.[9] His prayer led him from a normative to a transformative understanding of the eucharist. When Las Casas had come to see that the eucharist was being celebrated with "bread stolen from the poor," he was shocked and refused to celebrate for a time. That was not the end, however, but only the beginning of his life work.

In prayer he saw that the eucharistic mystery required him to commit himself to the work of seeking justice for the native peoples among the conquistadores and among the churchmen who rationalized the sins being committed in the name of the gospel. And when he had begun his new life, he celebrated eucharist again with the poor. Las Casas did not find in eucharistic liturgy the power to eliminate evil immediately and establish the reign of God. But transformed himself, he created space for justice and peace, hope and love. He learned in prayer the conditions under which it was possible for him to celebrate eucharist as a faithful disciple of Jesus.

Women today who are dealing with disappointment about the shape of the church, with disillusionment and the erosion of trust in what they thought was reliable may have a comparable question to bring to prayer. Under what conditions can I, as a woman who is a disciple of Jesus of Nazareth, join in celebrations of the eucharistic liturgy of the Roman rite? To what must I have committed myself when I leave the holy table? In my judgment, present disillusionment is grace offered to women and through women to the whole church. Holy discontent can lead to transformation.

Las Casas was virtually alone in his questioning. But a whole company of women who gather regularly for eucharistic liturgy is beginning to question the story of Jesus again in search for the living and life-giving God. Some men are among their number. Dare we believe there is power here not yet evident on the surface of things?

Looking into the tradition of eucharistic spirituality from another direction, Carolyn Walker Bynum has given us a fresh reading of the intense, often ecstatic, eucharistic spirituality of the fourteenth-century Beguine women in the Lowlands. Bynum's argument is complex, but its central insight is worth savoring.

In their eucharistic spirituality, late medieval women found not separation but continuity between their theologically disparaged bodiliness and the *humanitas Christi*. Contrary to medieval men's theological preoccupation with a realm of world-transcending spiritual power as the locus of divine mystery, the evidence is there that late medieval women knew a simpler mystery. As Bynum puts it, women's physicality had been presented to them in the tradition as a problem; their contemplative eucharistic experience led them to discover it as opportunity.[10]

While men institutionalized ways they could reach God by reversing what they were through manifestations of social and ecclesial power, through ritual acts of submission and cross dressing, women reached God, not by reversing their earthbound social identities, but by entering more fully into their own humanity.[11] Women mystics could see clearly that women as women were able to do what Christ did: bleed, feed, die, give life to others.[12] The Christ of the sacrament in continuity with the incarnate Christ proclaimed a great mystery: In bodily events lie revelations of grace.[13]

This eucharistically based self-understanding among women of the church did not die out, although it may have become unwelcome later among well-bred modern women and genteel novice directors. More than a decade ago an older sister of eastern European peasant heritage countered the fear of scandal that I had anticipated from a showing of Judy Chicago's "Dinner Party" in a general chapter program. She reported to the chapter delegates in accented speech, "When I was a young girl my mother told me that women's bodies were like the chalice. I had inside me a cup that held the blood of life, so I had to take good care of my body."

Ordinary women and the poor have often worn the clerical construction of reality lightly.[14] Poor women, outcast women, spiritually gifted women and prayerful women have always known a God whose mystery is not exhausted in the authoritative patriarchal, clerical rendering of Jesus' revelation. Why should two decades of neoclerical incoherence cause educated, faithful Catholic women to doubt that the eucharistic mystery affirms their personhood, dignity and power?

Bynum's rereading of late medieval women's distinctively nonclerical interpretation of the eucharist can help us. This was an understanding faithfully recorded and preserved, never condemned, esteemed in its day, long-forgotten, and now available for our reflection. It invites us to look again at the error of any narrow, surface-thin appropriation of eucharistic meaning.

It is the eucharistic Christ who has brought prayerful women to a depth of spiritual identity, insight and power generation after generation. The diary of your congregation's founder most likely witnesses to her confidence that eucharistic intimacy with Christ gave her the courage to continue her mission, even to withstand obstructionist officeholders in the church. Are we prepared to say these women were deceived, operating under delusions about the source of their power or the source of their imperatives?

The Roman Catholic eucharistic heritage is a rich, dense source of meaning and power for women. This meaning and power do not lie exclusively in the past; they have a present and future for those who trust themselves to eucharistic action in troubled times. To insist upon construing eucharist solely as a symbol of male power is to squander a known source of spiritual vitality in the Catholic community.

Where such impoverished constructions of the Catholic Church's eucharistic tradition have been accepted as the whole truth or the only significant truth, some Catholics have begun to identify themselves as post-Christian and to look elsewhere for the way, the truth and the life. Will a neopagan quasi-retrieval of rites of empowerment for women recreated from an undocumented past guarantee a better future for the human community than the service of the gospel and the eucharistic celebration of the mystery of salvation? Nobody has ever been able to prevent people from squandering real assets when the lure of fool's gold overtakes them, nor from risking a solid future on the futures market. Neoclericalism and neopaganism both look like fool's gold to me.

My conclusion is brief. Nothing of what I have said here is meant to deny that women's relation with the institutional church is indeed troubled. Everything I have said is meant to invite us to explore our living tradition of eucharistic spirituality openly and to enter into profound reflection on our ecclesial situation.

NOTES

This chapter was initially presented as an address to the LCWR annual assembly in Albuquerque, NM, in August of 1991.

1. Miri Rubin, *Corpus Christi: The Eucharist in Late Medieval Culture* (Cambridge: Cambridge University Press, 1991), 265.

2. 1983 Code of Canon Law, Canon 608; Canon 719.2.

3. See Carolyn Walker Bynum, *Holy Feast and Holy Fast* (Berkeley: University of California Press, 1987), and *Fragmentation and Redemption: Essays on Gender and the Human Body in Medieval Religion* (New York: Zone Books, 1991).

4. Rubin, 347.

5. General Instruction on the Roman Missal, 1-7; see also *Sacrosanctum Concilium*, 14.

6. *Sacrosanctum Concilium*, 28-29; General Instruction on the Roman Missal, 65-73, 257.

7. Herve-Marie Legrand, "The Presidency of the Eucharist According to the Ancient Tradition," *Worship* 53 (September, 1979), 413-38, reports a traditional basis for asking the question.

8. See, for example, Frank Henderson, "The Chrism Mass of Holy Thursday," in *Worship* 51 (March, 1977), 149-158; Peter Jeffery, "Mandatum Novum Do Vobis: Toward a Renewal of the Holy Thursday Footwashing Rite," in *Worship* 64 (March, 1990), 107-41.

9. Enrique Dussel, "The Bread of the Eucharistic Celebration as a Sign of Justice in the Community," in *Concilium* 152: *Can We Always Celebrate the Eucharist?*, Mary Collins and David Power, eds. (Edinburgh: T & T Clark Ltd., 1982). In that same number, see Elizabeth Schussler Fiorenza, "Table Sharing and the Celebration of the Eucharist."

10. Bynum, *Fragmentation*, 146-49.

11. *Ibid.*, 172.

12. *Ibid.*, 222.

13. *Ibid.*, 235.

14. *Ibid.*, 47, 53ff.

Religious Life in the U.S.— Understanding the Moment

Rembert G. Weakland, O.S.B.

Religious life is a lived ecclesial experience. It cannot be talked about in the abstract nor defined by absolute terms. It belongs to the heart of the church and is thus deeply ecclesial, but it has changed often in the history of the church according to the needs of the times. Whenever the church has tried to define it too narrowly, it has withered. It has flourished when it has been given a wide scope and permitted to regulate itself.

Religious life has deep biblical roots and is centered on the following or discipleship of Christ. Christ and the gifts of the Spirit are the root of all religious life; it is an ecclesial way of living out the gospel. Many biblical texts were brought forward in the past to prove this connection between religious life and the gospel. Now I believe it is more in keeping with biblical exegesis to see many, if not all, of those texts, as relating to all the baptized. Nevertheless, religious life remains rooted in a biblical image and ideal; it is a gift of the Spirit, and permits the religious to live out the following of Christ in a distinct way.

In the United States in the past, religious, both men and women, became closely tied to the history of the immigrant people and contributed to the religious and secular education of those people, so that Catholics could insert themselves well into the whole of the civic and business life of the nation. The last three decades, however, that is since Vatican Council II, have been crucial for the history of religious life in the United States. They have marked a turning point in that history. Although the past contribution of religious to the history of the church in the United States was enormous, it was somewhat limited, especially in the case of women, to school and hospitals. Now new ways and paths are opening up. It is a moment of searching, both for the church and also for religious.

The best way to begin a discussion about the place of the charism of religious and the role of religious congregations in the church in the United States today is to start with Vatican Council II and to describe

197

the new vision it gave the church. In doing so, however, one cannot just discuss the texts that refer to religious life itself. One must look at the whole spirit of the council and the new perspectives it brought. Religious entered into that new spirit with their whole beings. What they are today in the church—and what they will be—comes from their total acceptance of the vision of Vatican Council II and their desire to see it fulfilled.

RELIGIOUS LIFE AND VATICAN II

Vatican Council II marked a shift of emphasis and perspective with regard to both how the inner life of the church is conceived and how the church relates to the world around it.

The changes in the way the church perceived itself have affected all aspects of its inner life, not just with regard to hierarchy, laity, priests, and religious. For this reason, to talk about the general theme of religious life in the church in the United States today, it is necessary to outline first what those perspectives were that touched the inner life of the church, and secondly the ways in which that change of vision introduced by Vatican Council II influenced religious life. Five perspectives from Vatican Council II and how they influenced religious life in the United States will be described.

THE PEOPLE OF GOD

The primary document of the council that treats of the makeup of the church, *Lumen Gentium*,[1] first sets forth a vision of the whole, namely, the church seen as the People of God, before talking about the roles or different categories of members within the body. Some today would like to minimize the importance of this change of perspective. A fear has arisen with regard to this new approach. It springs out of a genuine concern that such a perspective could lead to a new "congregationalism" or to a false application to the inner life of the church of some of the democratic principles that come from Enlightenment philosophy. This tendency, it is feared, could work to the detriment of the church's tradition and history. In other words, it could lead to a denial of the hierarchical nature of the church.

This fear would be valid if one failed to read the subsequent chapters of *Lumen Gentium*. There the traditional hierarchical nature of the church is emphasized. The impact, however, of changing from a pyramid-image or hierarchical model of church, to a circle-image or community one as a beginning for a discussion on the nature of the church is in itself a major innovation. The added emphasis that the hierarchy finds its logical place within the circle of the People of God and is at the service of God for the well-being of those people, changes the way in which all the groups relate one to another. All members of the church now are seen as equal, at least in terms of full membership through baptism. Thus, all sense that they are responsible in one way or another for both the church's inner dynamics and its mission.

This new perspective entered very soon into religious life. Attitudes toward authority changed in religious life as well. Superiors were regarded primarily as serving the community and the mission of the congregation. They were more readily seen as animators or leaders who were at the service of the entire congregation and the church. Religious leaders tended to avoid authoritarian methods, sought to diffuse their authority by sharing it with others, and were very conscious of the errors of psychological dependency and infantilism.

It also became important in religious life in the United States that all the members of a community be involved in the dynamics that led up to the articulation of new goals and visions that were forged in subsequent general chapters. One could say that a renewal of collegial spirit rose up in religious congregations in the light of this insight of co-responsibility coming from the council.

THE ROLE OF THE BISHOP

One clear aspect of the documents of Vatican Council II is the renewal of and the new accent on the role of the bishop, both within the confines of his diocese and in his collegial responsibilities for the universal church. Many say this perspective was meant to complete the unfinished business of Vatican Council I and to complement the work done in that council on the role of the pope. In any case, the image of the local bishop was most certainly enhanced by Vatican Council II. The hierarchy is now seen primarily as occupying positions of service, and not posts of honor and prestige. They are regarded as being a part of the community and not above it. The pyramid exists within the circle and not outside of it. In addition, Vatican Council II spoke at length about the role of bishops and their relationship to the collegial governance of the whole church.

Unfortunately, in the documents of Vatican II there is not the same dynamic vision for priests and their ministry as there is for bishops and even for the laity. What is striking is that there is little new in Vatican Council II about the way in which priests and their ministry are treated. Some have observed that their role seems to be minimized by the council, even if a separate document is devoted to them. What is lacking is a compelling vision of priesthood for today, with new perspectives on how priesthood must also respond to the new model of church that the documents present.

This aspect or even deficiency of Vatican Council II with regard to priesthood may at first glance seem to have influenced religious life to a lesser degree. For religious institutes that consist mostly of priests it has had an impact that is not yet clear. One does hear, however, of a certain tension over the way in which candidates for the priesthood from religious orders are being trained as distinct from diocesan candidates. Since so many men religious are also clerical, this weakness of the council documents does not help the dialogue between religious life and clerical ministry.

The most direct impact, however, of this changed perspective with regard to the role of the bishop in the local church, is the new initiatives on the part of bishops to enter into the inner life of the religious communities. Documents since Vatican II have tried to make clear what these relationships should be and have modified and lessened perceptibly the older concept of exemption. Bishops are now asked to take a greater pastoral interest in the life of religious. Such an attitude can often be seen by religious as open interference in the inner life of the community, one that leads to a weakening of the religious authority within the community itself. Vatican Council II's emphasis on the stronger role of the bishop has led to this tension. It is more acute when the style of governance of the bishop of the local church contrasts sharply with that of the religious superior. If a bishop does not understand the dynamics of religious life, it can also lead to a stifling of the Spirit. If, in addition, the bishop unwisely supports within the community groups that take positions over against the lawful superior, it can lead to unfortunate inner turmoil in the community. Such appeals to the bishop from within the community have not been uncommon in this post-Vatican II period.

THE ROLE OF THE LAITY

There is definitely a new awareness of the role of the laity in church and world in the perspectives of Vatican Council II. The unequivocal call of all the baptized to holiness is very important. Vatican II does away with the "degrees of perfection" found in former teaching and sees the laity as truly called to holiness and as evangelizers in the world; they are the church *ad extra*.

Religious found themselves very much in tune with the thinking about the role of the laity in the church and the world. For a time they frequently saw their own role as that of training, encouraging, and helping the laity in taking those roles. Now they are more inclined to see the laity as co-workers and equals in the mission of the church. These new associations with the laity were important for the development of religious life in the United States after the council and continue to be so.

It was not clear in postconciliar thinking if members of religious congregations who were not ordained were to consider themselves as lay or clerical. They were often treated ambivalently, almost according to whim, when controversies arose.

THE ROLE OF RELIGIOUS

Religious, like priests, seemed to have fared less well in the council documents. In preparing the council documents on religious life, religious themselves did not play a significant role. They seemed then to take their historical place in the church for granted and did not articulate a new vision for themselves. It must be stated that religious welcomed the abolishing of the degrees of perfection, even if such a change may have seemed to diminish their prestige and privileged place within the church. The section of *Lumen Gentium* that dealt with religious life was accepted by religious as excellent. *Perfectae Caritatis*,[2] at the time of the council, seemed like an adequate document. Neither, however, came to terms with the new perspectives that make up the whole of the council's vision. Just as the priesthood did not receive from the council a new impetus, so the image of religious life did not shine forth as totally integrated into the newly defined mission of the church.

At times one wishes that the council, especially after *Gaudium et Spes*,[3] had returned to the role of religious. How do religious relate now to church and world in the light of the new way in which the whole church enters into dialogue with the same world? This question is not asked, neither for priests nor for religious. These deficiencies became very evident in the period following the council. Religious themselves wrestled with this vision of church and world as articulated by the council when they worked through their own statements of purpose in their general chapters. They eagerly picked up the theme of their new relationship to the world. That theme will be treated later as the postconciliar period is described.

HUMAN DEVELOPMENT

Additionally, one should not neglect a new perspective from Vatican Council II that placed emphasis on the importance of human development. This emphasis can be seen in *Gaudium et Spes*, but in other documents as well. Although the Council did not fall into the error of seeing the whole of human development from a purely physical or materialistic point of view, that is, it did not fall into a sterile "secular humanistic" analysis, it still saw the need to develop the whole of human potential if the spiritual dimension of the human person is to play its role. Faith tells us that the human person is created for an eschatological destiny but also that the final end is not obtained by jumping over this world. Rather how people have lived in this world, how they have related to it in every way, as fully developed human beings should, is an integral part of the eschaton.

Religious embraced this vision whole-heartedly. In fact, for religious much of the postconciliar period has been characterized by a concern for human and spiritual growth. I feel that this is one of the reasons, among many others, why women religious in the United States embraced the better aspects of the feminist movement. They saw in that social development a mirror of what they sought in their religious and spiritual lives. They knew that full personal growth, the development of their talents to the fullest, was the only correct way to contribute to the life of the church and its mission to the world. Such a perspective opened up for religious many new ways of contributing to the church and its mission.

THE CHURCH AND THIS WORLD

Vatican Council II brought a new perspective to how the church relates to the world. Perhaps no other change has affected the church in this postconciliar period in the United States as much as this one. The world, as perceived in *Gaudium et Spes*, is now seen more positively as in constant dialogue with the church. The church sees itself as having a common history with the world. The perspective is more ecumenical, but, in its own way, also more evangelical: the church cares for what happens in this world and wants to be a part of it and its history. It leaves its isolationism behind and takes up the role of being sacrament or witness to this world.

Religious were very much caught up in this new perspective and embraced it eagerly and totally. All of the first five perspectives—not just the texts of Vatican Council II themselves—affected religious life profoundly, especially in the United States, but none more so than the new involvement with the world. Some of the older terminology that came from the monastic tradition about "separation from the world" was abandoned by religious as inappropriate and meaningless in the new context. Orders that had an apostolic impulse from their origins saw in Vatican Council II a new way of bringing into focus their apostolic involvement with the world. They saw their charism vindicated by the council.

Many religious also decided that they could serve that world better as lay people and thus left religious communities to take up new work. This is often looked upon as a blemish on religious life in the postconciliar age. It could also be considered as a way in which religious life prepared for the life and work of the church important new active lay members, all very much imbued with the spirit of Vatican Council II. These former religious have played an important role in the postconciliar church in the United States, especially in the local churches.

One other point of clarification is necessary: religious, probably more than any other group within the church, took the council seriously and set forth all of their energies to implement its vision. Women religious in particular began to attend many theological and biblical seminars and courses, all in order to understand more clearly what Vatican Council II meant and to reflect on how to implement it better.

Many of these perspectives of Vatican Council II were reinforced by trends that had begun during and after World War II and that had given to Catholics in the United States a new position in their own society. The election for the first time of a Catholic president in the person of John Kennedy is evidence to the new group of Catholics taking their places in the political and social life of the nation. One could say that the effects of World War II on the Catholic population created fertile ground for introducing and even interpreting in an American sense the new perspectives of Vatican Council II.

Nevertheless, one would have to say that many in the U.S. church were not prepared for such dramatic new ways of seeing the inner life of the church and how it should relate to the world. Perhaps there were too many changes in too short a period of time, changes that had not been carefully prepared for by church leaders nor pastorally explained by its teachers.

POST-VATICAN II DEVELOPMENT

The postconciliar development of religious life in the United States has not been uniform. The basic concepts of the council were taken up in different ways. Nevertheless, this development is most important. At times it has been criticized, as if the Holy Spirit abandoned the church during these interim decades, but such an evaluation would be unfair and unjust. There also exists a tension among religious, one that is very regrettable, over the nature of the renewal asked for by Vatican Council II. The areas of difference will become apparent in what follows.

Renewal after the council was three-pronged and is based on the directives of the document *Perfectae Caritatis*. 1) The biblical roots of religious life were to inspire again the way of life that religious had chosen.

2) The charism of the founder was to be reexamined and permitted to fill again its place of inspiring religious today. 3) Accommodations to the needs of modern times were to be made. Religious at once set about to try to implement that three-pronged renewal.

CHARISM AND RELIGIOUS LIFE

Religious rightly saw their lives as falling into the category of charisms in the church, a category that St. Paul in his epistles wrote about so eloquently. They saw their lives as full of such gifts, freely given by the Holy Spirit. In examining the charism of the founder, they found much new inspiration for the living out of religious life in our day.

On the other hand, they also saw that the charism of the founder had been clarified and further determined through history by other members of the institute who followed in his or her footsteps. They also saw some of the difficulties that the original founders had had with the canonical structures of the church in their day and what compromises from the very beginning of the institute had to be made to satisfy both local bishops and the Holy See. Father Arrupe once said that the charism of Ignatius is important indeed, but one should not ignore the distinctive contributions to the history of the Jesuits made by the charisms of all the other Jesuit saints who followed.

In addition to the importance of the charism of the founder and of those other members of the institute who subsequently throughout history added insights and inspiration to the members, religious rightly began to see the importance of recognizing the charisms of the living members of their congregations and their gifts of the Spirit. They knew that these charisms were also gifts from that same Holy Spirit and should not be minimized or looked down on. This was an important development, since it gave more confidence to religious and was more biblical in its perspective.

It is noteworthy that official Vatican documents on religious life avoided the use of the term charism to describe the category in which religious life found itself in the church. Only the charism of the founder is mentioned. At times writers extended that concept to talk about the charism of an institute or congregation. Such terminology was debated at Vatican Council II before *Lumen Gentium* was written, but wisely avoided in the actual document, since, in the strict Pauline sense, the gifts of the Spirit are given to individuals, not to corporate or aggregate groups. Instead, institutes were seen as having several specific characteristics or qualities that flowed from the charism of the founder. Only thus, in a broad and imprecise sense, could one talk about the charism of an institute or of religious life in general. It is baptized human beings who receive charism from the Holy Spirit. They live out those charisms; they contribute to the life of the church through those charisms. The aggregate of similar charisms that correspond to the charism of the founder form the makeup of the religious institute.

A false dichotomy grew up in some later writings and in popular parlance in the United States between the charismatic aspect of the church and the hierarchical. In Pauline terminology the roles of leadership and administration in the church are also seen as charisms, gifts of the Holy Spirit. Religious had to learn that they were not the only ones who received such gifts. For example, bishops (people like Archbishop Oscar Romero) and lay people (like Dorothy Day) could be the recipients of prophetic charisms. Nevertheless, the realization that each religious is so gifted gave birth to a new, positive, and reassuring dynamic within the communities and provided at the general chapters of the congregations a sense of well-being and direction for the accommodations needed for modern times.

It could also be said that religious saw their charism as a prophetic one. Again, such a concept does not imply that bishops, popes, and laity could not receive a prophetic charism or be prophetic. It simply means that the way of life of such a religious should be in itself prophetic. For religious such prophecy stems out of the very nature of the way they live the gospel. It does not essentially consist in occasional utterances that challenge the People of God. It flows from their being.

Such a prophetic way of life could be seen in two ways, depending upon the reference point used. Historically, religious life has been seen as prophetic within the inner life of the church. Religious still saw the church as their prime prophetic audience. In addition, they saw that such prophecy could relate to the mission of the church to the world.

Their prophetic witness was a way of following Christ. No single person is capable of exhausting such a witness concerning who Christ was and is today. Religious select certain virtues or aspects of Christ's way of life and make them their own. By doing so they alert the church constantly to gospel values that could so easily get lost.

For example, celibacy is a gospel witness, a following of the example of Jesus Christ who was celibate. Celibacy remains within the church an example of the need to keep clearly in mind in the midst of all the cares and busyness of our day the fact that there are more important things than our programs and activities. It keeps the large goal of the next life before our eyes constantly. But such a witness within the church in our day and age also has a prophetic message to make to the secular society around us. It shows that there are more important aims and goals for the human person than the fulfilling of sexual desires. In a promiscuous world celibacy is prophetic by nature, much misunderstood, but, for a religious, essential to a full understanding of the nature of the Christian life.

Among the prophetic witnesses that religious have embraced in the postconciliar period, one that should be pointed out with emphasis, is the concern for the poor. This aligning of themselves with the poor is indeed prophetic and again witnesses to how Jesus himself related to the less fortunate. Religious see this as a part of their prophetic charism of poverty and detachment.

The way in which religious, especially religious women, have taken care of their elderly sisters is also a living witness to poverty and care for the weak, one much needed in our society.

For many religious congregations the charisms of the members were closely related to the apostolate or work that the founder sought to undertake. Today for many communities their apostolates seem to be more related to the natural talents and gifts of the members. This has caused a shift of emphasis away from corporate works to more personal contributions. The prophetic nature of the way of life itself remains the same, but it is lived out in different contexts according to the gifts and talents of the individual members. Such changes have often caused turmoil in communities and have not always been understood by the general Catholic population. Many religious did not do a good job in communicating their own inner struggles and values to the church at large in the United States. This relationship to corporate apostolates is also one of the distinguishing differences in renewal among the groups of religious after Vatican Council II.

The apostolates that religious once engaged in and that were often very closely related to the charism of the founder in the past century have been reexamined today. This has been especially true among women religious. Times have changed and such apostolates have also taken on new demands. In addition, religious have seen their numbers diminish and thus have found it more and more difficult to continue in some of the corporate works they once fulfilled. These discussions within religious institutes have not been easy ones. They have also caused some tensions between religious and local pastors and officials.

The renewal of obedience has been mostly biblical. Religious have seen themselves as being one with Christ in his *kenosis,* his emptying of self. They have also deepened their understanding of the meaning of Christ's obedience in accepting his Father's will that led to his sufferings and death on the cross. They have likewise rejoiced in their witness to his resurrection. They have not understood this witness of obedience as meaning that they should create more authoritarian structures. In fact, they have sought to make their communities more human and their mode of exercising authority more sensitive to the needs and gifts of the person. In this way they have hoped to avoid some of the pitfalls of some of the previous manifestations of religious life that could hold the members in an unhealthy dependency and that could crush human initiative and responsibility. Here, too, there have been different interpretations among religious congregations, and unfortunate tensions with Roman authorities have arisen.

One very sensitive point has been the need for an outward sign of the witness of religious life, such as through a distinctive dress or habit. Here, too, groups facing renewal differed, with some retaining a modified habit or veil, others simply trying to dress in a more simple and discreet style.

At times deeper and more serious tensions have arisen between the hierarchy and the prophetic witness of religious in the postconciliar period. Some of these tensions have involved, for example, the role of women in church and society. In particular, many religious women have received the kind of deeper theological training needed to reflect on and confront the delicate issues surrounding the role of women in church and society. They have thus entered more fully into the struggle within American society for more significant roles for women. Such tensions are inevitable and should be seen as a sign of life and growth, but they have also led to some very painful situations.

Religious continue to examine what their prophetic role should be within the church. Although they do not deny the importance of education, they no longer see themselves as just a less expensive work force for the educational endeavors of the church, but rather particularly as having a potentially broader scope and influence in church and world.

They have had to learn, too, that lay people can be gifted with prophetic witness to church and society and have tried their best to be supportive of such witnesses. In this respect religious have opened a new dialogue with laity on the way in which the laity can understand and continue in the church those specific characteristics and aspects of their institutes that flowed from the charism and intuitions of their founders.

RELIGIOUS AND THE WORLD: 1964–1980

Religious, especially women religious, took seriously the perspective of Vatican Council II and the insertion of the church into the life of the world. For many this corresponded to the charism of their founder, a charism that had been looked upon with suspicion in the past because it did not come out of the monastic model. In the postconciliar period the insertion of religious into the life of the world was made clear by subsequent church documents. This vision was best articulated by Pope Paul VI's apostolic letter entitled *Evangelica Testificatio* (1971).[4]

Pope Paul, it must be candidly admitted, was worried that religious could at times confuse the impulse of the world with the impulse of the Holy Spirit. He felt a need to outline again the renewal desired by the council and give some positive encouragement as well as articulate some needed cautions. Thus he examined first of all consecrated chastity, emphasizing the witness religious could give to church and world in that area. His treatment of poverty is remarkable and inspiring. He dwelt much on this witness in our day and accentuated the role of religious in hearing the cry of the poor and in responding to the need for social justice. He wrote:

> How then will the cry of the poor find an echo in your lives? That cry must, first of all, bar you from whatever would be a compromise with any form of social injustice. It obliges you also to awaken consciences to the drama of misery and to the demands of social justice made by the Gospel and the Church. It leads some of you to join the poor in their situation and to share their bitter cares. Furthermore, it calls many of your institutes to rededicate for the good of the poor some of their works —something which many have already done with generosity. §18

Pope Paul could not have been more affirming of the direction that religious, especially religious women, were taking. He spent four more paragraphs on this same theme and saw in this renewal the way in which religious should relate to the world.

When he dealt with "withdrawal from the world"—the classic term used in religious life—he interpreted it as the need to pass from excessive activity to recollection. He mentioned then the times of retreat and the need to get away from the hectic pace of today's world. In his concluding appeal he stated to religious:

> Deep understanding of present tendencies and of the needs of the modern world should cause your own sources of energy to spring up with renewed vigor and freshness. It is a sublime task in the measure that it is a difficult one. §51

He continued on in the same vein for several more paragraphs.

Religious in the United States responded well to this document, since it confirmed the direction they felt they were going in. Many had been influenced by similar thoughts expressed by Cardinal Suenens in a book that every religious woman in those days read carefully: *The Nun in the World*.[5] This positive book was the inspiration for much that happened among women religious in the United States in the early years of renewal after the council. It set a tone that was encouraging and exciting.

But there were shadows rising on the horizons. Concerns were voiced in Rome that this type of renewal often placed individual religious at the ambiguous and sensitive conjuncture between church and world, as the church in the United States began to deal more directly with social and political issues. Concerns were raised about the lack of visible signs of religious life in dress and community living. Authority structures in newly written constitutions of religious congregations were rejected by the Congregation for Religious in Rome as defusing authority too much. In general, tensions between religious congregations in the United States and the Roman Congregations seemed to multiply. In addition, Rome showed a certain uneasiness because of the large number of religious, especially women, who were seeking dispensations.

RELIGIOUS AND THE WORLD—1983

In *Lumen Gentium* there is no mention of secular institutes. *Perfectae Caritatis*, on the other hand, devotes a paragraph to them (§11). They were relatively new in the church at the time of Vatican Council II, having gained their first canonical approval in the 1940s, and were thus not well known to most of the bishops. It was still not clear at that time what the nature of some of the groups, such as the Opus Dei, would be. The decades following the council saw a rapid increase in these movements within the church and their growing importance. In Europe, they were playing a prominent role in the postconciliar renewal, both within the church and in the political arena. They also developed very close ties with the Vatican. It was clearly seen with time that the way in which the renewal of religious life in the United States was moving would cause a confusion between the two categories, namely between religious life and these new secular institutes that were springing up.

All of these concerns and the general apprehensions on the part of Rome with the development of religious life in the postconciliar period, especially in the United States, resulted in two documents in 1983 that have been central to all discussion since then. The edition of the *Code of Canon Law* and the *Essential Elements in the Church's Teaching on Religious Life*,[6] a document from the Congregation of Religious, appeared that year. The latter could be seen as a more thorough commentary on the former.

No documents on any theme issued during the implementation period after the council differ so remarkably from the treatment on the same subject found in Vatican Council II than these two documents.

Lumen Gentium and *Perfectae Caritatis* see religious life primarily as a following of Christ and a way of living the gospel. They are descriptive and encouraging, positive and supportive. Their reference to biblical roots, to the inspiration of the founder, to the need for accommodation were forward looking and full of trust in the Spirit. *Essential Elements* sees religious life primarily as a form of consecration to God. A new term not traditional in the church in the past to describe religious life, namely "consecrated life," is now introduced to embrace both secular and religious institutes. The three-pronged renewal of *Perfectae Caritatis* is not mentioned anymore. It is not without interest that *Essential Elements* defines first (in paragraph 9) what a secular institute is, namely, this consecration lived in the midst of the world. Only after establishing this definition of secular institutes does it go on to define religious life. This latter definition is made to contrast with that of secular institutes and so has none of the positive and encouraging dynamics found in previous documents, especially in *Evangelica Testificatio.*

The result, one must admit, is a kind of juridic straitjacket; a clear framework under the rubric of "consecrated life" is given first, with two distinct manifestations, one in the world and the other not so neatly defined. It seems clear that the theology of secular institutes wins out and a vagueness and uncertainty for religious life follows. In other words, what results is a description of a way of life that does not seem to spring from the lived reality of religious life in our day, but from a preconceived intellectual schematic framework that is more juridic, more external, and less inspiring.

Rather than affirm the development that had taken place since Vatican II concerning the whole relationship between religious and the world, it leaves that theological issue in abeyance. In a strange shift in logic, the question of distinctness from secular institutes becomes interpreted as meaning that religious life gives a public witness within the church. Religious would well have the feeling in reading this document that the older medieval model, one that is difficult to reconcile with Vatican Council II, has been again imposed upon them, making them theologically irrelevant in this postconciliar age.

Although there is much validity in the whole notion of "consecration" as it is explained in baptismal theology, its schematic use in this document seems forced, does not rise from the lived experience of religious, and is made to carry too much weight. Nevertheless, religious have accepted the new code and have tried bravely to reconcile their way of life with this newly imposed terminology. They know, however, that they do not fit so neatly into the categories outlined and continue to search for ways to explain to the church their inner desires and aims. Most of all, while they have accepted in faith these new concepts, they have not found them inspiring or liberating. The fact that the terms of *Essential Elements* and the code are not traditional means that the church must live with them for a time before seeing how well they correspond to the new reality.

FUTURE PERSPECTIVES

If one were to describe the way in which religious see themselves in today's church and world, several adjectives would come to mind.

They regard themselves, first of all, as *ecclesial*. Just as the church is a sign or sacrament to the world, so religious, as a part of that church, are also signs both within the church and to the world. They see themselves as very much involved in the mission of the church. They are not just a volunteer benevolent organization in society but are rooted in the faith community of believers. Their lives make no sense except when lived in the light of faith. Like Paul's image of the gifts building up the body of Christ, they see themselves and their gifts as given for the good of the whole church. They seek community among themselves and with all the baptized. They know that at times their role will not be an easy one in the church but that the church is their home.

They wish to give to the hierarchy the esteem and collaboration that are necessary for the mission of the church in its totality. They are not anti-clerical, nor religious free-thinkers. They, too, are searchers and acknowledge the important role of the hierarchy in that constant quest for truth and for God's will today. They look for the opportunities to speak to share their insights and experience. They desire, most of all, to contribute to the church and its mission the fruits of their charisms.

Religious life is also *christological*. Religious seek to imitate Christ and be one with him. For this reason they accept poverty for the kingdom and hope to identify themselves with the poorest and the voiceless. They know that no single way of life can totally witness to the fullness of Christ; thus they seek to keep alive in the Christian community aspects of Christian values that could of themselves be easily forgotten. Because of that sense of witness their lives involve radical commitments such as celibacy and poverty.

They do not feel they are better than other followers of Christ, even if their way of being disciples seems marked with very visible sacrifices. They want also to be witnesses of joy and resurrection. The roots of their way of life are always found in the gospel. They know they should be living "beatitudes." Just as Christ referred frequently to his Father and saw his own life as a fulfillment of the Father's will, so religious look to the larger destiny of the human person and this world.

Religious life is also *pneumatic.* Because it is the Holy Spirit who animates the church now and at all times, religious know that they must be in tune with that Spirit and discern where the Spirit is leading the church today. They know that they must listen to the voice of the Spirit through prayer and meditation, through reflection on the events of the world, through listening to each other and to the other members of the church, through dialogue with other believers and the world at large. In this way they seek to discern and respond to the actions of that Spirit in our midst. They know that their individual members are living temples of the Spirit and thus bearers of God's presence and message to this age.

Religious life is *charismatic.* It is a gift of the Holy Spirit for building up the church. It is not just an ornament. They know that the Spirit's charismatic gift involves prophecy in its deepest biblical sense. It is a witness to God's point of view, to the divine, to the spiritual realities that can so easily be smothered in our world. Regardless of the particular work or the particular devotion that may have been at the root of the charism of the founder, they know that these are all given by the Spirit for the benefit of the whole church. Freed up by celibacy and poverty, they can more easily respond to the promptings of the Spirit without counting the costs.

Religious life is *evangelizing.* Because of their baptism, religious know that they are bound up with the mission of the church. Their mission continues that of Jesus Christ. Through their role of being religious they participate fully in the mission of the church and especially in its evangelizing role. They too must bring Christ to the world, to culture, to society, to all aspects of human existence. In so many ways they can afford to be in the front lines of the church's evangelizing intent. Just as the church is by nature missionary, so too religious life must have the same dynamic, evangelizing thrust.

Because religious are very much tied up with Jesus Christ and with his discipleship, they must constantly be entering into Christ's paschal mystery to the fullest extent. Dying and rising again with Christ and in Christ is their basic spirituality. Perhaps at no period of history have they been called to a deeper participation in that mystery than today. They see clearly how they are dying with Christ at this moment. In hope and faith they also witness to his rising again. Religious live now out of a hope that is based on faith. Perhaps, because of the challenges that they now face, this moment is the crucial one for their witness to that hope. They know that the presence of the Holy Spirit will not be wanting in their midst.

NOTES

1. *The Documents of Vatican II*, W.M. Abbott and J. Gallagher, eds. (New York: Guild Press, 1966), "Dogmatic Constitution on the Church: *Lumen Gentium*," 14-96.

2. *The Documents of Vatican II*, "Decree on the Appropriate Renewal of the Religious Life: *Perfectae Caritatis*," 466-482.

3. *The Documents of Vatican II*, "Pastoral Constitution on the Church in the Modern World: *Gaudium et Spes*," 199-308.

4. Pope Paul VI, "The Evangelical Witness of the Religious Life: *Evangelica Testificatio*," *The Pope Speaks*, Vol. 16, No. 2 (Summer, 1971), 108-128.

5. Leon-Joseph Suenens, *The Nun in the World: New Dimensions in the Modern Apostlate* (Westminster, Md.: Newman Press, 1962).

6. "Essential Elements in Church Teaching on Religious Life": A Text of the Vatican Congregation for Religious and Secular Institutes, *Origins*, Vol. 13, No. 8 (July 7, 1983), 133-142.

Editor's Afterword

Paul J. Philibert, O.P.

The various perspectives that have been included in this book coincide to make it clear that religious life is now on the threshold of an important transformation. The anticipated changes will touch prayer and community life, formation, ministry, and roles of leadership. In these closing words, I would like to bring together some of the clearest signals from the work done by my colleagues in this volume. In doing so, I will address four different groups of persons: bishops, candidates for religious life, major superiors, and Catholic lay people.

TO THE BISHOPS:

The initiative for the 1994 synod was that of the Holy Father and his advisors. The synod itself is your own responsibility as the church's pastors. Speaking for my colleagues in religious life, I would like to focus upon a few points that are of particular concern for us. I hope that my comments will facilitate your understanding of some issues of central importance for North American religious.

First of all, I remind you of the extraordinary diversity of forms of religious life. At several points in this volume, we have commented upon the spectrum that reaches from enclosed contemplative monasteries to active apostolic institutes. Everything on the spectrum between these two poles not only has a different relation to apostolic involvement, but a particular tonality relative to the charism of the founder, the spirituality of the group, and the history of its cultural insertion in different geographical areas, language groups, and social milieux.

In our view, it would be unfortunate if one were to try to reduce religious life to a genus and species analysis. There is no simple common denominator that can be used as the generic form for religious life. Religious life arises genetically from the inspired, charismatic response to the gospel of a creative genius whose work is continued by a religious family of sisters and brothers beyond the original time and place of its foundation.

Many of the papers in this volume would argue that we may anticipate more diversity in the future rather than less, more creativity relative to apostolic solutions, and new approaches to the shaping of dedicated spiritual, religious, and apostolic life. We note that the vows are shaped by the institute's charism, not vice versa. As the CMSM Response to the Lineamenta put it: "Community life would express the specific charism religious had received, and they would formulate the vows according to their specific mission. The vows of poverty, chastity and obedience would be specific to particular forms of religious life."[1] This diversity, as we see it, is inspired by the Holy Spirit. It is God's gift to the church through religious institutes.

We believe that it is fair to say that no element in the church has been as responsive to the call for self-renewal and *aggiornamento* as religious have been. If there appears to be chaos or lack of operational clarity on the part of some groups of religious, it is important to acknowledge that in the span of the last thirty years we have been responding to cultural adjustments touching the influence of centuries.

In a certain sense, many of the tensions which have existed between some religious and some diocesan ordinaries have been due to the awkwardness that accompanies letting go of habitual attitudes and procedures for the sake of a renewed approach to pastoral life, piety, and religious community. Yet, in most cases, we would stand by the courage and perceptiveness of religious who have taken seriously the challenges of pastoral renewal in this country.

We note the often prophetic and courageous role of religious in the promotion of social justice in the renewal years. One of the most impressive signs of the "good fruit" of the renewal of religious life has been a reawakening of sensitivity to issues of justice mandated by the inspiration of our founders. The work of missionary outreach, the addressing of unjust social structures both here and in the mission field, and the search to involve lay collaborators in the justice agenda of our institutes are areas about which we are particularly proud, even as we recognize that not all members of our institutes have an equal enthusiasm for the demanding work of justice.[2] Yet this is an area where we have played an important role and where we will continue to be called to serve the church prophetically in the future.

For the last five years or more, American religious have been discussing the topic of refounding (mentioned in several places in this book). The key challenge in refounding is to lead the group back, in solidarity, to a keen appreciation of the contribution of the institute's "original inspiration" within the context of present time and place, and to act upon the demands of that renewed sense of the institute's charism. This is refounding in the sense that it engages all those members who are able to repossess the insight and enthusiasm of the early days.

For many American religious, their apostolic service has been an incarceration rather than an incarnation of their institute's charism. Eager to serve the local church, members of religious orders and congregations have often enough taken on roles in parishes, schools, or diocesan agencies which express pastoral generosity but which simultaneously drain energies away from the institute's focal responsibility as it struggles toward refounding.

We ask you bishops to understand this phenomenon. Religious are not just an additional personnel pool for the diocese, but also and especially communities charged by their history and charism to a particular expression of spirituality and apostolic presence according to the spirit of their founder and their institute's traditions. Often enough, it is religious themselves, habituated to pastoral service within the diocese, who are the most reluctant to respond to the call to retune the pastoral expression of their lives to the refounding theme. Nevertheless, this is an important issue for religious that will continue to influence the work of transformation in the years ahead.

As your co-workers in the pastoral field, we respect the difficulty of your position of administration. You too are caught in a "mission or maintenance" dilemma many times. We certainly expect that you will easily understand the anguish and the difficult choices which we face in the administration of our own pastoral personnel. As many of the authors here have articulated one way or another, however, most of us believe that the problems of personnel shortages and reprioritizing of institutional commitments can honestly be seen as a work of divine providence and a call to a new awareness of the emergence of God's kingdom in our time and our situation.

Many major superiors of both women and men continue to feel that a genuine and substantial dialogue with their diocesan ordinaries is still lacking in their regions. The record is very mixed on this score, since there are very positive examples of open and productive collaboration between religious superiors and bishops, but equally unfortunate cases where what is meant to be a dialogue has become little more than the visitation of the bishop to a gathering of religious superiors to lay down the law. At this moment of the church's evolution, we believe that it would be a failure of responsibility to neglect continued foundational conversation about the ecclesial meaning of our form of life that goes beyond juridical issues and nostalgia for days gone by and enters into discussion of our mutual interests for the church's cultural vitality and gospel realism. We dare to hope that the Synod of 1994 will promote the deepening of exactly this kind of dialogue.

We want to express our thanks to you bishops both for the time and energy which you have devoted to preparing for the synod within the National Conference of Bishops, in regional meetings with religious superiors, and in preparation for the actual synod event. You may be certain of our prayers for the meetings in Rome and that you will be graced by the special guidance of the Holy Spirit. May God's Spirit lead us all into a deeper understanding of God's will and providence for religious in these last years of this millennium.

TO CANDIDATES CONSIDERING ENTRY
INTO RELIGIOUS LIFE

If you have been guided somehow to read this volume, I would like to address some words of encouragement to you. It may be dismaying for someone contemplating the beginning of a life of religious service to recognize how complicated that life is and how many different considerations may be raised to address its future prospects. But with confidence and conviction, I invite you to move ahead in responding to the call to gospel service. You have experienced your call as a fascination with this form of life and as a special awareness of your spiritual life and of your hope to be a life-giving presence in this world.

You must keep your eye on the gospel. The word of God has primacy over all our customs, all our history, and all our present limitations. As Donald Senior's essay in this book states so clearly, your call is a call to discipleship. Above all else, it is God's Spirit that calls you to faith and to a generous response to the person and preaching of Jesus the Lord. That is the heart of your vocation.

Your enthusiasm and your dreams will be important for the future of religious life. The energy that you bring to the common life, worship, and apostolate of the institute to which you feel called is the future energy of religious life in our country. The dreams and hopes which you conceive for a meaningful Christian existence are the potential shape of the institute you are about to enter.

It has always been the case that religious life is renewed from within. Our institutions, no matter how old or venerable they may be, are always changing in significant ways because of the talent and vision of those who enter, become stable members, and later become the leaders for the future development of our institutes. I do not want to encourage megalomaniacs among those reflecting upon entering religious life—that is, don't come with the idea that you're going to turn everything around by your own dogmatic whims. But I do want everyone thinking seriously about religious life to reflect carefully about the fact that they have the power to make a difference for the better by their entering the life.

Finally, remember that the church has many times had to be responsive to change. We find ourselves at a moment in which there is a tremendous gap between the popular culture and the moral and spiritual teaching of the church. But the church will move faithfully into a new age. And you may be certain that the dedicated Christian life of Catholic religious will be alive and generative, as a source of transformation, as Christians move into a new millennium.

I hope that you will be able to read the analyis contained in this book not as a diagnosis of death and confusion, but as a recognition of the power of God's providence and God's Holy Spirit. You should know that in our communities, we pray daily for those of you who are preparing to enter our ranks. With humility, we invite you and welcome you.

TO MAJOR SUPERIORS

Obviously major superiors function as agents of unity in this time when there are so many forces of division within religious life as well as within the church. Throughout this volume, we have contrasted certain tendencies in living religious life in a time of renewal, suggesting perhaps that such divisions occur principally between one type of institute and another. But, in fact, almost all these tendencies or divisions exist within almost every institute—indeed, within every province or monastery of each institute. It is essential for you as superiors (no matter what title your own particular institute uses to identify your role of administration) to accept the role of servant through loving communication with each member. Often this is extremely difficult, since many religious have authority problems and are put off by the very role superiors must play as coordinators of the institute's common good. But the need for someone to be in dynamic communication with every member of the community is a matter of the greatest urgency.

As Howard Gray points out so clearly in his chapter, the fundamental urgency for a superior is to keep a focus on mission. You can become overwhelmed by the maintenance issues: personnel problems and finances can eat up all your days. Yet in fact the major contribution that you will make in your time of leadership within your institutes will be on the basis of your capacity to identify, communicate, and serve the charism that is the heart and soul of your orders and congregations. This will allow a continued emphasis upon new life: both the new life of the mission endeavors as well as the new life of those who are coming to us as candidates in these latter days.

Many of the pages of this book call us to a pragmatic realism about the meaning of the vows. While many older religious were catechized in the vows with a stress on asceticism and renunciation, the biblical and theological sense of the vows reflected in these studies is quite different. The following of Jesus does not require either Jansenism or Manicheism of us—God is not calling us to be connoisseurs of unhappiness—our own or others'. We still have to find ways to express the age-old wisdom of religious disciplines whose objective was spiritual intensity and moral integrity for the sake of discipleship. Unless we do—unless we accept responsibility to continually examine the sources for spiritual transformation of ourselves and our members—our quest for gospel authenticity will be short-changed by individualistic ego trips in place of a collaborative struggle for the coming of the kingdom of God.

The focus of our life of Christian dedication is vision and compassion. Obedience calls the whole community to listen (and to aid one another in listening) to the word of God. Poverty is for the sake of freedom with an eye to mercy. Chastity, like poverty, makes a certain rare quality of freedom possible but also, as Donald Senior says above, "Celibate chastity becomes a Christian option only because consuming passion for God takes over one's life."

As superiors, it falls to you to find ways to articulate the core realities of religious life and the charism of your institute that guides their being lived out. It will take courage to become vulnerable enough to speak forthrightly about vision. But your voice on the essentials will make possible a dialogue that is urgently needed—a dialogue that will not take place in all likelihood unless you initiate it.

In their many presentations about their research on the future of U.S. religious life, David Nygren and Miriam Ukeritis have often stressed that in their view we have now a ten-year period of grace in which to address what we have learned about the possibilities for survival and transformation of religious institutes in this country. Many houses, provinces, and even institutes may not survive this ten-year period of opportunity. Or, as Sean Sammon says above, some may survive in only a marginal existence or a weakened state. What we need to assess is what we want to do about the realities that face us: can we enable the future or will we dig into entrenched habits from the past?

The key issues before us, I think, are charism and solidarity. As our authors—especially Howard Gray, Paul Hennessy, Margaret Brennan, and Donna Markham—have noted, what we are about for the sake of the kingdom of God is too important to be the preserve of vowed religious exclusively. Each institute has a responsibility now to give intentional priority to lay formation and collaboration in ministry and spirituality, thus sharing its charism. Equally challenging and equally important, we are called to collaboration with other institutes both for an analysis of the actual pastoral needs of the local churches and for pastoral cooperation to meet those needs in ways which we can no longer do by ourselves.

To thrive in your difficult role as a major superior, you must own the mystery that you are chosen. Many of you have been chosen by your institute's members directly, some through a representative process, and others by appointment of a superior or general council. But you are also chosen by God. This dimension of providence in the role that you serve has great value. The affirmation of grace is the only energy that can enable you to bear up under the demands of an office so overwhelming.

The networking of the LCWR and CMSM leadership regions is a great blessing to most major superiors. It is immensely helpful to meet in a context of prayer and mutual support in order to share honestly the frustrations and the dreams that each of us must live with. This volume grew out of LCWR and CMSM activities. It is my hope that it will be an invitation to some of you who have not yet become familiars of the conferences' activities to profit from the benefits that they have to offer.

TO CATHOLIC LAY PEOPLE

If you have labored through this volume on a topic rarely dealt with in such detail among lay audiences, let me address a few words especially to you. For me it is of the greatest importance that lay people should understand the meaning of religious life. The life we lead as members of approved institutes of religious sisters, brothers, and priests in the Roman Catholic Church is meant above all to be a sign of solidarity with and concern for you.

We have not entered this life to separate ourselves or to choose a way that is spiritually or socially better than that of any of you. At the heart of our choice, there lies our own undeniable conviction that God is asking us to be responsive to grace in a vocation to contemplative prayer and apostolic compassion.

But our commitment to the Christian life is not an effort at separation, but solidarity. Paul Hennessy's article explores the theme of charism. This is of the greatest importance at this time. By charism, we mean the spiritual sense or key idea that inspired the founder of a religious institute and which has been handed on as the guiding principle for the life and action of members of the religious order or congregation through the ages. This charism governs the way we live, pray, and minister.

We are beginning to recognize in a way very different from previous generations that this charism is something meant to be shared, not hoarded. It is not destined to influence the spirituality and apostolate exclusively of vowed religious, but also to be the inspiration and the guide of the lives of many lay persons as well.

It is in everyone's interest for the laity in the Roman Catholic Church to become more deeply involved in their awareness of God, a satisfying relation of prayer, and a generous exercise of their gifts for the corporal works of mercy. The church, as Pope John Paul II so frequently indicates in his writings, is about to come into a new age which will be characterized by the full spiritual and apostolic development of the laity.

The universal call of all the baptized to holiness was made brilliantly clear by the teaching of Vatican II. The Constitution on the Church, §40, states with emphasis: "The Lord Jesus, the divine Teacher and Model of all perfection, preached holiness of life to each and every one of His disciples, regardless of their situation.... Thus it is evident to everyone that all the faithful of Christ of whatever rank or status are called to the fullness of the Christian life and to the perfection of charity. By this holiness a more human way of life is promoted even in this earthly society."[3]

In the reconsideration of the evangelical counsels (which form the basis for the vows which religious profess) you can see a place for yourself. The core of obedience is cultivating a heart that learns to listen deeply to the voice of God made manifest in gospel reading, reflection, conscientious dialogue, and careful discernment. The point of evangelical poverty is a readiness to follow God's call, wherever it leads—a readiness facilitated by freedom from overconcern for earthly goods. In chastity, the key value is a passion for God and a freedom of heart to serve the family of Jesus.

In proportionately different ways, you as laity are called to realize these same values. In these evangelical values we have a basis for solidarity in the conviction that the gospel is the true meaning of our human existence. For our commitment as religious to make the sense to society that we want it to make, it is important for you to understand and participate in this ecclesial reality.

It is clear, too, if you have followed the arguments of our authors, that there will be more apostolic options available to you. We believe that this is God's doing, and not just an unfortunate consequence of our inability to keep business as usual functioning (relative to numbers of vocations and institutional supports). The time has come for us to be in serious dialogue with you about your understanding of this new moment of church life.

Perhaps in this century you have seen religious principally as pastoral workers who happened to live in community. Our lifetime engagement in a formation process aimed at authentic realization of the dynamics of Christian community—such as Kevin Seasoltz describes above—may not have been so evident to you as observers of our religious lives. Yet, if the age of transformation succeeds, you will see religious more principally as people on fire with good news about their experience of God's love and Christ's call to them, and you will find that they will be restless to have you know and share in the charism—evangelization, compassion, healing, hospitality—that is the passion of their lives. The time has come to talk of such things.

You will have to be patient if our conversation is frequently skewed by nostalgia for the past that we know better than the uncharted future, or if we do not know how to assist you adequately to enter into our frequently complicated rules of conversation about charism and ministry. We will have to count on you to do your part to articulate your vocation to lay and family sanctity. We will have to cooperate as partners in a transformed church.

Finally, know that you are respected by religious for the integrity of your own Christian life where and as you are. You are the leaven in the dough which is your own family, community, and work experience in a process of transformation. Like you, we religious wait and wonder about the future shape of the church as well as the future shape of our own particular ecclesial situation. Let us pray for one another as we move into this future. It will be a time of many graces and many opportunities for the gospel.

NOTES

1. CMSM, "Religious Orders Amid Cultural Realities," *Origins*, 22:42 (Apr. 1, 1993), 725.

2. David J. Nygren and Miriam D. Ukeritis, "The Religious Life Futures Project: Executive Summary," *Review for Religious*, 52:1(Jan.-Feb., 1993), 6-55. Cf., esp., 23.

3. *The Documents of Vatican II*, "The Church," 66-7, §40.